The Army of the Kingdom of Italy, 1805–1814

Uniforms, Organization, Campaigns

Second Edition, fully revised and expanded

Stephen Ede-Borrett

HELION & COMPANY

Helion & Company Limited
Unit 8 Amherst Business Centre
Budbrooke Road
Warwick
CV34 5WE
England
Tel. 01926 499 619
Email: info@helion.co.uk
Website: www.helion.co.uk
Twitter: @helionbooks
Visit our blog http://blog.helion.co.uk/

Published by Helion & Company 2024
Designed and typeset by Mary Woolley, Battlefield Design (www.battlefield-design.co.uk)
Cover designed by Paul Hewitt, Battlefield Design (www.battlefield-design.co.uk)

ISBN 978-1-804514-42-9

British Library Cataloguing-in-Publication Data.
A catalogue record for this book is available from the British Library.

Contents

Preface to First Edition

This work is not intended to be a detailed study of the service and history of the Army of the Kingdom of Italy, although they are both covered superficially. Neither is it intended as an history of Italy or even the Kingdom during this period.[1] It is primarily a work of uniformology – a study of the changes in the uniforms and equipment of the units of the Army of the Kingdom of Italy (NB NOT, in Napoleonic terms, the Army of Italy, on which see below), and for completeness those parts of the Navy who served alongside that Army in land campaigns.

The format for each unit that I have chosen to use is that formulated by the late W. J. Rawkins in his books published by Anschluss Publishing. Over the years I have seen many ways of presenting this information but his is, in my opinion, undoubtedly the best and, in the vein of Isaac Newton, I readily acknowledge the debt that I owe him in copying his format.

I have tried not to be pedantic over many details of a uniform and state that this source is right and this one wrong – uniformology is not such an exact science. In many cases it is highly probable that both original sources may be correct and that variations in many aspects of a uniform changed from issue to issue, or even tailor to tailor, and may thus have often been seen alongside each other. This may have been the period of elegant uniform but Colonels still followed their personal whims on many things, strict precise uniformity simply did not exist in most units and many old or outdated items of uniform or equipment continued to be issued until stocks were exhausted. What are given here are, therefore, both the regulations (when they existed - the Kingdom's Army seemed remarkably lax on such things, however those that existed were usually, although not always, quite clear) and many of the numerous recorded variations to them.

While there are *brief* overviews of each unit's organisational changes during the period these were frequent and, particularly in the Royal Guard, were at best barely completed before the next was ordered. It is also worth noting that the theoretical establishments were rarely achieved, as some of the actual strengths quoted will amply show.

Many obsolete patterns of uniforms from the Army of the abolished Republics continued to be worn, again particularly in the Royal Guard, until 1806/1807 whatever the new regulations might say (a similar situation existed in almost all armies of almost every era). I have not tried to cover these 'older' uniforms since to do so would increase the size of this work exponentially to no real effect and they are thus mentioned only in passing. It is, however, hoped that these earlier uniforms may be covered in a later volume on the Armies of the Italian Republics.

While much of this material has been collected over many years my thanks must go particularly to those authors whose works are cited in the Bibliography, especially Piero Crociano, whose series in the long-gone and much lamented English-language *Tradition Magazine* first sparked my interest in the Kingdom of Italy and whose work provided the skeleton for me to build on. Also to Art Etchells and to Laurent Claudet for sharing the fruits of their researches and their libraries, to Peter Heath of Anschluss Publishing the publisher of W. J. Rawkins' books, and to Fabrice and Sophie Dalamare of Uniformologie who found so many of the illustrations and sources that I have used. My thanks also to my partner Mary, who has patiently read the manuscript and corrected many of my errors, but as always any errors that remain are totally down to me.

Lastly my apologies to native speakers of Italian, my own Italian is very basic and I apologise if I have mangled your language at any point.

Stephen Ede-Borrett
London April 2021

1 For this I would highly recommend Juan Carlos Carmigniani and Gilles Boué (Marie-France Renwick trans.), *Napoleon and Italy : A Military History of Napoleonic Italy, 1805–1815* (Paris: Histoire & Collections, 2016).

Preface to Second Edition

My thanks to Helion for the opportunity to update this study. Thankfully there are no major corrections to the first edition (except for a few corrections of the misspelling of Italian ranks), which was a relief, but there is a lot of additional information that has come to light since I wrote the first edition, and the inclusion of a large number of additional colour illustrations will, hopefully, make this work even more useful to uniformologists, historians and wargamers. I have also taken the opportunity to include, with thanks to Brown University Library's Anne S. K. Brown collection, the wonderful paintings from the 'Otto Manuscript'. I have not gone into great detail about this manuscript as to do so in 'competition' to the excellent work of Guy C. Dempsey would seem inadequate – I would therefore recommend anyone interested to check out Guy Dempsey's book cited in the Bibliography.

I would reiterate my thanks to Art Etchells and Lauren Claudet as well as Fabrice and Sophie Dalamare but I would also like to thank Bruno Mugnai for tidying up some of my poor Italian and also Duncan Rogers, Charles Singleton, Andrew Bamford and Serena Jones for all of their help they have given, and, of course, my ever tolerant partner Mary. Needless to say (but I will say it anyway) any mistakes that remain are my responsibility.

Stephen Ede-Borrett
London
April 2024

This book is respectfully dedicated to

Bridget Bentley
Kesh Kotecha
Sarah Thompson
Juliet Bugby

My friends.
They were good times, thankyou.

And to my partner
Mary Duff
Without whose encouragement it would probably never have been finished
and to the boss, Caroline, feline extraordinaire, who helped as only cats can.

Note on Terminology and Unit Titles

Throughout I have used Italian military terminology for ranks, titles and section headings, although occasionally not in the body text but only when exact equivalents exist (i.e. you will occasionally find "Captain" not '*Capitano*' and '1st Regiment' and not '*1º Reggimento*', et cetera).

My reasoning behind this is to maintain a consistency that is usually lacking in English-language works on the Italian Army whereby '*sotto tenente*' would become '2nd lieutenant', '*fanteria*' would become 'infantry' (or even 'foot') but '*Cacciatori a Cavallo*' would at best become simply '*Chasseurs a Cheval*', in itself a French term not an English one! It is thus easier and clearer to use the original Italian.

An anomaly worth mentioning is that I have used the French term 'sabre-briquet' for the infantry pattern short sword. There is no really accurate translation of this term (it literally translates as 'lighter sabre') and the weapon was a direct and exact copy of that in use by the French Army, so the French term seems appropriate.

The English equivalents of the original Italian are immediately obvious in most cases but included below is a glossary of Italian to English ranks and titles that may occasionally be of help. It is also useful to bear in mind that the command structure and rank titles were often copied from the French Army on which the Army of the Kingdom of Italy was modelled.

Italian	**English**	**Notes**
Aiutante	Adjutant	to a Battalion
Aiutante-Sottufficiale	Adjutant N.C.O.	to a Company
Ammiraglio	Admiral	
Artigliere	Gunner	
Primo Artigliere	1st Class Gunner	
Autista	Driver	of limbers of artillery, supply wagons, et cetera
Bracciante	Worker	Literally 'labourer'
Brigadiere	Corporal	Cavalry
Cacciatore	Chasseur	Centre Company, Light Infantry
Capitano	Captain	
Capo di Squadrone	Squadron Commander	Roughly a Major
Capo di Battaglione	Battalion Commander	Roughly a Lieutenant-Colonel
Carabinieri	Grenadier	In the light regiments
Chirurge Maggiore	Surgeon-Major	Regimental senior surgeon
Chirurge	Surgeon	
Comandante	Commander	Naval rank
Cornette	Hornist	
Caporale	Corporal	Infantry
Caporole-Furiere	Quartermaster Corporal	to a Company

Caporale-Tamburo	Corporal-Drummer	Responsible for the drummers of a unit.
Colonnello	Colonel	
Colonnello Sotto	No Equivalent	A rank somewhere between Colonel and Lt-Colonel
Contrammiraglio	Rear Admiral	
Generale di Brigata	Brigadier-General	
Generale di Divisione	Major General	
Furiere	Quartermaster	
Fuciliere	Private	Centre company soldier, line regiments
Granatiere	Grenadier	Elite company soldier
Maggiore	Major	
Maestro Artigiano	Master-Artisans	on a Regimental staff
Maniscalo	Farrier	
Musicanti	Bandsmen	
Porta Aquila	Eagle Bearer	a title NOT a rank, the holder would have held a military rank in addition
Quartier Mastro	Quartermaster	to a Battalion or Regiment.
Sergente	Sergeant	
Sergente Maggiore	Sergeant-Major	
Sotto-Chirurgo	Assistant Surgeon	
Sotto Tenente	2nd Lieutenant	roughly the equivalent of the British rank of Ensign, still in use as a rank in the British Army of the Napoleonic Wars
Sottufficiale	N.C.O.	
Tenete	Lieutenant	
Tamburo	Drummer	
Tamburo Maggiore	Drum Major	Responsible for both Drummers and Musicians within a unit. The next in line above the Caporale-Tamburo
Tromba-Maggiori	Trumpet-Major	
Trombettiere	Trumpeter	
Veterinario	Veterinarian	
Vice Ammiraglio	Vice Admiral	
Volteggiatore	Private	Light company soldier (in all infantry regiments)
Zappatore	Sapper	

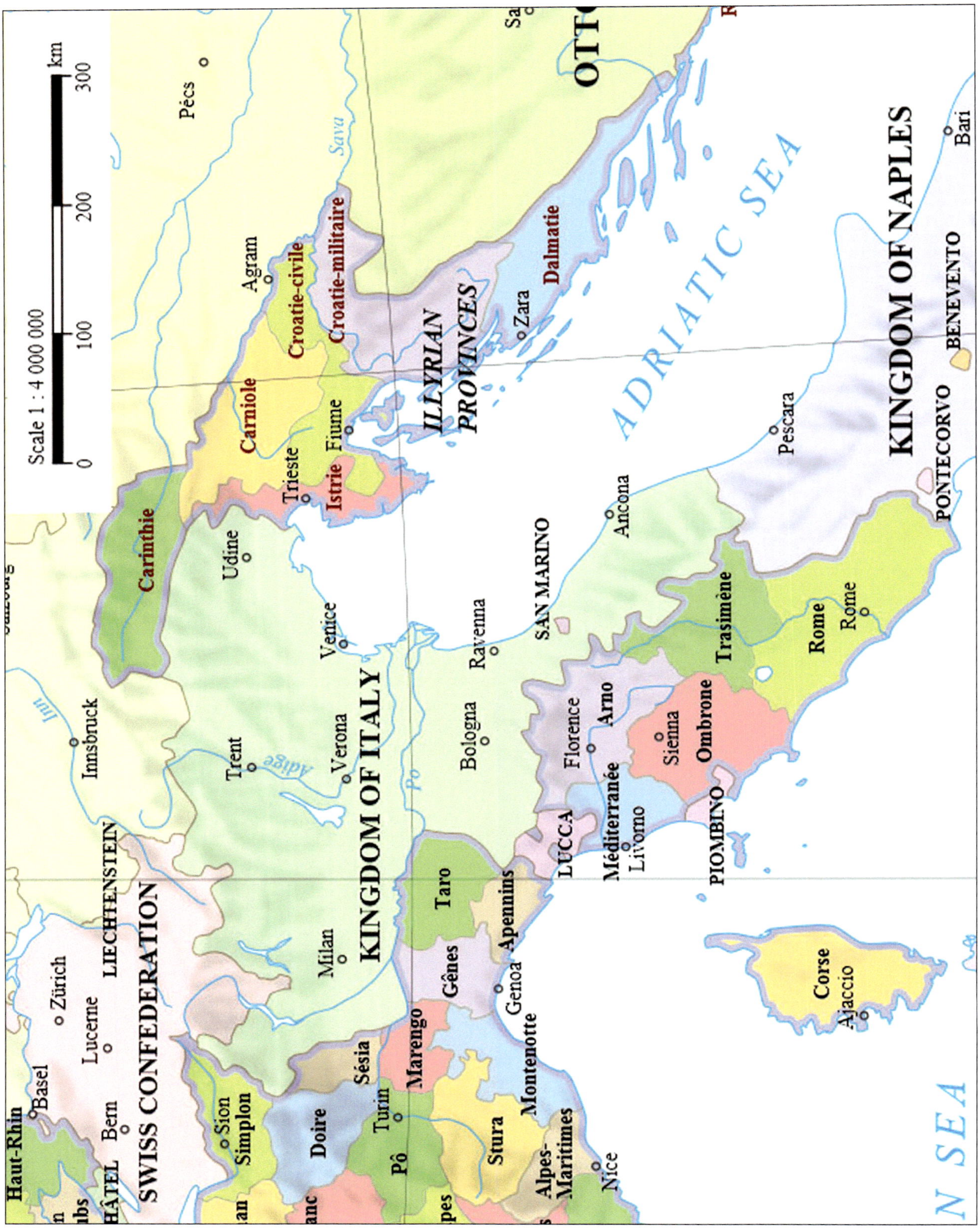

The Kingdom of Italy in 1812
Detail from a map by Andrein via Wikipedia Commons

Introduction
The Napoleonic Kingdom of Italy, 1805–1814

The Kingdom of Italy came into being on 17 March 1805, when the Italian Republic was dissolved, and Napoleon, who had been President of the Republic, was elevated to the throne as the new Kingdom's monarch. The 24-year-old Eugène de Beauharnais, Napoleon's stepson, was nominated as Viceroy. Napoleon was crowned with the Iron Crown of Lombardy in Milan Cathedral on 26 May 1805 and took the full title of "Emperor of the French and King of Italy".

The Republic ceased to exist upon the creation of the Kingdom but its Constitution was never formally abolished although a series of Constitutional Statutes completely altered it:

The first, proclaimed on 19 March just two days after the creation of the Kingdom, when Napoleon was declared King, established that the monarchy was to be hereditary and the King's sons would succeed to the throne, even if the French and the Italian crowns were separated after Napoleon's death.

The second, dated 29 March, regulated the Regency, the major Officials of the Kingdom, and the oaths to be taken by the Army, the Civil Service, and the populace.

In practice, however, the third Statute of 5 June 1805 was the new Constitution of the Kingdom: the King was to be Head of State, and had the full powers of government; in his absence, his powers were in the hands of the Viceroy; respectively these were Napoleon and Eugène de Beauharnais. The *Consulta*, Legislative Council, and speakers, were all merged into a new Council of State, whose recommendations and motions were advisory only, and not binding on either the Head of State or the Viceroy. The legislative body, the old Parliament, theoretically remained in being, or at least it was not formally abolished, but after 1805 it was not called again.

By a Statute of 16 February 1806 the proclamation of 19 March of the previous year was amended and Eugène and his heirs were nominated as the heirs to the Kingdom upon Napoleon's death.

The last of the important Statutes was that of 21 September 1808, which created a new nobility of dukes, counts and barons; and two further Statutes, of 15 March 1810, established an annuity for the members of the Royal Family.

The Kingdom of Italy initially comprised the territories of the old Italian Republic: the former Duchies of Milan, Mantua, and Modena, with the western part of the Republic of Venice, part of the Papal States in The Romagna, and the province of Novara. After the defeat of the Third Coalition and the subsequent Treaty of Pressburg of 1 May 1806, Austria surrendered the remaining part of the Venetian territories, including Istria and Dalmatia down to Cattaro (today Kotor). All of these were incorporated in the Kingdom of Italy, although at the same time Massa and Carrara were transferred to the Principality of Lucca and Piombino, ruled by Elisa Bonaparte.[1] Then, on 24 May 1806, The Duchy of Guastalla was annexed and added to the Kingdom.

By the Convention of Fontainebleau with Austria of 10 October 1807, Italy ceded Monfalcone to Austria and gained Gradisca, putting the new border on the River Isonzo.

In Spring 1808 *Maréchal* Marmont annexed the Republic of Ragusa, which was then added to the Kingdom, and on 2 April 1808, following the dissolution of the Papal States, the Kingdom annexed the present-day Marches.

This was the Kingdom at its maximum extent, with 6,700,000 inhabitants and 2,155 Cities, Towns and Villages.

The final changes to the Kingdom's borders came following the defeat of Austria in 1809. Napoleon and Maximilian, King of Bavaria, signed the Treaty of Paris on 28 February 1810, deciding an exchange of territories which also involved the Kingdom of Italy: Bavaria ceded

Coat of Arms of the Kingdom of Italy
(Image created by 'Sodacan' under a Wikimedia Creative Commons Licence)

1 Maria Anna Elisa Bonaparte Baciocchi Levoy (3 January 1777 – 7 August 1820), younger sister of Napoleon, Emperor of the French and King of Italy. She was the only one of Napoleon's sisters to hold independent political power.

the Southern Tyrol to the Kingdom of Italy, which in its turn ceded Istria and Dalmatia (with Ragusa) to France.

Napoleon abdicated the throne of the Kingdom of Italy on 11 April 1814 at the same time as he abdicated the throne of France. Eugène was on the Mincio with the Army and attempted to have himself crowned as his father's successor but there was little enthusiasm from the Senate and on 20 April a Provisional Regency Government was appointed. Three days later Eugène surrendered and was exiled to Bavaria. On 28 April the Austrians occupied Milan and over the next month the previous monarchies in Modena, Romagna and Piedmont were re-established. The remaining territories of the Kingdom were annexed by Austria on 12 June 1814; no vestiges of the Napoleonic Kingdom of Italy were allowed to survive.

The Armée d'Italie

It should be noted that in the Orders of Battle of the French armies of the First Empire the Armée d'Italie was *not* the Army of the Kingdom of Italy, although it invariably included the main field units of that Army. The *Armée d'Italie* was a mainly French force stationed in what was, post 1805 the Kingdom of Italy, primarily to keep a 'watch' on the Austrian Empire who between 1791 and 1815 spent a greater period at war with France than any other Country, excepting only Great Britain.

The status reports of the Armée d'Italie amply demonstrate this:[2]

The status reports of the Armée d'Italie

Date	Total Strength	French	Italian	
1805, Vendémiare 8	65,257	60,191	5,066	
1806, April 1	56,653	50,143	6,510	
1807, September 15	95,093	76,609	18,484	
1808, July 1	75,799	57,257	18,542	
1809, April 1	108,542	77,543	28,285	+ 2,714 Neapolitans
1814, January 15	45,025[3]			

The Iron Crown of Lombardy

Throughout the Kingdom of Italy's existence The Iron Crown of Lombardy featured strongly in its iconography. Tradition states that the Iron Crown was made for Theodelinda, Queen of the Lombards (c.570–628),[4] and was supposed to incorporate the iron from one of the nails of the True Cross. Theodelinda's Crown was made of six separate plates of gold, set with precious gems, over an iron circlet structure, hence the term "Iron Crown".

Upon Theodelinda's death in 628, the Crown was deposited in Monza Cathedral (along with a*[nother]* piece of the True Cross), where it is still preserved. When Charlemagne took the throne of Lombardy in 774 the Iron Crown was used for his Coronation, and this tradition was continued at the subsequent coronations of Holy Roman Emperors when they were crowned King of Lombardy; it was thus natural that Napoleon should also do so.

The Iron Crown of Lombardy.
Note that this is what the Crown *actually* looks like, although when used as a badge by the Kingdom's Army it was shown with a 'spiked' upper edge. It was also depicted with the 'spiked' upper edge on the Kingdom's Coat of Arms. Interestingly it is shown in this accurate form on the Commemorative Medal struck to celebrate Napoleon's Coronation as King of Italy (photograph ©James Steakley, photographed in the Theodelinda Chapel of the cathedral of Monza, CC BY-SA 3.0, https://commons.wikimedia.org/w/index.php?curid=5403306)

2 From Juan Carlos Carmigniani and Gilles Boué ,(Marie-France Renwick, trans.). *Napoleon and Italy : A Military History of Napoleonic Italy, 1805–1815*, (Paris : Histoire & Collections, 2016), p.221. Also see Appendix III.

3 The last, and incomplete, status report of the Armée d'Italie.

4 Theodelinda, Queen of the Lombards, was the daughter of Herzog Garibald I of Bavaria. In 558 she married Authari, King of the Lombards, and after his death in 590 his successor, Agilulfas, the following year. She exerted a great amount of influence in restoring Nicene Christianity to a position of primacy in Italy against its rival, Arian Christianity. She built a number of churches throughout Lombardy and Tuscany, including the Cathedral of Monza, dedicated to Saint John the Baptist.

Italy in the Napoleonic Period, 1796–1814

From *The Encyclopaedia Britannica* 1911 Edition[1]

The campaign of 1796 which led to the awakening of the Italian people to a new consciousness of unity and strength is detailed in the article 'Napoleonic Campaigns'. Here we can attempt only a general survey of the events, political, civic and social, which heralded the Risorgimento in its first phase. It is desirable in the first place to realise the condition of Italy at the time when the irruption of the French and the expulsion of the Austrians opened up a new political vista for that oppressed and divided people.

For many generations Italy had been bandied to and fro between the Habsburgs and the Bourbons. The decline of French influence at the close of the reign of Louis XIV left the Habsburgs and the Spanish Bourbons without serious rivals. The former possessed the rich duchies of Milan (including Mantua) and Tuscany; while through a marriage alliance with the house of Este of Modena (the Archduke Ferdinand had married the heiress of Modena) its influence over that duchy was supreme. It also had a few fiefs in Piedmont and in Genoese territory. By marrying her daughter, Maria Amelia, to the young duke of Parma, and another daughter, Maria Carolina, to Ferdinand of Naples, Maria Theresa consolidated Habsburg influence in the north and south of the peninsula. The Spanish Bourbons held Naples and Sicily, as well as the Duchy of Parma. Of the nominally independent states the chief were the Kingdom of Sardinia, ruled over by the house of Savoy, and comprising Piedmont, the isle of Sardinia and nominally Savoy and Nice, though the two provinces last named had virtually been lost to the monarchy since the campaign of 1793. Equally extensive, but less important in the political sphere, were the Papal States and Venetia, the former torpid under the obscurantist rule of Pope and cardinals, the latter enervated by luxury and the policy of unmanly complaisance long pursued by doge and council. The ancient rival of Venice, Genoa, was likewise far gone in decline.

The small states, Lucca and San Marino, completed the map of Italy. The worst-governed part of the peninsula was the south, where feudalism lay heavily on the cultivators and corruption pervaded all ranks. Milan and Piedmont were comparatively well governed; but repugnance to Austrian rule in the former case, and the contagion of French Jacobinical opinions in the latter, brought those populations into increasing hostility to the rulers. The democratic propaganda, which was permeating all the large towns of the peninsula, then led to the formation of numerous and powerful clubs and secret societies; and the throne of Victor Amadeus III, of the house of Savoy, soon began to totter under the blows delivered by the French troops at the mountain barriers of his Kingdom and under the insidious assaults of the friends of liberty at Turin. Plotting was rife at Milan, as also at Bologna, where the memory of old liberties predisposed men to cast off clerical rule and led to the first rising on behalf of Italian liberty in the year 1794. At Palermo the Sicilians struggled hard to establish a Republic in place of the odious government of an alien dynasty. The anathemas of the Pope, the bravery of Piedmontese and Austrians, and the subsidies of Great Britain failed to keep the league of Italian princes against France intact. The Gran Duca di Tuscany was the first of the European sovereigns who made peace with, and recognised the French Republic, early in 1795. The first fortnight of Napoleon's campaign of 1796 detached Sardinia from alliance with Austria and England. The enthusiasm of the Italians for the young Corsican "liberator" greatly helped his progress. Two months later Ferdinand of Naples sought for an armistice, the central duchies were easily overrun, and, early in 1797, Pope Pius VI was fain to sign terms of peace with Bonaparte at Tolentino, practically ceding the northern part of his states, known as the Legations. The surrender of the last Habsburg stronghold, Mantua, on the 2nd of February 1797 left the field clear for the erection of new political institutions.

Already the men of Reggio, Modena and Bologna had declared for a democratic policy, in which feudalism and clerical rule should have no place, and in which manhood suffrage, together with other rights promised by Bonaparte to the men of Milan in May 1796, should form the basis of a new order of things. In taking this step the Modenese and Romagnols had the encouragement of Bonaparte, despite the orders which the French directory sent to him in a contrary sense. The result was the formation of an assembly at Modena which abolished feudal dues and customs, declared for manhood suffrage and established the Cispadane Republic (October 1796).

The close of Bonaparte's victorious campaign against the Archduke Charles in 1797 enabled him to mature those designs respecting Venice. On a far higher level was his conduct towards the Milanese. While the French directory saw in that province little more than a district which might be plundered and bargained for, Bonaparte, though by no means remiss in the exaction of gold and of artistic treasures, was laying the foundation of a friendly republic. During his sojourn at the castle of Montebello or Mombello, near Milan, he commissioned several of the leading men of northern Italy to draw up a project of Constitution and list of reforms for that province.

1 London 1911, accessed through Project Gutenberg. https://www.gutenberg.org/files/41343/41343-h/41343-h.htm

Meanwhile he took care to curb the excesses of the Italian Jacobins and to encourage the Moderates, who were favourable to the French connexion as promising a guarantee against Austrian domination and internal anarchy. He summed up his conduct in the letter of the 8th May 1797 to the French directory, "I cool the hot heads here and warm the cool ones." The Transpadane Republic, or, as it was soon called, the Cisalpine Republic, began its organised life on the 9th July 1797, with a brilliant festival at Milan. The Constitution was modelled on that of the French directory, and, lest there should be a majority of clerical or Jacobinical deputies, the French Republic through its general, Bonaparte, nominated and appointed the first deputies and administrators of the new government. In the same month it was joined by the Cispadane Republic; and the terms of the treaty of Campo Formio (October 17, 1797), while fatal to the political life of Venice, awarded to this now considerable state the Venetian territories west of the river Adige. A month later, under the pretence of stilling the civil strifes in the Valtelline, Bonaparte absorbed that Swiss district in the Cisalpine Republic, which thus included all the lands between Como and Verona on the north, and Rimini on the south.

Early in the year 1798 the Austrians, in pursuance of the scheme of partition agreed on at Campo Formio, entered Venice and brought to an end its era of independence which had lasted some 1100 years. Venice with its mainland territories east of the Adige, inclusive of Austria and Dalmatian, went to the Habsburgs, while the Venetian isles of the Adriatic (the Ionian Isles) and the Venetian fleet went to strengthen France for that eastern expedition on which Bonaparte had already set his heart. Venice not only paid the costs of the war to the two chief belligerents, but her naval resources also helped to launch the young general on his career of eastern adventure. Her former rival, Genoa, had also been compelled, in June 1797, to bow before the young conqueror, and had undergone at his hands a remodelling on the lines already followed at Milan. The new Genoese Republic, French in all but name, was renamed the Ligurian Republic.

Before he set sail for Egypt, the French had taken possession of Rome. Already masters of the papal fortress of Ancon, they began openly to challenge the Pope's authority at the Eternal City itself. Joseph Bonaparte, then French envoy to the Vatican, encouraged democratic manifestations; and one of them, at the close of 1797, led to a scuffle in which a French general, Duphot, was killed. The French directory at once ordered its general, Berthier, to march to Rome: the Roman democrats proclaimed a Republic on the 15th February 1798, and on their invitation Berthier and his troops marched in. The Pope, Pius VI, was forthwith hauled away to Siena and a year later to Valence in the south of France, where he died. Thus fell the temporal power. The "liberators" of Rome thereupon proceeded to plunder the city in a way which brought shame on their cause and disgrace (perhaps not wholly deserved) on the general left in command, Masséna.

These events brought revolution to the gates of the Kingdom of Naples, the worst-governed part of Italy, where the boorish King, Ferdinand IV (*il rè lazzarone*, he was termed), and his whimsical consort, Maria Carolina, scarcely held in check the discontent of their own subjects. A British fleet under Nelson, sent into the Mediterranean in May 1798 primarily for their defence, checkmated the designs of Bonaparte in Egypt, and then, returning to Naples, encouraged that court to adopt a spirited policy. It is now known that the influence of Nelson and of the British ambassador, Sir William Hamilton, and Lady Hamilton precipitated the rupture between Naples and France. The results were disastrous. The Neapolitan troops at first occupied Rome, but, being badly handled by their leader, the Austrian general, Mack, they were soon scattered in flight; and the Republican troops under General Championnet, after crushing the stubborn resistance of the lazzaroni, made their way into Naples and proclaimed the Parthenopaean Republic (January 23, 1799). The Neapolitan Democrats chose five of their leading men to be directors, and tithes and feudal dues and customs were abolished. Much good work was done by the Republicans with his army beyond the river Mincio, ten days earlier during their brief tenure of power, but it soon came to an end owing to the course of events which favoured a reaction against France. The directors of Paris, not content with overrunning and plundering Switzerland, had outraged German sentiment in many ways. Further, at the close of 1798 they virtually compelled the young King of Sardinia, Charles Emmanuel IV, to abdicate at Turin. He retired to the island of Sardinia, while the French despoiled Piedmont, thereby adding fuel to the resentment rapidly growing against them in every part of Europe.

The outcome of it all was the War of the Second Coalition, in which Russia, Austria, Great Britain, Naples and some secondary states of Germany took part. The incursion of an Austro-Russian Army, led by that strange but magnetic being, Suvarov, decided the campaign in northern Italy. The French, poorly handled by Schérer and Sérurier, were everywhere beaten, especially at Magnano (April 5) and Cassano (April 27). Milan and Turin fell before the allies, and Moreau, who took over the command, had much difficulty in making his way to the Genoese coast-line. There he awaited the arrival of Macdonald with the army of Naples. That general, Championnet's successor, had been compelled by these reverses and by the threatening pressure of Nelson's fleet to evacuate Naples and central Italy. In many parts the peasants and townsfolk, enraged by the licence of the French, hung on his flank and rear. The Republics set up by the French at Naples, Rome and Milan collapsed as soon as the French troops retired; and a reaction in favour of clerical and Austrian influence set in with great violence. For the events which then occurred at Naples, so compromising to the reputation of Nelson. Sir William Hamilton was subsequently recalled in a manner closely resembling a disgrace, and his place was taken by Paget, who behaved with more dignity and tact.

Meanwhile Macdonald, after struggling through central Italy, had defeated an Austrian force at Modena (June 12, 1799), but Suvarov was able by swift movements utterly to overthrow him at the Trebbia (June 17–19). The wreck of his force drifted away helplessly towards Genoa. A month later the ambitious young general, Joubert, who took over Moreau's command and rallied part of Macdonald's following, was utterly routed by the Austro-Russian Army at Novi (August 15) with the loss of 12,000 men. Joubert perished in the battle. The growing friction between Austria and Russia led to the transference of Suvarov and his Russians to Switzerland, with results which were to be fatal to the allies in that quarter. But in Italy the Austrian successes continued Melas defeated Championnet near Coni on the 4th November; and a little later the French garrisons at Ancona and Coni surrendered. The tricolour, which floated triumphantly over all the strongholds of Italy early in the year, at its close waved only over Genoa, where Masséna prepared for a stubborn defence. Nice and Savoy also seemed at the mercy of the invaders. Everywhere the old order of things was restored. The death of the aged Pope Pius VI at Valence (August 29, 1799) deprived the French of whatever advantage they had hoped to gain by dragging him into exile; on the 24th March 1800 the conclave, assembled for greater security on the island of San Giorgio at Venice, elected a new pontiff, Pius VII.

Such was the position of affairs when Bonaparte returned from Egypt and landed at Fréjus. The contrast presented by his triumphs, whether real or imaginary, to the reverses sustained by the armies of the French directory, was fatal to that body and to popular institutions in France. After the coup d'état of Brumaire (November 1799) he, as First Consul, began to organise an expedition against the Austrians (Russia having now retired from the coalition), in northern Italy. The campaign culminating at Marengo was the result. By that triumph (due to Desaix and Kellermann rather than directly to him), Bonaparte consolidated his own position in France and again laid Italy at his feet. The Austrian general, Melas, signed an armistice whereby he was to retire on the 4th June, Masséna had been compelled by hunger to capitulate at Genoa; but the success at Marengo, followed up by that of Macdonald in north Italy, and Moreau at Hohenlinden (December 2, 1800), brought Emperor Francis to sue for peace which was finally concluded at Lunéville on the 9th February 1801. The Cisalpine and Ligurian Republics (reconstituted soon after Marengo) were recognised by Austria on condition that they were independent of France. The rule of Pius VII over the Papal States was admitted; and Italian affairs were arranged much as they were at Campo Formio: Modena and Tuscany now reverted to French control, their former rulers being promised compensation in Germany. Naples, easily worsted by the French, under Miollis, left the British alliance, and made peace by the treaty of Florence (March 1801), agreeing to withdraw her troops from the Papal States, to cede Piombino and the Presidii (in Tuscany) to France and to close her ports to British ships and commerce. King Ferdinand also had to accept a French garrison at Taranto, and other points in the south.

Other changes took place in that year, all of them in favour of France. By complex and secret bargaining with the court of Madrid, Bonaparte procured the cession to France of Louisiana, in North America, and Parma; while the duke of Parma (husband of an Infanta of Spain) was promoted by him to the duchy of Tuscany, now Italy, renamed the Kingdom of Etruria. Piedmont was declared to be a military division at the disposal of France (April 2 1801); and on the 21st September 1802, Bonaparte, then First Consul for life, issued a Decree for its definitive incorporation in the French Republic. About that time, too, Elba fell into the hands of Napoleon. Piedmont was organised in six departments on the model of those of France, and a number of French veterans were settled by Napoleon in and near the fortress of Alessandria. Besides copying the Roman habit of planting military colonies, the First Consul imitated the old conquerors of the world by extending and completing the road-system of his outlying districts, especially at those important passes, the Mont Cenis and Simplon. He greatly improved the rough track over the Simplon Pass, so that, when finished in 1807, it was practicable for artillery. Milan was the terminus of the road, and the construction of the Foro Buonaparte and the completion of the cathedral added dignity to the Lombard capital. The Corniche road was improved; and public works in various parts of Piedmont, and the Cisalpine and Ligurian Republics attested the foresight and wisdom of the great organiser of industry and quickener of human energies. The universities of Pavia and Bologna were reopened and made great progress in this time of peace and growing prosperity. Somewhat later the Pavia canal was begun in order to connect Lake Como with the Adriatic for barge-traffic.

The personal nature of the tie binding Italy to France was illustrated by a curious incident of the winter of 1802–1803. Bonaparte, now First Consul for life, felt strong enough to impose his will on the Cisalpine Republic and to set at defiance one of the stipulations of the treaty of Lunéville. On the pretext of consolidating that Republic, he invited 450 of its leading men to come to Lyons to a Consulta. In reality he and his agents had already provided for the passing of proposals which were agreeable to him. The deputies having been dazzled by fêtes and reviews, Talleyrand and Marescalchi, ministers of foreign affairs at Paris and Milan, plied them with hints as to the course to be followed by the Consulta; and, despite the rage of the more democratic of their number, everything corresponded to the wishes of the First Consul. It remained to find a chief. Very many were in favour of Count Melzi, a Lombard noble, who had been chief of the executive at Milan; but again Talleyrand and French agents set to work on behalf of their master, with the result that he was elected president for ten years. He accepted that office because, as he frankly informed the deputies, he had found no one who "for his services rendered to his country, his authority with the people and his separation from party has deserved such an office." Melzi was elected vice-president with merely honorary functions. The Constitution comprised a Consulta charged with executive duties, a legislative body of 150 members and a court charged with the maintenance of the fundamental laws. These three bodies were to be chosen by three electoral colleges consisting of (a) landed proprietors, (b) learned men and clerics, (c) merchants and traders, holding their sessions biennially at Milan, Bologna and Brescia respectively. In practice the Consulta could override the legislature; and, as the *Consulta* was little more than the organ of the president, the whole Constitution may be pronounced as autocratic as that of France after the changes brought about by Bonaparte in August 1802. Finally we must note that the Cisalpine now took the name of the Italian Republic, and that by a concordat with the Pope, Bonaparte regulated its relations to the Holy See in a manner analogous to that adopted in the famous French concordat promulgated at Easter 1802. It remains to add that the Ligurian Republic and that of Lucca remodelled their constitutions in a way somewhat similar to that of the Cisalpine.

Bonaparte's ascendancy did not pass unchallenged. Many of the Italians retained their enthusiasm for democracy and National Kingdom independence. In 1803 movements in these directions took place at Rimini, Brescia and Bologna; but they were sharply repressed, and most Italians came to acquiesce in the Napoleonic supremacy as inevitable and indeed beneficial. The complete disregard shown by Napoleon for one of the chief conditions of the treaty of Lunéville (February 1801) – that stipulating for the independence of the Ligurian and Cisalpine Republics – became more and more apparent every year. Alike in political and commercial affairs they were for all practical purposes dependencies of France. Finally, after the proclamation of the French Empire (May 18, 1804) Napoleon proposed to place his brother Joseph over the Italian state, which now took the title of Kingdom of Italy. On Joseph declining, Napoleon finally decided to accept the Crown which Melzi, Marescalchi, Serbelloni and others begged him to assume. Accordingly, on the 26th May 1805, in the cathedral at Milan, he crowned himself with the Iron Crown of the old Lombard kings, using the traditional formula, "God gave it me: let him beware who touches it." On the 7th June he appointed his step-son, Eugène Beauharnais, to be Viceroy. Eugène soon found that his chief duty was to enforce the will of Napoleon. The legislature at Milan having ventured to alter some details of taxation, Eugène received the following rule of conduct from his step-father: "Your system of government is simple: the Emperor wills it to be thus." Republicanism was now everywhere discouraged. The little Republic of Lucca, along with Piombino, was now awarded as a principality by the Emperor to Elisa Bonaparte and her husband, Bacciocchi. In June 1805 there came a last and intolerable affront to the Emperors of Austria and Russia, who at that very time were seeking to put bounds to Napoleon's ambition and to redress the balance of power. The French Emperor, at the supposed request of the doge of Genoa, declared the Ligurian Republic to be an integral part of the French Empire. This defiance to the sovereigns of Russia and Austria rekindled the flames of war. The third coalition was formed between Great Britain, Russia and Austria, Naples soon joining its ranks. While Masséna pursued the Austrians into their own lands at the close of 1805, Italian forces under Eugène and Gouvion St Cyr held their ground against allied forces landed at Naples. After Austerlitz (December 2, 1805) Austria made peace by the treaty of Pressburg, ceding to the Kingdom of Italy her part of Venetia along with the provinces of Istria and Dalmatia. Napoleon then turned fiercely against Maria Carolina of Naples upbraiding her with her "perfidy" He sent Joseph Bonaparte and Masséna southwards with a strong column, compelled the Anglo-Russian forces to evacuate Naples, and occupied the south of the peninsula with little opposition except at the fortress of Gaeta. The Bourbon court sailed away to Palermo, where it remained for eight years under the protection afforded by the British fleet and a British Army of occupation. On the 15th February 1806 Joseph Bonaparte entered Naples in triumph, his troops capturing there two hundred pieces of cannon. Gaeta, however, held out stoutly against the French. Sir Sidney Smith with a British squadron captured Capri (February 1806), and the peasants of the Abruzzi and Calabria soon began to give trouble. Worst of all was the arrival of a small British force in Calabria under Sir John Stuart, which beat off with heavy loss an attack imprudently delivered by General Réynier on level ground near the village of Maida (July 4). The steady volleys of Kempt's light infantry were fatal to the French, who fell back in disorder under a bayonet charge of the victors, with the loss of some 2700 men. Calabria now rose in revolt against King Joseph, and the peasants dealt out savage reprisals to the French troops. On the 18th July, however, Gaeta surrendered to Masséna, and that Marshal, now moving rapidly southwards, extricated Réynier, crushed the Bourbon rising in Calabria with great barbarity, and compelled the British force to re-embark for Sicily. At Palermo Queen Maria Carolina continued to make vehement but futile efforts for the overthrow of King Joseph. It is more important to observe that under Joseph and his ministers or advisers, including the Frenchmen Roederer, Dumas, Miot de Melito and the Corsican Saliceti, great progress was made in abolishing feudal laws and customs, in reforming the judicial procedure and criminal laws on the model of the Code Napoléon, and in attempting the beginnings of elementary education. More questionable was Joseph's policy in closing and confiscating the property of 213 of the richer monasteries of the land. The monks were pensioned off, but though the confiscated property helped to fill the empty coffers of the state, the measure aroused widespread alarm and resentment among that superstitious people.

The peace of Tilsit (July 7 1807) enabled Napoleon to press on his projects for securing the command of the Mediterranean, thenceforth a fundamental axiom of his policy. Consequently, in the autumn of 1807 he urged on Joseph the adoption of vigorous measures for the capture of Sicily. Already, in the negotiations with England during the summer of 1806, the Emperor had shown his sense of the extreme importance of gaining possession of that island, which indeed caused the breakdown of the peace proposals then being considered; and now he ordered French squadrons into the Mediterranean in order to secure Corfu and Sicily. His plans respecting Corfu succeeded. That island and some of the adjacent isles fell into the hands of the French (some of them were captured by British troops in 1809–10); but Sicily remained unassailable. Capri, however, fell to the French on the 18th October 1808, shortly after the arrival at Naples of the new King, Murat.

This ambitious Marshal, brother-in-law of Napoleon, foiled in his hope of gaining the Crown of Spain, received that of Naples in the summer of 1808, Joseph Bonaparte being moved from Naples to Madrid. This arrangement pleased neither of the relatives of the Emperor; but his will now was law on the continent. Joseph left Naples on the 23rd May 1808; but it was not until the 6th September that Joachim Murat made his entry. A fortnight later his consort Caroline arrived, and soon showed a vigour and restlessness of spirit which frequently clashed with the dictates of her brother, the Emperor and the showy, unsteady policy of her consort. The Spanish National rising of 1808 and thereafter the Peninsular War diverted Napoleon's attention from the affairs of south Italy. In June 1809, during his campaign against Austria, Sir John Stuart with an Anglo-Sicilian force sailed northwards, captured Ischia and threw Murat into great alarm; but on the news of the Austrian defeat at Wagram, Stuart sailed back again.

It is now time to turn to the affairs of central Italy. Early in 1808 Napoleon proceeded with plans which he had secretly concerted after the treaty of Tilsit for transferring the Infanta of Spain who, after the death of her consort, reigned at Florence on behalf of her young son, Charles Louis, from her Kingdom of Etruria to the little principality of Entre Douroe of Portugal. Etruria reverted to the French Empire, but the Spanish princess and her son did not receive the promised indemnity. Elisa Bonaparte and her husband, Bacciocchi, rulers of Lucca and Piombino, became the heads of the administration in Tuscany, Elisa showing decided governing capacity. The last part of the peninsula to undergo the Gallicizing influence was the papal dominion. For some time past the relations between Napoleon and the Pope, Pius VII, had been severely strained, chiefly because the Emperor insisted papacy, on controlling the church, both in France and in the Kingdom of Italy, in a way inconsistent with the traditions of the Vatican, but also because the pontiff refused to grant the divorce between Jerome Bonaparte and the former Miss Patterson on which Napoleon early in the year 1806 laid so much stress. These and other disputes led the Emperor, as successor of Charlemagne, to treat the Pope in a very highhanded way. "Your Holiness (he wrote) is sovereign of Rome, but I am its Emperor"; and he threatened to annul the presumed donation of Rome by Charlemagne, unless the Pope yielded implicit obedience to him in all temporal affairs. He further exploited the Charlemagne tradition for the benefit of the Continental System, that great engine of commercial war by which he hoped to assure the ruin of England. This aim prompted the annexation of Tuscany, and his intervention in the affairs of the Papal States. To this the Pope assented under pressure from Napoleon; but the latter soon found other pretexts for intervention, and in February 1808 a French column under Miollis occupied Rome, and deposed the papal authorities. Against this violence Pius VII protested in vain. Napoleon sought to push matters to an extreme, and on the 2nd April he adopted the rigorous measure of annexing to the Kingdom of Italy the papal provinces of Ancona, Papal Urbino, Macerata and Camerina. This measure, which seemed to the pious an act of sacrilege, and to Italian patriots an outrage on the only independent sovereign of the peninsula, sufficed for the present. The outbreak of war in Spain, followed by the rupture with Austria in the Spring of 1809, distracted the attention of the Emperor. But after the occupation of Vienna the conqueror dated from that capital on the 17th May 1809 a Decree virtually annexing Rome and the Patrimonium Petri to the French Empire. Here again he cited the action of Charlemagne, his "august predecessor," who had merely given "certain domains to the bishops of

Rome as fiefs, though Rome did not thereby cease to be part of his empire." In reply the Pope prepared a bull of excommunication against those who should infringe the prerogatives of the Holy See in this matter. Thereupon the French general, Miollis, who still occupied Rome, caused the Pope to be arrested and carried him away northwards into Tuscany, thence to Savona; finally he was taken, at Napoleon's orders, to Fontainebleau. Thus, a second time, fell the temporal power of the papacy. By an Imperial Decree of the 17th February 1810, Rome and the neighbouring districts, including Spoleto, became part of the French Empire. Rome thenceforth figured as its second city, and entered upon a new life under the administration of French officials. The Roman territory was divided into two departments – the Tiber and Trasimenus; the Code Napoléon was introduced, public works were set on foot and great advance was made in the material sphere. Nevertheless the harshness with which the Emperor treated the Roman clergy and suppressed the monasteries caused deep resentment to the orthodox.

There is no need to detail the fortunes of the Napoleonic states in Italy. One and all they underwent the influences emanating from Paris; and in respect to civil administration, law, judicial procedure education and public works they all experienced great benefits, the results of which never wholly disappeared. On the other hand, they suffered from the rigorous measures of the Continental System, which seriously crippled trade at the ports and were not compensated by the increased facilities for trade with France which Napoleon opened up. The drain of men to supply his armies in Germany, Spain and Russia was also a serious loss. A powerful Italian Corps marched under Eugène Beauharnais to Moscow, and distinguished itself at Malo-Jaroslavitz, as also during the horrors of the retreat in the closing weeks of 1812. It is said that out of 27,000 Italians who entered Russia with Eugène, only 333 saw their country again. That campaign marked the beginning of the end for the Napoleonic domination in Italy as else-where. Murat, left in command of the Grand Army at Vilna, abandoned his charge and in the next year made overtures to the allies who coalesced against Napoleon. For his vacillations at this time and his final fate, here it must suffice to say that the uncertainty caused by his policy in 1813–1814 had no small share in embarrassing Napoleon and in precipitating the downfall of his power in Italy. Eugène Beauharnais, Viceroy of the Kingdom of Italy, showed both constancy and courage; but after the battle of Leipzig (October 16–19, 1813) his power crumbled away under the assaults of the now victorious Austrians. By an arrangement with Bavaria, they were able to march through Tirol and down the valley of the Adige in force, and overpowered the troops of Eugène whose position was fatally compromised by the defection of Murat and the dissensions among the Italians. Very many of them, distrusting both of these kings, sought to act independently in favour of an Italian Republic. Lord William Bentinck with an Anglo-Sicilian force landed at Leghorn on the 8th March 1814, and issued a proclamation to the Italians bidding them rise against Napoleon in the interests of their own freedom. A little later he gained possession of Genoa. Amidst these schisms the defence of Italy collapsed. On the 16th April 1814 Eugène, on hearing of Napoleon's overthrow at Paris, signed an armistice at Mantua by which he was enabled to send away the French troops beyond the Alps and entrust himself to the consideration of the allies. The Austrians, under General Bellegarde, entered Milan without resistance; and this event precluded the restoration of the old political order.

The arrangements made by the allies in accordance with the treaty of Paris (June 12, 1814) and the Final Act of the congress of Vienna (June 9, 1815), imposed on Italy boundaries which, roughly speaking, corresponded to those of the pre-Napoleonic era. To the Kingdom of Sardinia, now reconstituted under Victor Emmanuel I, France ceded its old provinces, Savoy and Nice; and the allies, especially Great Britain and Austria, insisted on the addition to that monarchy of the territories of the former Republic of Genoa, in respect of which the King took the title of Duke of Genoa, in order to strengthen it for the duty of acting as a buffer state between France and the smaller states of central Italy. Austria recovered the Milanese, and all the possessions of the old Venetian Republic on the mainland, including Istria and Dalmatia. The Ionian Islands, formerly belonging to Venice, were, by a treaty signed at Paris on the 5th November 1815, placed under the protection of Great Britain. By an instrument signed on the 24th April 1815, the Austrian territories in north Italy were erected into the Kingdom of Lombardo-Venetia, which, though an integral part of the Austrian Empire, was to enjoy a separate administration, the symbol of its separate individuality being the Coronation of the Emperors with the ancient Iron Crown of Lombardy ("Proclamation de l'Empereur d'Autriche, &c.," April 7, 1815, State Papers, ii. 906). Francis IV, son of the Archduke Ferdinand of Austria and Maria Beatrice, daughter of Ercole Rinaldo, the last of the Estensi, was reinstated as duke of Modena. Parma and Piacenza were assigned to Marie Louise, daughter of the Austrian Emperor and wife of Napoleon, 'on behalf of her son, the little Napoleon,' but by subsequent arrangements (1816–1817) the duchy was to revert at her death to the Bourbons of Parma, then reigning at Lucca. Tuscany was restored to the Gran Duca Ferdinand III of Habsburg-Lorraine. The Duchy of Lucca was given to Marie Louise of Bourbon-Parma, who, at the death of Marie Louise of Austria, would return to Parma, when Lucca would be handed over to Tuscany. The Pope, Pius VII, who had long been kept under restraint by Napoleon at Fontainebleau, returned to Rome in May 1814, and was recognised by the congress of Vienna (not without some demur on the part of Austria) as the sovereign of all the former possessions of the Holy See. Ferdinand IV of Naples, not long after the death of his consort, Maria Carolina, in Austria, returned from Sicily to take possession of his dominions on the mainland. He received them back in their entirety at the hands of the powers, who recognised his new title of Ferdinand I of the Two Sicilies. The rash attempt of Murat in the autumn of 1815, which led to his death at Pizzo in Calabria, enabled the Bourbon dynasty to crush malcontents with all the greater severity. The reaction, which was dull and heavy in the dominions of the Pope and of Victor Emmanuel, systematically harsh in the Austrian states of the north, and comparatively mild in Parma and Tuscany, excited the greatest loathing in southern Italy and Sicily, because there it was directed by a dynasty which had aroused feelings of hatred mingled with contempt.

There were special reasons why Sicily should harbour these feelings against the Bourbons. During eight years (1806–1814) the chief places of the island had been garrisoned by British troops; and the commander of the force which upheld the tottering rule of Ferdinand at Palermo naturally had great authority. The British government, which awarded a large annual subsidy to the King and Queen at Palermo, claimed to have some control over the administration. Lord William Bentinck finally took over large administrative powers, seeing that Ferdinand, owing to his dullness, and Maria Carolina, owing to her very suspicious intrigues with Napoleon, could never be trusted. The contest between the royal power and that of the Sicilian estates threatened to bring matters to a deadlock, until in 1812, under the impulse of Lord William Bentinck, a Constitution modelled largely on that of England was passed by the estates. After the retirement of the British troops in 1814 the Constitution lapsed, and the royal authority became once more absolute. But the memory of the benefits conferred by "the English Constitution" remained fresh and green amidst the arid waste of repression which followed. It lived on as one of the impalpable but powerful influences which spurred on the Sicilians and the democrats of Naples to the efforts which they put forth in 1821, 1830, 1848 and 1860.

This result, accruing from British intervention, was in some respects similar to that exerted by Napoleon on the Italians of the mainland. The brutalities of Austria's white coats in the north, the unintelligent repression then characteristic of the house of Savoy, the petty spite of the duke of Modena, the medieval obscurantism of Pope and cardinals in the middle of the peninsula and the clownish excesses of Ferdinand in the south, could not blot out from the minds of the Italians the recollection of the benefits derived from the just laws, vigorous administration and enlightened aims of the great emperor. The hard but salutary training which they had undergone at his hands had taught them that they were the equals of the northern races both in the council chamber and on the field of battle. It had further revealed to them that truth, which once grasped can never be forgotten, that, despite differences of climate, character and speech, they were in all essentials a nation.

J HL. R.

[John Horace Round, M.A., LL.D. (Edin.)]

Eugène Rose de Beauharnais, Viceroy of Italy

Top: Eugène from a contemporary illustration by Albrecht Adam in a simplified version of full dress. As always with the Prince he is shown with his distinctive affectation of the buttoning of his coat. The orange, edged green, sash visible below the coats is that of the *Gran Croce dell'Ordine della Croce di Ferro* (Grand Cross of the Order of the Iron Cross), the star on his left breast is the same Order. The medal on the red ribbon is the Légion d'Honneur. The coat tails are decorated with gold Imperial Eagles. The baton in his right hand while resembling that of a Maréchal de France is not formally so, although it does appear near identical.

Bottom Left: Eugène in the full dress uniform of *Viceré d'Italia* (*Vice-roi d'Italie* /Viceroy of Italy). The honours and decorations are as above.

Bottom Right: Eugène, again from an illustration by Albrecht Adam, in a simplified campaign dress worn in Russia in 1812. Again note the distinctive coat fastening and the sash of the Order of the Iron Crown. He is holding a telescope in his right hand, not a baton. Note the simplified shabraque from the full dress version.

1

Generali (General Officers) & Staff

As with many, perhaps most, of the uniforms of the Army of the Kingdom of Italy those of the Italian General Officers closely followed the pattern of that worn by their French equivalents. However, the basic colour of the uniform for the Italian General Officers and Staff was dark green in place of the French blue.

Again, as with the *Generali*, the uniform of the *Aiutanti* and staff echoed that of their French counterparts.

Eugène Rose de Beauharnais, Viceroy of Italy

(Paris, 3 September 1781 – Munich, 21 February 1824)[1]

1805	
7 June	Proclaimed Viceroy of Italy
13 December	Promoted to Major General in the French Army
1806	
3 January	Appointed Commander-in-Chief of the Armée d'Italie
1809	
16 April	Battle of Sacile
14 June	Battle of Raab
5/6 July	Battle of Wagram
1812	
18 April	Leaves Milan for the Russian campaign as commander of IV Corps of the Grande Armée (see Appendix)
19 August	Battle of Smolensk
7 September	Battle of Borodino
24 October	Battle of Maloyaroslavets
1813	
16 January	Appointed Commander of the Grande Armée when Murat left the Army to return to Naples
5 April	Battle of Möckern
1 / 2 May	Battle of Lützen
22 November	Eugène refuses the Allies' offers to abandon Napoleon
1814	
8 February	Battle of the Mincio
16 April	Signs the Armistice at Milan
23 April	Surrenders the Army at Mantua. (Napoleon had abdicated on 11 April)

Tomb of Eugène de Beauharnais, in the Church of St Michael, in Munich, sculpted by Bertel Thorvaldsen. The inscription reads
heic placide ossa cubant
EUGENII NAPOLEONIS
regis Italiae vice quondam gerentis
nat. Lutet Pariside d. III sept. MDCCLXXXI
def. Monachii d. XXI febr. MDCCCXXIV
monumentum posuit vidua moerens
AUGUSTA AMALIA
Maximil. Jos. Bav. regis filia
(Photo, José Luiz, of São Paulo, Brazil. Reproduced by permission under a Wikipedia Commons Licence)

Son and heir of Alexandre de Beauharnais and Josephine Tascher de la Pagerie, later the wife of Napoleon. Eugène became Napoleon's adopted son and heir to the throne of the Kingdom of Italy, although not to the Imperial Title, even though officially known as His Imperial Highness

1 Eugène is buried in The Church of St Michael in Munich. He had been created Herzog von Leuchtenberg by his father-in-law Maximilian I Joseph, King of Bavaria on 14 November 1817. The title became extinct with the death of the 8th Duke, Sergei Georgievich, in Rome in 1974, although the title is claimed by the line of Nicolas Alexander Fritz de Beauharnais (b.1933), through a morganatic marriage.

from December 1804. He was created Prince de Venise on 30 March 1806 and became heir to the Grand Duchy of Frankfurt in 1810, and thus became Großherzog when Karl von Dalberg, Archbishop of Regensburg and Großherzog abdicated on 26 October 1813. Although as the Grand Duchy was then occupied by the Allies the title was no more than nominal.

In 1806 Eugène married Augusta, the daughter of Maximilian, King of Bavaria, and was created Herzog von Leuchtenberg by his father-in-law. The title became extinct in 1974 with the death of Sergei the 8th Herzog, although it is claimed by the Leuchtenberg family through a morganatic marriage.

Eugène de Beauharnais at the Battle of Borodino (7 September 1812). Engraving by Albrecht Adam and published in Munich c. 1820, after a sketch made at the time. Eugène is clearly shown with his coat buttoned/unbuttoned in his customary eccentric style. (Anne S. K. Brown Military Collection, Brown University Library, reproduced with thanks)

Uniform

Eugène is shown in a portrait by Richter[2] in a uniform essentially that described below for General Officers but with gold lace on the bicorne, a dark blue coat with a dark blue collar, both embroidered with gold oak leaf design, and all buttons gilt. The oak leaf embroidery covers the front of the coat, along both sides of the opening, and also follows around the lower edge and down into the tails. The heavy bullion-fringed epaulettes are gold. He does not wear a sash and the narrow red waist belt is laced gold with a gilt clasp. His sword has a gilt hilt, gilt sword-strap and knot, and gilt scabbard. Richter shows Eugène wearing a dark blue cloak over the coat but there is no indication of lining colour for either cloak or coat.

Eugène de Beauharnais, Duke of Leuchtenberg, post 1815. Artist unknown (Public Domain)

Richard Knötel's plate of Eugène in *Grosse Uniformenkunde*[3] shows a somewhat simpler uniform, taken from an illustration by Albrecht Adam of Eugène in campaign dress during the 1812 campaign, in contrast to Richter's portrait showing Gala or Full Dress. The coat has the oak leaf embroidery only on the collar of the dark blue coat which has black Polish cuffs edged with two lines of gold piping, and black turnbacks with gold eagle badges. The horse furniture is a red shabraque with a wide gold lace just inside the edge and gold fringe along the very edge; the red double pistol holster covers have a similar edging. Another illustration by Albrecht Adam of Eugène in 1812 shows essentially the same uniform but with dark blue breeches in place of white.

In both Richter's portrait and Knötel's plate the Viceroy is shown with all but the lower two buttons of the coat undone to show a white shirt beneath and the red sash of the *Légion d'Honneur* worn *under* the coat. Albrecht Adam shows a similar conceit in his illustrations of

2 Johann Heinri Richter, 1803–1845. Painting in the Leuchtenberg Collection in Munich.
3 Richard Knötel, *Grosse Uniformenkunde*, (Rathenow: Max Babeuzien, 1890–1914). Band III, Nr 58.

Eugène in 1812 confirming that this is almost certainly how the Viceroy usually appeared.

A contemporary picture by Lejeune shows Eugène at Borodino again in essentially the same uniform as that shown by Albrecht Adam including the eccentricity of it being fastened by only the lower two buttons,[4] obviously a personal conceit of Eugène.

In the collection of the Musée National des Châteaux Malmaison et de Bois-Préau is the coat that Eugène is traditionally said to have worn during the campaign of 1812 in Russia. This conforms to that shown in Richter's portrait in all respects, and it confirms Richter's showing of seven large buttons on the front instead of the customary nine. The cuffs, which cannot be seen on the Richter portrait, are of 'Polish' cut – a variation that may simply have been Eugène's personal preference – with no buttons. The lining is the same dark blue colour as the coat.[5]

Aide-de-Camp to the Viceroy

The aides-de-camp to the Viceroy wore the uniform of an *Aiutante* (see below) with the epaulettes of a *Capo di Battaglione* and a silver aiguillette on the right shoulder. The cuffs of the coat were trimmed with silver lace; the breeches were dark green decorated with silver lace Hungarian knots on the thighs and a wide silver stripe on the outer seam. The waistcoat was light blue with silver lace at the front and lower edges, and silver frogging at each button and buttonhole. The boots were Hungarian pattern with silver lace trim and tassels. Horse furniture followed that for the Aiutanti, again see below.

Albert Rigondaud, 'Rigo Le Plumet' *Peintre Officiel de l'Armee*, confirms all details of the full dress uniform of the Viceroy's aides but on the undress/campaign surtout (see below) he shows a broad silver lace edging to the collar, along the lower edge of the coat and around the turnbacks, and on the plain cuffs.[6]

An illustration of an ADC to Eugène and dated to c1811 shows an alternative, Hussar style, uniform

Headwear

Black/brown colpack with a red bag, unusually hanging on the right-hand side, with silver piping and tassel. Tall white plume at the front above a National cockade. Silver metal chin scales.

Coat

Red, hussar style dolman with mid-blue collar edged with broad white/silver lace, mid-blue pointed cuffs with four broad white/silver lace chevrons above. White silver lace frogging and three rows of silver buttons.

Red pelisse edged in white fur, four white/silver broad lace chevrons on the sleeves. White/silver frogging and silver buttons.

Blue and white barrel sash with white/silver cords.

Breeches, et cetera

Mid-blue overalls with two broad white/silver stripes down the outside and blue straps under the boot. NB there is no evidence of leather inserts.

Equipment

Black boots, but because they are worn underneath overalls the pattern is unknown. Dark red cartouche box strap edged in a broad silver lace worn over the left shoulder. On the front is a silver heart-shaped plate with silver chains attaching the plate to another higher up. The cartouche box cannot be seen but speculation would suggest that this would have been the small cavalry style, perhaps in red leather rather than black.

Straight cavalry sabre with a brass, single-bar hilt carried in an all steel scabbard from a white waist belt, mainly hidden by the barrel sash, and white suspension straps. White sword-knot and tassel.

Horse Furniture

Because the figure is shown dismounted there is no evidence of horse furniture. This may have been a similar pattern to that used by the *Aiutante* which appears to have been of a general style used throughout the Staff.

A list of Eugène's eight Aides at Borodino together with short biographies of each is given by Dr F. G. Hourtoulle in *Borodino The Moskova : The Battle for the Redoubts*.[7]

Generali

(General Officers)

Headwear

General officers wore a black bicorne, often velvet faced in full dress, trimmed at the upper edge with elaborate silver lace, which usually incorporated a laurel and oak leaf design, and with silver tassels at the outer tips. Beneath the large National cockade was a silver rosette secured by

4 F. G. Hourtoulle, *Borodino The Moskova : The Battle for the Redoubts*, (Paris: Histoire & Collections, 2000), p.87.

5 The coat is not on display but was shown in the exhibition 'Eugène de Beauharnais, un Prince Européen' at the Musée, which ran from 9 October 2022 to 9 January 2023 at the Châteaux of Malmaison & Bois-Préau..

6 Albert Rigondaud, Rigo Le Plumet, *Le Plumet* series of plates, Pl.108, *Aides de Camp du Vice-Roi d'Italie, 1812*, (Louannec: Privately Published, 1960–1980).

7 F. G. Hourtoulle, *Borodino The Moskova : The Battle for the Redoubts*, (Paris: Histoire & Collections, 2000), p.87.

Richard Knötel, *Grosse Uniformenkunde, Band III* (Rathenow: Max Babeuzien, 1893), Plate III / 58
From Left: Eugène, *Generali, Aiutanti, Commissari di Guerra* attached to the *Guardia Reale*. (Author's Collection)

a wide, deep silver cockade strap which almost reached the lower edge of the hat and was finished with a silver button. The outer edges of the bicorne were trimmed with a feather trim, silver for the Viceroy, white for a *Generale di Divisione* and black for a *Generale di Brigata*. For parade dress the hat was further decorated with a tall white feather plume with short red and green feathers at the base.

Coat

The coat was of a cut similar to that of the regulation coat of French Generals: single-breasted, surtout style with high upright collar, plain squared cuffs and long tails without turnbacks but open at the rear with a double vent. This coat was dark green lined red, with red collar and cuffs. It was closed at the front with nine silver buttons embossed with the Imperial Eagle. The front of the coat was trimmed with elaborate silver embroidery extending down to the edge and a similar embroidery decorated both sides of the rear vents. The same embroidery embellished the upper and front edge of the collar and upper edge of the cuffs. Nine batons of the embroidery sometimes also appeared on the coat's breast, each baton running out from a button or buttonhole. Epaulettes were silver with thick crescents and heavy bullion fringe; the straps were lace embroidered and decorated with three stars for a *Generale di Divisione* and two for a *Generale di Brigata*.

The silver silk waist sash was knotted at the left hip and ended with heavy silver bullion tassels for both the Viceroy and for *Generali*. The silver sash for *Generale di Divisione* was worked through with diagonal red stripes, and for the *Generale di Brigata* was worked through with light blue stripes.

Breeches, Et cetera

Breeches were white and worn with high, cuffed, heavy cavalry style boots with brass spurs. *Generali*' dark green, high-collared greatcoats were of the cavalry pattern with silver lace on the edges of the collar and shoulder straps.

Equipment

Waist belts were of the light cavalry pattern in black leather edged with silver braid and with a silvered 'S' buckle and silver fittings. The regulation sword had a gilded hilt (when worn, many officers wore privately purchased swords of their own choice of pattern, as in the French Army the 'Mameluke style' was popular), the sword-knot followed the colouring of the waist sash. Scabbards were silver-plated steel, or black leather with gilt fittings.

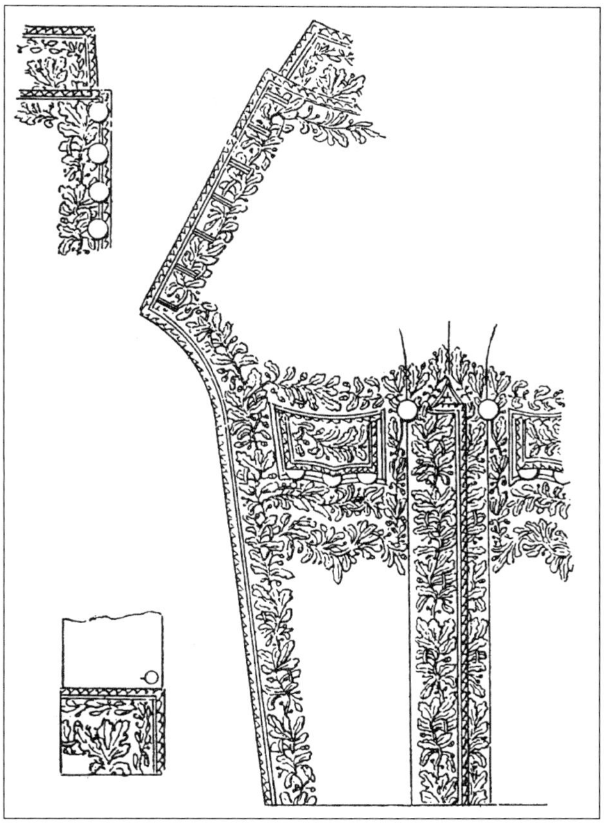

Detail of the lacing on the full dress coats of *Generali*
The buttons were probably of the same design as worn by the Guard: an Imperial Eagle below the Imperial Crown. On the breast of the Eagle was an oval design within which was a star crowned with the Iron Crown. NB although I have been unable to confirm this from any contemporary source. (H. Malibran, *Guide à l'Usage des Artistes et des Costumiers*, Paris: Combet et Cie, 1907)

Close up detail of the collar and cuff lace.
(H. Malibran, *Guide à l'Usage des Artistes et des Costumiers*, Paris: Combet et Cie, 1907)

Horse Furniture

Generali' shabraques were similar to those of dragoon officers and of dark green cloth with a double wide silver lace trim piped silver at the outer edge, each stripe separated by a welt of dark green, the triple pistol holster covers were decorated in the same way. The Viceroy used a shabraque of the same pattern but with the addition of a heavy bullion fringe at the very outer edge. Saddles and harness were black leather, the latter trimmed with silver lace. All buckles and fittings were silver-plated.

General Pino

Pino is depicted in an unpublished study by Louis de Beaufort "after Boisselier", in an otherwise unique uniform, but its very uniqueness makes it worth recording:

Headwear

A brass dragoon pattern helmet with brown fur turban and a black shiny leather peak bound in brass and with brass chin scales. The houpette is white and the helmet has a tall red plume at the left side mounted in a brass socket.

Coat

Dark blue habit style with white squared lapels, white collar and white turnbacks, all piped white. The cuffs cannot be seen in the illustration because Pino is wearing white gauntlet-cuffed gloves. All buttons are brass and the epaulettes are full, heavy-fringed pattern in gold. Over his right shoulder he is wearing the red silk sash edged green of the *Légion d'Honneur*.

Breeches, Etc

White waistcoat with brass buttons, white breeches and black heavy cavalry pattern boots.

Equipment

White waist belt over the waistcoat with a large square buckle. Heavy cavalry pattern sword with brass hilt and a gilt sword-knot and tassel in an all steel scabbard carried from white slings with brass buckles.

Aiutante-Comandante

(Aide-de-Camp Commandant)

Headwear

Black bicorne edged silver with cockade and cockade strap as for *Generali*.

Coat

In full dress *Aiutante-Comandante* wore a dark green, long tailed habit with pointed lapels and plain cuffs without cuff flaps. The coat had dark green facings piped silver, and red unpiped turnbacks. The collar was decorated with two horizontal batons of lace, each with a small button at the front; the cuffs had similar batons of vertical lace with a silver button at the top.

On campaign the above coat was usually replaced with the undress coat: the usual pattern surtout with facings as above. This coat was also worn when not on duty and for "walking-out dress".

The silver epaulettes of a full *Colonnello* were worn on both patterns of coat.

Breeches, Et cetera

Breeches and waistcoats were white for parade and full dress and dark green for campaign dress; buttons were silver. Boots were of the cuffed heavy cavalry pattern with silvered spurs. Greatcoats were of the dark green cavalry pattern with silver batons on the collar, as on the coat.

Equipment

Light cavalry sabre with silvered or gilded hilt, silver sword-knot and tassel, black leather scabbard with gilt fittings. The sword was worn from an hussar style belt of black leather with silver lace trim and silvered fittings.

Horse Furniture

Was the same pattern as that used by *Generali* with a double, wide silver band at the edge of the shabraque.

Aiutanti

(Aides-de-Camp)

Aiutante, full dress c. 1810. Described simply as 'Italie' and 'Agutante' this is an Aiutante in full dress. Although the lapels were regulated as sky blue the variant shown here of dark green piped sky blue does not seem an unlikely 'personalisation' or it may even have been a common variant. (Vinkhuijzen Collection, General Research Division, New York Public Library Digital Collections. Public Domain)

Headwear

Black bicorne hat with national cockade and silver cockade strap and tassels. The plume was coloured to indicate the staff level to which the officer was assigned (see below).

Coat

The full dress coat was a dark green short tailed habit-vest, with pointed lapels, Polish cuffs and 'a la Soubise' pockets. The coat had collar, cuffs and lapels of sky blue and turnbacks of dark green piped sky blue, the pockets were piped sky blue.

In undress and on campaign *Aiutanti* wore a dark green surtout coat with collar, cuffs, turnbacks and piping as on the full dress coat.

Epaulettes of rank were worn on both patterns of coat and the arm sash of an *Aiutante* was tied above the elbow on the left arm with the tassels hanging on the outside of the arm. This sash, and the plume of the bicorne, was coloured to denote the staff level to which the ADC was assigned (note, not the officer's actual, personal rank).

	Sash	Plume
Brigade	Sky blue trimmed silver	Sky blue over green
Division	Red trimmed silver	Sky blue over red
Corps / Army	White trimmed silver	Sky blue over red

Breeches, Et cetera

The breeches were green with silver Hungarian knots on the thighs and a silver stripe along the outer seam. The waistcoat was sky blue with silver lace 'frogging' and trim for parade, and plain dark green for undress and campaign. The boots were Hungarian pattern with silver lace and tassel.

Equipment

Waist belts were black leather and sabres were of the pattern used by officers of the light cavalry, with a silver sword-knot and tassel.

Horse Furniture

As for the *Aiutante-Comandante* but with a single wide silver lace band.

Revisori Militari

(Military Auditors)

Revisori Militari, who were exclusively officers, were a part of the General Staff and were, as the name implies, responsible for checking the accounts of the Army.

Headwear

Black bicorne with National cockade and a silver cockade strap and tassels.

Coat

The coat was of the same cut as that of the General Officers but was bright red, with dark green collar and plain round cuffs and piping to the horizontal pockets. There was a single line of silver lace at the edge of the collar and the cuffs and on the pockets. Like the Generals' coat it had no turnbacks. All buttons were silvered. Inspectors (*Ispettori*) wore a light blue sash, with silver fringe, around the waist over the coat. Sub-Inspectors (*Sotto Ispettori*) had a green sash with a gold fringe.

Revisiori attached to the Guard wore a silver aiguillette on the right shoulder.

Breeches, Et cetera

Breeches and waistcoats were white for parade and full dress and dark green for campaign dress; again buttons were silver. Boots were of the cuffed heavy cavalry pattern with silvered spurs.

Equipment

Officers' pattern sword with silvered or gilded hilt, silver sword-knot and tassel, black leather scabbard with gilt fittings. The sword was carried on a black leather waist belt with silver lace trim and silvered fittings, worn under the coat and over the waistcoat.

Horse Furniture

The shabraque and pistol holsters were of the same pattern as that used by General Officers but in red with wide silver lace edge.

Revisore Capo

(Chief Auditor)

The uniform was generally the same as above but with some minor additional decoration.

Headwear

As above with the addition of silver lace along the edge and white feather plumes.

Coat

The coat was of the same colouring and cut as the *Revisori* but had double silver lace on the collar and a silver 'oak leaf' design lace down the front of the coat and around the cuffs and the edges of the coat's tails. His sash was red with a silver fringe.

Commissari di Guerra

(Military Commissaries)

Commissari di Guerra were responsible for arranging and organising quarters and the supply services for the Army both on campaign and during peacetime. The uniform was generally similar in cut and style to the *Revisori Militari.*

Headwear

Black bicorne with National cockade and a silver cockade strap and tassels

Coat

The coat, of the same cut as that of the *Generali*, was light blue with a bright red collar and plain round cuffs and piping to the horizontal pockets. Like the *Generali*' and the *Revisori*' coats it had no turnbacks. The coat fastened with nine silvered buttons.

Commissari on the General Staff had a double silver lace edge to the collar, cuffs and pockets and the silver oak leaf pattern lace on the front of the coat and around the tails.

Commissari attached to Divisions had a single silver lace on the collar, cuffs and pockets.

Commissari 'Ordinari' had silver lace only on the collar and cuffs.

Commissari Aiutanti had silver lace only on the collar but with a narrow dark green lace inside it.

As with the *Revisori*, *Commissari* attached to the *Guardia* had a silver aiguillette at the right shoulder.

Breeches, Et cetera

Breeches and waistcoats were white for parade and full dress and dark green for campaign dress; again buttons were silver. Boots were of the cuffed, heavy cavalry pattern with silvered spurs.

Equipment

Officers' pattern sword with silvered or gilded hilt, silver sword-knot and tassel, black leather scabbard with gilt fittings. The sword was carried on a black leather waist belt with silver lace trim and silvered fittings, worn under the coat and over the waistcoat.

Horse Furniture

The shabraque and pistol holsters were of the same pattern as that used by *Generali* and *Revisori Militari* but were light blue with silver lace.

Engravings (hand coloured) of the Army of Italy in review (Public Domain)
top: 1805, centre: 1807, bottom: 1812
These engravings are three of the five (the remaining two show the Armies of the various pre-Kingdom Republics) that were published in Alesandro Zanoli, *Sulla Milizia Cisalpino-Italiana. Cenni Storico Statistici dal 1796 al 1814*, (Milan: Borroni e Scotti, 1845).
This series of engravings is remarkably accurate and are perhaps the first post-Napoleonic celebrations of the Kingdom's Army. The *Pompiero* of the *Pompieri Della Città di Milano* (centre of illustration 009 with his back to the viewer) was copied essentially unchanged by Knötel for his plate III / 45 (see below). Most other units on these plates can also be easily identified.

2
Guardia Reale (The Royal Guard)

The *Guardia Reale* of the Kingdom of Italy came into existence by a Royal Decree of 20 June 1805. Outwardly it appears to have been organised on the same lines as the French *Garde Impériale* with most of the units corresponding with those of that body although this superficial similarity is illusory albeit that the *Guardia Reale* was, like the *Garde Impériale*, a self-contained force of all arms.

The Decree creating the *Guardia Reale* gave it an initial structure of three defined parts:

Guardie d'Onore (Guards of Honour)
Guardie Veliti (Velite Guards)
Guardie della Linea (Guards of the Line)

More detail on each individual unit is given below under the appropriate section but it should be noted that the first two were essentially training schools for officers whereas only the latter followed the French *Garde Impériale* system of recruiting veterans from the line into an elite combat unit, albeit that, as its title suggests, it was the least prestigious of the three.

To be eligible for admission to the Regiments of the *Guardie della Linea* a recruit was supposed to have had five years service and a good disciplinary record but as these units absorbed the Presidential Guard units (see below) initially at least they were composed of men who had no service record and had simply joined the latter direct from civilian life.

Throughout its existence the *Guardia Reale*, and to a lesser extent the line regiments, contained a number of French officers. Initially these French officers were considered senior to any Italian officer of the same rank, regardless of length of service. However by a Decree of 21 May 1808 Eugène set out that French and Italian officers were to be considered equal, with seniority determined only by length of service of rank.

The Units of the *Guardia Reale*. Plate 48 of Dr Lienhart & R. Humbert, *Les Uniformes de l'Armée Française. Recueil d'Ordonnances de 1690 à 1894, Volume 5*, (Leipzig: Ruhl 1894). (Author's Collection)

2 (1) Cavalry of the *Guardia Reale*

Organisation

The cavalry of the *Guardia Reale* comprised:

> *Guardia Reale d'Onore* of 4, later 5, companies.
> *Dragoni Della Guardia Reale*, of 2 squadrons.
> *Gendarmeria Scelta Della Guardia Reale* of 1 company strength.

The personal escort for the Viceroy was customarily provided by the *Dragoni Della Guardia Reale* and not by the *Guardia Reale d'Onore* as might have been expected – an unkind observer might perhaps suggest that Eugène felt safer if his escort was provided by the regular army proper...

Guardia Reale d'Onore

(Royal Guards of Honour)

History and Organisation

The unit[1] had its origins in the City Guards of Honour that had escorted Napoleon on his entry into Italy even before the Kingdom was proclaimed.[2] These aristocratic bodies were not strictly military units in any sense but were akin to the local landed classes dressing in military uniform to feel important for the day. Napoleon disbanded these local groups with the intention of using their manpower to form the *Guardia Reale d'Onore* and tie himself closer to the aristocracy of his new Kingdom, and that aristocracy to him likewise..

The four, later five, companies of the *Guardia Reale d'Onore della Guardia Reale* were each recruited from one of the four principal Departments of the Kingdom and bore the subsidiary title of that department. The recruiting Departments were:

1st Company *'Milano'*:	Olona, Agogna, Lario, Adda
2nd Company *'Bologna'*:	Reno, Crostolo, Panaro, Mincio
3rd Company *'Brescia'*:	Serio, Alto Po, Mella, Adige
4th Company *'Romagna'*:	Rubicone, Basso Po

In 1806, when the Venetian territories were absorbed into the Kingdom of Italy, a 5th Company *'Venezia'* was raised from the Departments created within the new territory.

The Regiment[3] was considered as a training school for officers and the other ranks as 'officer cadets' who could be promoted into the line cavalry regiments with the rank of *Sotto Tenente* after two years' service.

All rank and file were required to be literate in both Italian and French and have a private income of at least 1,200 Milan Lira per year, which, as in the Velites (see below), was to be paid to the State. The initial voluntary enlistment from the sons of the wealthy proved to be unpopular and enlistment was therefore subsequently made compulsory for any who fulfilled the criteria. Discipline and duties were light and even rank and file *guardia* of the companies had their own grooms, probably for this reason the unit proved less than successful when it participated in the field in 1809 and 1812.

The officers of *Guardia Reale d'Onore*, as with the officers of the French *Garde Impériale*, held a double rank of grading over the line officers, thus a *Sotto Tenente* of the *Guardia Reale d'Onore* ranked as a *Capitano* in the line, et cetera.

The Company establishment was laid out in a Decree of 6 August 1805 as

1 *Capitano*	1 *Tenente*
1 *Sotto Tenente*	1 *Maresciallo d'Alloggio Capo*
4 *Marescialli d'Alloggio*	1 *Brigadiere Furiere*
8 *Brigadieri*	1 *Maniscalo*
2 *Trombettieri*	1 *Tamburino*
86 *Guardie*	

Within this establishment 3 *brigadieri*, 36 *guardie*, and the *tamburo* were to be dismounted.

The *trombettieri*, the *tamburo* and the *maniscalo* were recruited from the line cavalry and were not *Guardia* in the same sense as the troopers.

All companies were commanded only by their own officers and there was no form of regimental organisation or overall command, a situation that added to the chaotic affairs and lack of discipline of the unit – or more strictly, units. To overcome this the *Regolamento di Disciplina Interna ed Administrazione Della R. Guardie d'Onore*[4] were issued on 7 August 1806 and *Gaetano Battaglia*, the Capitano of the 1st Company *'Milano'*, was given overall command of the five companies with the acting rank

1 It is not technically correct to refer to the Companies as a "unit" before 1806, or even perhaps 1808, since they existed as separate Companies but it is so much more convenient to do so, for which I ask the reader's indulgence.

2 Similar local *Gardes d'Honneur* existed throughout France and even in the Netherlands. They frequently seized the honour of escorting The Emperor when he was in their area, militarily though they were insignificant.

3 Whether the Companies should ever truly be considered as a 'Regiment', even after the creation of the Staff in 1808, is arguable but again it is a convenient shorthand to refer to them as such, for which I beg the reader's indulgence.

4 'Regulations of Internal Discipline and Administration….'

of *maggiore* and with the intention that they should be commanded as a single unit.

On 30 March 1807 a company of grooms was formally added to the regimental establishment. The company was formed as five squads of 25, each under a *Capo Spose* ('Head Groom') and each squad was assigned to a specific company.

Finally, on 14 March 1808 a small Regimental Staff of *chirurge*, assistant *chirurge* and a *veterinario* was created, and then later in the same year a second *tenente* was added to the *1°* Company allowing Battaglia to command the Regiment with less responsibility for his own company. At the same time it was decided that all members of the companies were to be mounted which also resulted in the *tamburo* being removed from the company establishments.

Despite all of these theoretical establishments, in 1809 the unit could only raise enough personnel for a single composite company to accompany the army into the field. In July 1807 the *Guardia Reale d'Onore* mustered a strength of only 374 all ranks against an establishment of 535 (see Appendix II for the illustrative strength of the Guard). However when the Army of Italy joined the *Grand Armée* for the Russian campaign of 1812 the five companies were essentially at establishment.

In 1813 the *Guardia Reale d'Onore* who returned from the campaign in Russia were transferred into the line as officers of the reformed Army, and only a single company was raised for the new Army. This single company had a new establishment of:

1 *Capitano*	2 *Tenente*
2 *Sotto Tenente*	1 *Maresciallo d'Alloggio Capo*
6 *Marescialli d'Alloggio*	1 *Brigadiere Furiere*
10 *Brigadieri*	2 *Maniscalo*
1 *Brigadiere Trombettiere*	3 *Trombettieri*
124 *Guardie*	

It was uniformed as the 4th Company *'Romagna'*.

On 16 May 1814, the *Guardie d'Onore* was the first unit of the Royal Guard to be formally disbanded, having already transferred the majority of its personnel to other units.

In the ten years of its existence a total of 895 men had passed through its ranks of whom:

450 were promoted to Officers in other units
106 were discharged for wounds or illness
193 were killed or taken prisoner (mainly in Russia)

Service

1805	
November	Observation Corps against Venice.
1809	One composite company drawn from all troops joined the Army after the Battle of Sacile on 16 April.
8 May	Battle of the Piave
14 June	Battle of Raab
5 July	Battle of Wagram (108 officers and men). No officer casualties, killed or wounded, are recorded during the campaign.
1812	
7 September	Battle of Borodino
24 October	Battle of Maloyaroslavetz
16 November	Battle of Krasnoi[5]
28 November	Battle of the Beresina?
1812	
	During the campaign Martinien records as "Killed or Disappeared"[6]
	5 *Capitani*
	13 *Tenenti* (2 of whom were killed in action)
	1 *Chirurge* (killed in action)
1813–1814	
	Various skirmishes during the defence of the Kingdom but no officers are recorded as killed or wounded during these campaigns
1814	
8 February	Battle of the Mincio (119 officers and men)

5 The 'Battle of Krasnoi' was actually a series of large skirmishes fought between 15 November and 18 November . Casualty returns suggest that that the Army of the Kingdom was heavily involved in the fighting on the 16th.

6 Aristide Martinien, *Tableaux par Corps et par Batailles des Officiers Tués et Blessés Pendant les Guerres de l'Empire 1805–1815*, (Paris: Henri-Charles Lauvazelle, 1899), p.692.

Guardia Reale d'Onore, c. 1806
The four companies of *Guardia Reale d'Onore* in early 1806 before the raising of the 5° Company *'Venezia'*. Left to right the figures are 1° Company *'Milano'*, 2° Company *'Bologna'*, 3° Company *'Brescia'*, 4° Company *'Romagna'*. While at a cursorily glance the footwear appears to be gaiters and boots the artist had actually depicted the heavy cavalry boot. Note that all four are wearing a black bicorne and not the elaborate *Guardia d'Onore* helmet. Undated but it is likely that this illustration is actually from late 1805 or the first half of 1806. (Contemporary illustration by 'CM' in the Anne S. K. Brown Military Collection, Brown University Library)

Uniform

From late 1805 until 1810,[7] at the very latest, each company of the Guards had a unique uniform. While much of the general equipment was the same as that in use post 1810, and described below, the 1805 coats were :-

1st Company *'Milano'*:	Red coat with blue collar, lapels, cuffs and turnbacks, silver buttons and eagles on the turnbacks.
2nd Company *'Bologna'*:	White coat with blue facings.
3rd Company *'Brescia'*:	Blue coat with crimson facings.
4th Company *'Romagna'*:	Green coat faced red.
5th Company *'Venezia'*:	Green coat faced orange.

Initially buttonholes were piped silver although this distinction was officially abolished in August 1806. Horse furniture appears to have been of the company facing colour, piped silver. *Trombettieri* generally wore reversed colours but a contemporary illustration shows a *trombettiere* in a yellow coat faced light blue and with a white helmet crest, unfortunately the company is not recorded, although 'Bologna' would seem the most likely and it is possible that the illustration is *c.* 1811 and not from the early period.

Guardia Reale d'Onore, Milano c. 1805–1809
Dated 1809 in the Anne S. K. Brown Collection the series by 'CM' is actually probably earlier, perhaps 1805–1806. (Contemporary illustration by 'CM' in the Anne S. K. Brown Military Collection, Brown University Library)

7 Alain Pigeard, 'Les Gardes d'Honneur du Royaume d'Italie', in *Tradition No.117, Janvier 1997*, (Paris: Tradition, 1996), pp.12–16 gives a date of 1812 for this change but all other sources consulted put it much earlier.

Guardia Reale d'Onore, Bologna c. 1805–1810, and Trumpeter *c.* 1811–12. Two studies by Henri Boisselier of the uniforms of the Company before the adoption of the green coat by all five companies *c.* 1810. The silver/white lace on the buttonholes is noteworthy, as is the fact that the Company is shown wearing a black bicorne throughout the early period. It is possible that the helmet may not have been worn in anything but full dress or may not even have been fully taken into use until after 1810. (Watercolours in the Author's Collection)

The 'traditional' uniform was introduced as a cost reduction exercise as many families were unwilling to pay the high cost of equipping their sons, resulting in the Guards being severely understrength even at the beginning of 1809. The new uniform was laid down by Decree and thus is more completely documented. Since the coats were issued annually the 'change' would have been fairly swiftly effected

Headwear

The helmet was brass (similar in appearance to that worn by the French Carabiniers after the 1810 dress regulations) with a black woollen caterpillar crest, the lower portion of the helmet, excluding the peak, was a steel 'band' with a crowned[8] 'N' in brass at the front. The peak, chin scales and plume holder were brass and in full dress a white plume was worn at the left-hand side. The brass crest holder comb was in the form of an Eagle with swept back wings; the wings formed the side of the crest, the chest the front of the crest and the eagle's head protruded forward below the caterpillar crest. While some examples of this elaborate helmet actually survive it is arguable how widespread its use really was after 1807, however at some point before 1812 this helmet with its elaborate crest holder had definitively been replaced with the more usual plain brass one. This change may have been at the same time as the change of coat colour but would, no doubt, have taken some time to 'work through' the whole unit since helmets, unlike coats, were not replaced annually.

The *Pokalem* pattern fatigue caps were dark green with piping of the company colour. After 1808 a unique pattern of fatigue cap seems to have come into use; it was similar in appearance to the German *Feldmutz* with soft crown and wide headband and a small patch at the crown from which a short cord and tassel hung, the colouring was the same as for the *Pokalem*.

Coat

The full dress coat was the uniform pattern dark green habit, with the lapels, cuffs and turnbacks of the facing colour, a dark green collar and dark green three-pointed cuff flaps piped with the company facing colour, pockets

8 "crowned" in any reference to the Kingdom of Italy's Army means, of course, with the Iron Crown of Lombardy, not the French Imperial Crown.

Trooper's Helmet *Guardia Reale d'Onore*
Brass skull, Steel turban edged in brass, Brass 'N' and crown, Black woollen caterpillar crest, Brass crest holder and chin scales, Black leather peak bound in brass. (Private Collection, ©photo courtesy of Laurent Claudet)

were piped in the company facing colour. The collar and cuffs both had two narrow white horizontal batons of lace. There were similar lace batons on the lapel buttonholes. Red contra-epaulettes were worn on both shoulders with brass scaled straps, and with a white aiguillette on the right shoulder. All buttons were pewter/white metal.

The undress uniform, also worn on campaign for everyday wear (although the *Guardie d'Onore* would have worn full dress coats into action), was a dark green surtout coat with collar, cuffs, turnbacks and piping as for the habit coat. Epaulettes, et cetera were the same as those worn on the full dress coat and were probably the same items simply transferred from that coat.

Company Facings and Distinctive Colour:

1st Company *'Milano'*	Pink
2nd Company *'Bologna'*	Yellow
3rd Company *'Brescia'*	Buff
4th Company *'Romagna'*	Red
5th Company *'Venezia'*	Orange

Breeches, Et cetera

Breeches and waistcoats were white and boots were of the cuffed, heavy cavalry pattern with blackened iron spurs. White overall trousers were worn with the fatigue coat and after 1810 heavy grey cloth overall trousers with black leather inserts and cuffs and a single row of cloth covered buttons on the outer seam were worn with the surtout coat in campaign dress order.

The dark green greatcoat had a facing colour lining and trim to the edge of the collar and cape, and white metal buttons. Gauntlets were whitened leather.

Equipment

The cartridge box was worn on a white leather belt over the left shoulder and had a large, open brass buckle behind the left shoulder. The cartridge box lid was decorated with a brass crowned eagle badge. The waist belt was white with a closed brass buckle, embossed with a grenade badge. The Regiment's sabres were of a unique pattern having a brass, three bar hilt with the Iron Crown in pierced relief at the side of the basket and they had white sword-straps and knots. Scabbards were polished steel.

Knötel Plate III/29, *Guardia Reale d'Onore* 1812. From Left: Guard, Officer, *trombettiere*, Guard, Officer. (Author's Collection)

Guardia Reale d'Onore, Bologna c1812. These studies by Boisselier, companion pieces to the above, show the new uniform taken into use in 1810. Noticeable, and certainly not in the regulations, the officer is shown continuing to use the earlier buttonhole lace. Note the cloak folded with the yellow facing uppermost on top of the valise and that the *trombettiere* is still depicted with a yellow faced cloak even though *his* facings were actually blue. NB although the second plate is titled 'Brescia', the yellow facings show that this is in fact 'Bologna' – for Boisselier's study of 'Brescia' see below. (Watercolours in the Author's Collection)

Trooper's Sword *Guardia Reale d'Onore*. Buff leather covered hilt bound with brass wire. Steel guard and scabbard. Red cloth 'pad' below the hilt where it rests against the scabbard. (Private Collection, ©photo courtesy of Laurent Claudet)

Officers & N.C.O.s

N.C.O.'s rank was indicated by diagonal bars worn above the cuff in the same way as those worn throughout the Army, vizt:

Trombettiere Maggiori	Two silver bars, piped red
Maresciallo d'Alloggio Capo	Two silver bars, piped red
Marescialli d'Alloggio	A single silver bar, piped red
Brigadieri:	Two white woollen bars piped red.

The aiguillette was mixed silver and red for the senior grades.

Officers' helmets were gilt with silver-plated base, the crowned 'N' was also gilt metal. The coat was the same cut as the rank and file but of finer cloth and with silver rank epaulettes and aiguillettes. All lace was silver. Senior officers used the silver oak leaf design on the collar, cuffs and lapels. Surtouts and stable jackets were as for the men with the addition of officers' rank distinctions. Breeches and waistcoats were white. Belts were white in full dress and black leather for campaign. The cartridge box was decorated with silver lace. The sabre was of the same pattern as the troopers with a gilded hilt and the brass scabbard had black leather inserts. Officers' greatcoats were dark green with wide silver lace trim to the cape and silver piping on the body.

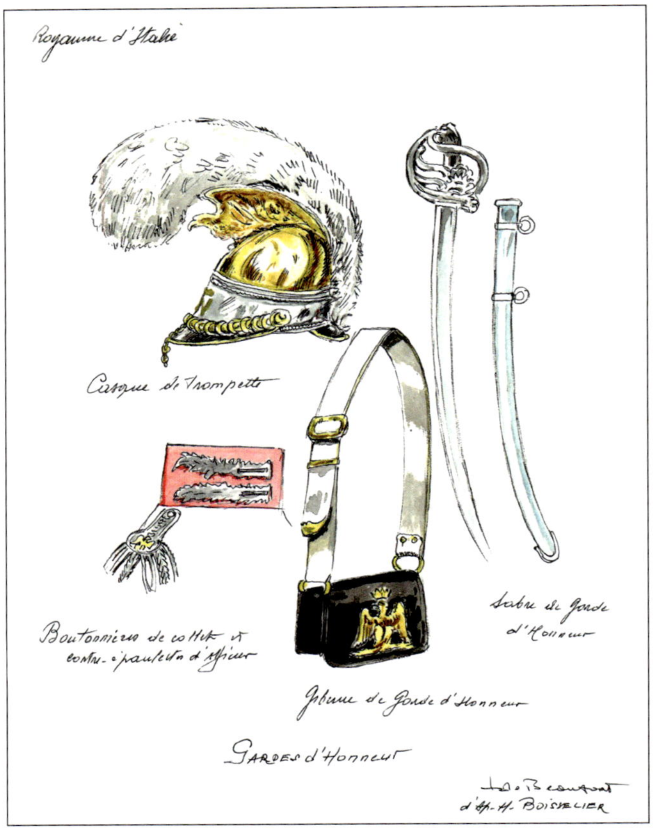

Guardia Reale d'Onore. Details of Equipment. (Watercolour by Henri Boisselier in the Author's Collection)

Musicanti

Initially at least *trombettieri* probably wore coats of reversed colours with white lace on the collar and cuffs and white aiguillettes, although it should be pointed out that this is based on very slight information. The helmet was the same as that for the troopers with a red crest and a plume of either red or facing colour.

Trumpets were brass with silver cords (mixed sky blue and silver for the 2nd and 5th Companies). Trumpet banners were of a 'swallow-tail' design of the troop facing colour with silver fringes. On the obverse the banners had the Iron Crown and laurels all in silver; on the reverse was a laurel wreath encircling the motto 'GUARDIE REALI / D'ONORE', again all in silver.

By 1810/early 1811 the *trombettieri* had adopted a new uniform. Although this was broadly similar to the above and the new uniform coat was still in 'reversed colours', it had sky blue facings and plain white aiguillettes for all companies, the helmet had a white crest (one illustration shows a *trombettiere* of the 5th Company *'Venezia'* with an orange crest) and a white plume.

The Musée de l'Armée in Paris has a late-period helmet of a *trombettieri* from the Regiment in its collection (the troop is unknown) which has a white crest and in all respects, except one, is identical to the trooper's helmet illustrated above. The exception is in the chinscales and the associated boss: the boss is a simple round, indented disc (although this may be the 'underneath' of the lion's head boss) while the chinscales are larger and of a simple oval design, rather than the scalloped edges shown on the example in the photographs of a helmet above.

The *tamburi* were uniformed the same as *trombettieri* although a contemporary illustration shows the *tamburo* of the *1° 'Milano'* company wearing below-knee black gaiters. It appears likely that this may have been repeated across the other companies.

Guardia Reale d'Onore, 'Brescia', 1811–1812. The uniform post the 1810 'regulation' with the facing colour usually described as 'buff' showing a distinct orange hue. The uniform is essentially that laid down in 1810 although the *trombettieri'* red crest is otherwise unrecorded. Also note the grey button-down overalls for wear on the march; these would usually be removed before action. (Watercolour by Henri Boisselier in the Author's Collection)

Horse Furniture

Troopers' shabraques were of the 1805 pattern as used by both the Guard and the line dragoons. These were dark green with a wide outer lace inside which was narrow white piping. The rear corners were decorated with white crowns. The dark green square valise and the double pistol holsters were both trimmed the same as the shabraque. When not in use, the greatcoat was strapped to the top of the portmanteau with the red lining uppermost, except on full dress parades when it appears not to have been carried.

Trombettieri' shabraques were either of the same pattern as the troop or, as some contemporary illustrations show, of the facing colour; both were edged white with an outer piping of facing colour.

Officers' shabraques were dark green with a double wide silver lace stripe along the edge, and a narrow dark green piping along the edges of each stripe. The crowns in the rear corners were of silver embroidery. The pistol holster covers were triple layer and dark green, trimmed in the same manner as the shabraque.

Each company rode a distinctive colour of horses:

1st Company	blacks
2nd Company	bays
3rd Company	blacks
4th Company	bays
5th Company	chestnuts with white socks

Trombettieri of all companies rode the customary greys.

Bivouac of the Guardia Reale d'Onore. Note the unique pattern of fatigue cap. Contemporary engraving from Albrecht Adan et al, *Voyage Pittoresque Et Militaire De Willenberg En Prusse Jusqu'à Moscou Fait En 1812 : Pris Sur Le Terrain Même*, (Munich: Hermann & Barth, 1828). (Public Domain)

Bivouac of the Guardia Reale d'Onore, Marienpol 26 June 1812. Engraving after a contemporary sketch from Albrecht Adan et al, *Voyage Pittoresque Et Militaire De Willenberg En Prusse Jusqu'à Moscou Fait En 1812 : Pris Sur Le Terrain Même*, (Munich: Hermann & Barth, 1828).
Note the mixture of practical service dress and the full dress of the Guard who has obviously just come off duty. (Public Domain)

Dragoni Della Guardia Reale

(Dragoons of the Royal Guard)

History and Organisation

Although the Decree of 20 June 1805 that created the regiment ordered that it was to be recruited from men of the line cavalry of at least five years service and an unblemished record, the *Dragoni Della Guardia Reale* was actually raised by the merging of the two existing cavalry units of the Presidential Guard – the *Granatieri a Cavallo* (who formed the first two companies of the *Dragoni)* and the *Cacciatori di Cavalli* (who formed the second two). Subsequent recruits, however, followed the criteria set down in the 20 June 1805 Decree.

The constituent units of the Regiment were in France when Napoleon was crowned Emperor, and at the time organised as a single squadron of four companies, when they returned to Italy in late 1805 they were organised with a small Regimental Staff and two squadrons each of two companies. The formal establishment of the Regiment was, however, not laid down until 21 May 1808, although it may actually have been similar, if not identical, since 1805. See Appendix II for actual strength return in July 1807, which is illustrative of some part of the establishment.

Knötel Plate III / 18, *Dragoner-Regiment der Königlichen Garde*, 1812 (*Dragoni Della Guardia Reale, 1812*). (Author's Collection)

The May 1808 order set out the Regiment's establishment as :

Regimental Staff	
1 *Colonnello*	1 *Capo Squadrone*
1 *Aiutante Maggiore*	1 *Quartiermaistro Tesoriere*
1 *Sottoaiutante Maggiore*	1 *Portastendardo*
2 *Ufficiali di Sanita*	1 *Sotto Tenente Istruttore*
1 *Veterinario*	1 *Vammastro*
1 *Trombettiere Maggiori*	1 *Brigadiere Trombettiere*
6 *Maestro-artigiani*	(Master craftsmen: boot maker, tailor, breeches maker, armourer, saddler?)[9]
Company Establishment	
1 *Capitano*	2 *Tenente* (1 *1° Classe*, 1 *2° Classe*)
2 *Sotto Tenente*	1 *Maresciallo d'Alloggio Capo*
4 *Marescialli d'Alloggio*	1 *Ottantadue Dragoni*
8 *Brigadieri*	1 *Maniscalo*
2 *Trombettieri*	1 *Tambure*
82 *Dragooni*	

Initially the *Maniscalo* on the staff, and the *tambure* and 22 *dragoni* of each Company, were to be dismounted. By August 1811 the dismounted section had disappeared at which time all ranks are recorded as being mounted and a fifth company was also added to the establishment in that month to act as a depot (although I have been unable to discover the exact date). On 18 November of the same year the company establishment for all companies was raised to 140, including 40 *dragoni 2° Classe*.

In 1813, after returning from the Russian campaign, the Regiment was reformed with a reduced establishment of four companies.

An order of 11 August 1808 set out that the Regiment should be mounted on bay horses, except for the *trombettieri* who were to ride greys.

Service

1809	Joined the Army on 16 April, after the Battle of Sacile
8 May	Battle of the Piave
14 June	Battle of Raab (1 Capitano wounded)
5 July	Battle of Wagram (248 officers and men)
1812	
7 September	Battle of Borodino
24 October	Battle of Maloyaroslavetz
16 November	Battle of Krasnoi
28 November	Battle of the Beresina?
	During the campaign Martinien records "Killed or Disappeared"[10] 2 *Capitani*, 5 *Tenenti*, 1 *Chirurge*
13 December	Skirmish near Kowne (1 *Tenente* wounded)
1813–1814	Defence of the Kingdom of Italy
1813	
16 September	Skirmish at Weisselburg (1 *Capitano*, 2 *Tenenti* wounded)
27 November	Skirmish at Leguano (2 *Tenenti* wounded)
1814	
8 February	Battle of the Mincio (289 officers and men. 2 *Capitani*, 2 *Tenenti* wounded)

Uniform

The uniform of the *Dragoni Della Guardia Reale* was formally laid down in a Decree dated 15 April 1806, prior to which they had worn the uniform of their old units of the Presidential Guard, but as items needed replacement these were of the new *Dragoni Della Guardia Reale* patterns when the older was not in store. The resultant appearance must have been somewhat 'untidy' to say the least. A single contemporary painting records an otherwise unrecorded simplification of the uniform in 1813, but in the absence of any other confirmation I have not repeated this here.

Headwear

The helmet worn by the *Dragoni Della Guardia Reale* was of the same pattern as that of the French and Italian line dragoon regiments. The helmet was brass, with a brass crest embossed with a 'shell' design at the side and embossed on the front with an Italian Eagle bearing a star, with an 'N' surmounted by the Crown of Lombardy at its

9 I have not found the profession of this sixth individual, although all records of the establishment agree that there were six.

10 Aristide Martinien, *Tableaux par Corps et par Batailles des Officiers Tués et Blessés Pendant les Guerres de l'Empire 1805–1815*, (Paris: Henri-Charles Lavauzelle, 1899), p.694.

Dragoni Della Guardia Reale during the 1812 campaign in Russia. Contemporary hand coloured engraving from Albrecht Adam et al, *Voyage Pittoresque Et Militaire De Willenberg En Prusse Jusqu'à Moscou Fait En 1812 : Pris Sur Le Terrain Même*, (Munich: Hermann & Barth, 1828). (Public Domain)

*Dragoni Della Guardia Reale, c.*1812
Dated to c. 1812 this contemporary (or copy of a contemporary?) illustration shows, left to right, *trombettiere*, officer, *zappatore*(?), and two *dragoni*. The centre figure must be presumed to be a sapper since the *Dragoni* did not have an elite company, this is the only indication of a sapper's uniform that I have seen and *zappatore* do not appear on the establishment. It is possible that this is an error on the artist's part and he has confused the Regiment with that of the Line *Dragoni* who did have sappers although the uniform shown is that of the *Guardia*, the other possibility is that the artist presumed the existence of a *zappatore*. (Vinkhuijzen Collection, General Research Division, New York Public Library Digital Collections. Public Domain)

centre. The horsehair tail and houpette were black and the turban was leopard skin, extending over the peak which was trimmed with a narrow brass edging. Chin scales were brass and the full dress plume was red. Fatigue caps were dark green with red piping and grenade badge. Although usually of the *Pokalem* pattern the older line pattern is also illustrated suggesting that, as so often, older stocks continued to be used and issued.

Coat

The dark green coat was the usual pattern in the Army and of the same cut as that worn by the two line dragoon regiments. It had a dark green collar without piping, white lapels and red 'Brandenburg cuffs' with white three-pointed cuff flaps.[11] The turnbacks were red with white grenade badges mounted on a green cloth backing that showed as a narrow edge to the badge, by 1812 however (and I have been unable to find a date for the change) the turnback badges were a white 'Iron Crown' device. Red contra-epaulettes were worn on both shoulders with brass scaled straps and with a white aiguillette on the right shoulder. All buttons were pewter and embossed with a crowned 'N' (the crown was, of course, the Iron Crown of Lombardy).

To protect and preserve the expensive full dress coat, on campaign the regiment wore a dark green surtout coat with a green collar piped red, all other facings and details were as for the habit.

Breeches, Et cetera

The breeches and waistcoat were white with pewter buttons (smaller versions of those on the coat). The boots were of the cuffed, heavy cavalry pattern with steel spurs. Greatcoats were dark green, with a dark green collar, all lined red. The greatcoats are sometimes shown with red piping at the edges and along the edge of the collar, although this could simply be the lining showing. Buttons were white metal. Gauntlets were whitened leather,

11 A surviving coat has dark green cuffs and cuff flaps, both unpiped. This variation is not otherwise recorded.

Equipment

A whitened leather pouch belt was worn over the left shoulder supporting a black leather cartridge box; the belt had a large, open, brass buckle behind the shoulder. The cartridge box lid was decorated with a brass crowned eagle badge. The waist belt was white with a closed brass buckle, embossed with a grenade badge. The straight heavy cavalry sword had a three bar hilt and a white sword-knot and tassel; it was carried in a brass scabbard with black inserts on double slings from the waist belt. On campaign the belt was often worn over the right shoulder, and with the pouch belt, thus gave the appearance of cross belts.

The musket was a shorter version of the same weapon as that carried by the infantry, and was of the same bore, thus it was a true musket and not a cavalry carbine. The infantry musket was bound and fitted in steel but it appears that the *Dragoni Della Guardia Reale* had a variant bound and fitted with brass as used by the French *Garde Impériale*. The musket had a whitened leather sling with a brass buckle. When mounted, the *dragoni* carried their muskets in a bucket, butt downward, on the right side of the saddle.

Officers & N.C.O.s

N.C.O.'s rank was indicated by diagonal bars worn above the cuff in the same way as those worn throughout the Army, vizt:

Trombetta-Maggiori	Two silver bars, piped red
Maresciallo d'Alloggio Capo	Two silver bars, piped red
Marescialli d'Alloggio	A single silver bar, piped red
Brigadieri	Two white woollen bars piped red.

The aiguillette was mixed silver and red for the senior grades.

The officer's helmet was the same pattern as the troopers' but all brass was gilded.

The coat was of the same cut as the rest of the unit with silver epaulettes of rank, silver aiguillettes and turnback badges and silver cords worn on the right shoulder. Belts were white for full dress and black leather for campaign

Dragoni Della Guardia Reale, Officer 1805. The use of double pistol holster covers in place of the usual triple cover may be related to the early date and the use of older equipment although it is possible, albeit unlikely, that it was an error on Boisseiler's part. (Watercolour by Henri Boisselier in the Author's Collection)

Dragoni Della Guardia Reale, *Colonello* and *Capitano*, 1811–1812. Note the eccentric personalisation of fringing that the *Colonello* has added to his pistol holsters and saddlecloth. The latter also appears to have rounded, rather than pointed, rear corners. (Watercolour by Henri Boisselier in the Author's Collection)

wear. Officers' greatcoats were dark green, double-breasted and trimmed with silver lace on the collar and edge.

Officers wore silver epaulettes to show ranks in a sequence identical throughout the Army

Colonello / Colonello Sotto	Two silver bullion-fringed epaulettes
Maggiore	As above but with gold straps.
Capo Battaglione	Silver bullion fringe epaulette on the right shoulder, contre-epaulette on the left.
Capitano	As above but fine fringed epaulette
Tenente	As above but with a narrow red stripe along the straps
Sotto Tenente	As above but with two red stripes

The *Aiutante*, usually (although not necessarily) a *Capitano*, wore the *Capitano* epaulettes of rank but on opposite shoulders.

Trombettieri

The *trombettieri*' helmets were the same pattern as that of other ranks but with a red mane black houpette and sky blue plume. Fatigue caps were sky blue with white piping and white grenade badge.

The *trombettieri* wore a sky blue habit with red collar, lapels, turnbacks, cuffs and cuff flaps. The epaulettes were the same as worn by the troopers with a mixed red and white aiguillette. The collar, lapels and cuffs were trimmed with 3cm of silver lace and the buttonholes were edged with silver lace with small tassels on the inside ends. The pockets were piped red. The two buttons at the rear waist of the coat had a silver lace 'trefoil' pattern around them. The pockets were piped red. The turnbacks badge was a white grenade. All buttons were pewter.

For campaign dress *trombettieri* used a sky blue surtout with all facings as for the habit and narrow silver lace on the collar and cuffs.

Breeches and boots were as for the other ranks, waistcoats were white with pewter buttons

The trumpets were brass with white or mixed white and crimson cords, and the crimson trumpet banner was square with silver fringes at all four edges, and embroidered with an Imperial Eagle surrounded by a laurel, all in silver.

Belts and swords were the same as those used by the troopers but the sword-knot was red. Greatcoats were sky blue with a white lining.

Horse Furniture

The dark green shabraque was the 1805 pattern used by the line *dragoni*, with double pistol holster covers and black leather saddle. The shabraque had white lace piped in dark green, and the pistol holsters were decorated the same. The rear corners of the shabraque had an embroidered white grenade badge. The valise was dark green with white lace, and when not in use, the greatcoat was strapped to the top of the portmanteau with the red lining uppermost.

Dragoni Della Guardia Reale, Dragoon and Trumpeter, 1811–1812. Uniformed following regulations but note the method of carrying the dragoon musket, this was longer than the standard cavalry carbine and could not therefore be carried on a swivel and belt. Dragoons in the French Army carried their muskets in the same way.

The design on the trumpet banner is unclear here but it is shown in a line drawing which appeared in *Carnet de la Sabretache 1971*, plate 59. The banner was red and of a swallow-tail form, fringed in silver. The design showed the Imperial Eagle surmounted by an Imperial Crown and with the star and Iron Crown disc on its chest. Above this was a three part scroll in white with the legend GUARDIA / REALE / ITALIANA in black. In each corner of the banner was a grenade badge. All embroidery was in silver.

Note that on the 'detail' illustration of a helmet of a senior officer the leopard skin turban extends across the peak. (Watercolour by Henri Boisselier in the Author's Collection)

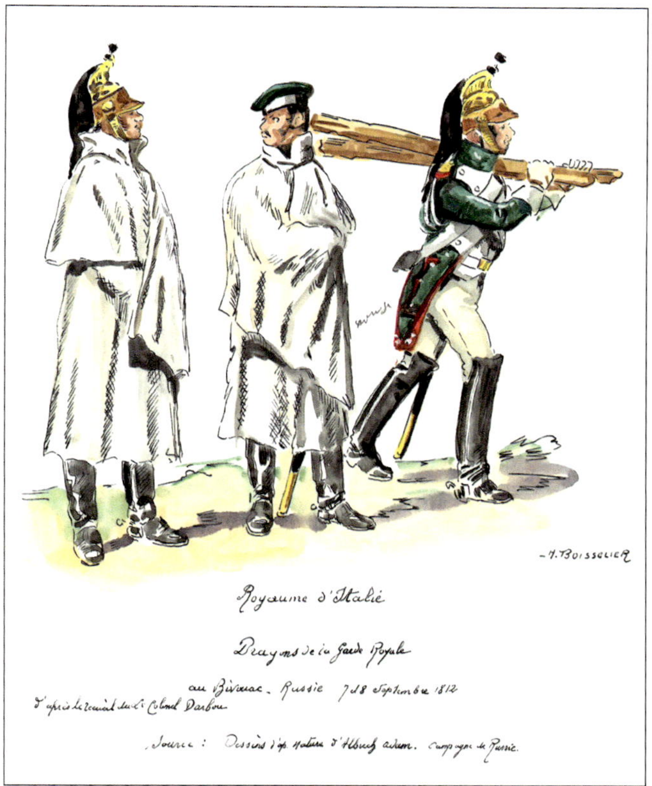

Dragoni Della Guardia Reale, *Dragoni* 1812
Dragoni in regulation overcoat/cloak. Essentially these figures confirm the contemporary work of Albrecht Adam. (Watercolour by Henri Boisselier in the Author's Collection)

Dragoni Della Guardia Reale, *Dragoni* 1812
Left: Officer in full dress (see text).
Centre: *Trombettiere* in full dress. The appearance of this *trombettiere* is virtually identical to that of a *trompette* of the French *Garde Impériale* save only for the red mane on the helmet, which may (and this is pure speculation) have been the reason for its adoption. The absence of turnback badges is probably an error on the artist's part.
Right: *Dragone* in stable dress wearing the greatcoat/cape. Note that he is not wearing his (expensive) coat, note also the pattern of the fatigue cap, and the fullness of the greatcoat which would, when mounted, also provide some protection for the flanks of the horse.
(Watercolour by Henri Boisselier in the Author's Collection)

Officers' shabraques were dark green with a double silver lace edging each piped red, the outer twice the width of the inner.

Trombettieri' shabraques were the same as those of the officers but with white lace in place of the silver. The valise was sky blue trimmed with white.

By an Order of 11 August 1808 the Regiment was to be mounted on bay horses with *trombettieri* on the traditional greys.

Gendarmeria Scelta Della Guardia Reale

(Elite Gendarmes of the Royal Guard)

History and Organisation

The *Gendarmeria Scelta* was organised as only a single, very weak, company and was formally raised by a Decree of 6 September 1808 for police and security duties within the Royal Palace, and the Royal Guard's Camp when on campaign. From the creation of the Kingdom until 1807 the unit's duties had been carried out by a detachment of the *Gendarmerie d'Elite* of the French *Garde Impériale* but when these were recalled to France at the

Dragoni Della Guardia Reale, Dragoni 1805
Dated 1809 in the Anne S. K. Brown Collection the series by 'CM' is actually probably earlier, perhaps 1805–1806, although as there were no uniform changes such dating, in this case, is academic only. The rosette at the horse's head does not appear to be regulation but may be purely something given to this individual. (Contemporary illustration by 'CM' in the Anne S. K. Brown Military Collection, Brown University Library)

end of 1807, Eugène retained two officers and twenty-five gendarmes in Italy who became the nucleus of the *Gendarmeria Scelta*.

The *Gendarmeria*'s full establishment was three officers (sources vary as to the commander's rank, either a *Capo di Squadrone* or a *Capitano*), three *sergenti*,[12] four *brigadieri*, one *trombettiere*, one *maniscalo* and fifty-five *gendarmi*.[13] For administrative purposes the *Gendarmeria Scelta* were attached to the *Dragoni della Guardia* as a "sub-division".

Gendarmeria Scelta Della Guardia Reale, c1810. The similarity to the *Gendarmes d'Elite* of the French *Garde Impériale* is clearly visible in this illustration but given the close relationship to them at their raising (see the information in the text) this is perhaps not surprising. The only difference from the uniform of 1812 is the colouring – after c1812 the dark blue coat, saddlecloth, et cetera were all changed to dark green. (Vinkhuijzen Collection, General Research Division, New York Public Library Digital Collections. Public Domain)

12 Literally "Deputy Marshals", equivalent in effect to sergeants.
13 Originally recruited one from each of the 30 Departments, plus the twenty-five French Gendarmes.

Service

The *Gendarmeria Scelta* was not a field combat unit although it was present with the Army at most, if not all, of its actions even if it generally served at Headquarters. *Tenente* Durand of the *Gendarmeria* was wounded at Raab on 14 June 1809, although this is the only recorded officer casualty during any of the Army's campaigns.

Uniform

The uniform of the company of *Gendarmeria* was not laid down in the 1808 Decree and, almost by default, they were initially uniformed almost identically to their counterparts of French *Garde Impériale*, whose men had provided the original cadre of the unit.

Headwear

The headwear was a black peaked bearskin without front plate; the chin scales were brass and the shiny leather peak was bound in brass. The patch at the rear was crimson with a white grenade. The full dress cords were white and the plume, worn above the National cockade on the left of the cap, was red.

For service on foot the *Gendarmeria Scelta* wore the black bicorne with National cockade and a red carrot-shaped pompom. Fatigue caps were dark blue with crimson piping and tassels.

Coat

The dark blue habit had crimson collar, lapels, cuffs, cuff flaps and turnbacks, all piped dark blue. The pockets were piped in crimson and the turnback devices were white grenades. A white, fringed epaulette was worn on the right shoulder and a trefoil epaulette and an aiguillette on the left. All buttons were pewter. Before 1813 (perhaps when the unit was reformed after the campaign in Russia?) the coat was changed to dark green in place of the blue but all other details remained the same.

Breeches, Et cetera

Waistcoats were buff coloured cloth but the breeches were soft buff leather. Boots were of the high, heavy cavalry pattern with steel spurs. On foot the *Gendarmeria Scelta* wore high, black gaiters with cloth covered buttons.

Greatcoats were dark blue with white metal buttons and crimson lining. I have come across no confirmation that the greatcoats changed to dark green in line with the coat, but given the longevity of such items even if intended it is unlikely that it came into effect before the fall of the Kingdom. Gauntlets were white with buff cuffs.

Equipment

Equipment was of the same pattern as that in use by the *Dragoni della Guardia* except that the *Gendarmeria* wore the light cavalry pattern waist belt and carried the light cavalry pattern sabre, with a white sword-knot and tassel. All belts were buff leather edged white, again in the same manner as the Gendarmes of the French *Garde Impériale*.

Officers & N.C.O.s

All rank distinctions and badges were the same as those used by the Royal Guard's infantry. Officers' belts were buff leather edged silver and their dark blue greatcoats were trimmed silver along the edge of the cape and perhaps on the cuffs. Officers carried the light cavalry pattern sabre with a silver sword-knot and tassel. The sub-division's commander wore a white plume in his bearskin.

Musicanti

The *trombettiere'* uniform was generally of the same appearance as that of the rest of the unit although of a different colouring. The cords of the bearskin were mixed crimson and white and the plume was crimson tipped white. The coat was crimson with crimson collar, light blue cuffs, lapels, turnbacks and piping on the pockets and silver lace on the collar lapels and turnbacks. The aiguillette and epaulette were mixed light blue and white. The *trombettiere'* cloak was light blue lined crimson. Trumpets were brass with mixed crimson and white cords.

Horse Furniture

The dark blue shabraques were of the *Dragoni della Guardia* pattern with triple holster covers; both holster covers and shabraque were edged with a wide white lace piped crimson and the shabraque had white grenades at the rear corners. The valise was dark blue with white trim. The *trombettieri'* shabraques were of the same pattern and were crimson with white edging piped dark blue. Officers had silver lace piped dark blue in place of the white piped crimson and silver grenades in the rear corners. It is *possible*[14] that the dark blue changed to dark green at the same time as the regiment's coat colour changed.

14 Aesthetically it would seem more pleasing to the eye, and that was often important particularly in elite units.

2 (2), Infantry of the *Guardia Reale*

Reggimento di Fanteria della Guardia Reale

(The Infantry Regiments of the Royal Guard)

History and Organisation

The senior Regiment of Infantry of the *Guardia Reale* was created by the Decree of 26 June 1805 and was created from, and absorbed, the units of *Granatieri* and *Cacciatori della Guardia del Presidente*[15] (the Presidential Guard) of the defunct Italian Republic.

Although often considered as two units the *Granatieri* and *Cacciatori* were officially the 1st and 2nd battalions respectively of the same regiment and shared a single Regimental Staff.

Knötel Plate III / 59, Infantry of the *Guardia Reale*, 1812. (Author's Collection)

The Regimental strength was laid down as a Regimental Staff and two battalions, each of five companies, and an Order of 14 March 1808 confirmed the establishments as

Regimental Staff	
1 *Colonnello*	1 *Maggiore*
2 *Capo Battaglione*	2 *Aiutanti-Maggiori*
2 *Sottoaiutanti-Maggiori*	1 *Quartiermaistro*
2 *Ufficialo di Santa*	2 *Aquile-Alfiori*
1 *Vammastro*[16]	1 *Tamburo Maggiore*
1 *Caporale-Tamburo*	30 *Musicanti*
4 *Maestro-Artigiani* (master craftsmen: bootmaker, tailor, breeches maker, armourer)	
Company Establishment	
1 *Capitano*	1 *Tenente 1ª Classe*
1 *Tenente 2ª Classe*	1 *Sotto Tenente*
1 *Sergente Maggiore*	4 *Sergenti*
1 *Quartiermaistro*	8 *Caporali*
3 *Tamburi*	2 *Zappatori*
82 *Soldati*	

A Decree of 16 October 1808 increased the Company establishment to 140 officers and men.

On 12 April 1811, an artillery company was added to the Regiment, with two 3pdr pieces, drawn by eight horses each.

In the rebuilding and reorganisation of the *Guardia Reale* in 1813 following its near-complete destruction in Russia the *Carabinieri* battalion (ex *Cacciatori*) was disbanded. The survivors were drafted into the *Granatieri* and the *Carabinieri* battalion itself was replaced in the establishment with a second battalion of *Granatieri*, the Regiment then formally became the *Granatieri a Piedi della Guardia Reale.*

Throughout the Regiment's existence the 5th Company appears to have existed as essentially a depot company, rather than a field company.

It is perhaps worth noting that the uniform of this regiment was not laid down in the initial decrees and at first its personnel continued to wear the uniform of the old *Guardia del Presidente* although the uniform quickly evolved into a copy of that worn by the French *Garde Impériale*. Most of the differences, particularly for the *Granatieri*, could have been achieved simply by altering current equipment rather than the expense of issuing new. The old *Guardia del Presidente* uniform of

15 These two battalions each had an establishment of eight companies totalling 546 men making them somewhat larger that the new *Guardia Reale* units and the creation of the new unit resulted in an excess of officers and N.C.O.s, many of whom entered the line regiments.

16 Apparently unique to the *Guardia*, this was an N.C.O. in charge of the regimental wagons.

the *Cacciatori* was replaced by one resembling that of the *Granatieri* by an Order dated 15 April 1806.

Granatieri a Piedi Della Guardia Reale

(Foot Grenadiers of the Royal Guard)

Service

1805	
14 October	Surrender at Ulm
2 December	Battle of Austerlitz
1809	Joined the Army after the Battle of Sacile on 16 April.
27 to 30 April	Battle of Caldiero
8 May	Battle of the Piave
14 June	Battle of Raab
5 July	Battle of Wagram (343 officers and men)
1812	
7 September	Battle of Borodino
24 October	Battle of Maloyaroslavetz
16 November	Battle of Krasnoi
28 November	Battle of the Beresina ?
	During the campaign Martinien records "Killed or Disappeared"[17] 1 *Capitano*, 11 *Tenenti*, 2 *Chirurgi*
1813–1814	Defence of the Kingdom of Italy
1813	
5 May	Skirmish at Gesdorf (1 *Capitano* wounded)
1814	
8 February	Battle of the Mincio (522 officers and men)
16 February	Skirmish at Salo (2 *Capitani* and 2 *Tenenti* wounded)

Uniform

Headwear

From at least mid-1806 the *Granatieri* wore a black bearskin of a pattern identical to that of the Grenadiers of French *Garde Impériale* but with a white metal plate embossed with the Imperial Eagle with the letters R and I on either side. The patch at the rear of the bonnet was red with a white cross, replaced from 1809–10 with a white grenade. The full dress cords and flounders were white. The National cockade was worn on the left side of the bearskin and, in full dress, this was surmounted by a tall red plume.

When the regiment was created in 1805 it continued to wear the bearskin of the previous *Guardia del Presidente*, which was similar to the above but had a shiny black leather peak, a brass plate embossed with a grenade and double cords. Given the usual contemporary habit of the reuse of obsolete equipment so far as it was possible, it is probable that many of these bearskins were 'adapted' to reflect the new pattern and continued in use until they were worn out or lost. Perhaps it would not be unrealistic to have seen some companies with the peakless bearskin and others wearing bearskins with peaks throughout 1805 and early 1806 as the 'updating' of these proceeded throughout the Regiment until eventually everyone had the new version, or something that equated closely to it. The 'Weiland manuscript', dated to c.1806, shows a

Granatieri a Piedi Della Guardia Reale, c1806
Although sometimes dated to 1812 the white cross on the patch at the rear shows this dates to 1810 or earlier. The plates of the *fanteria di linea reggimenti* (see below) indicate that these paintings may have been made around early 1806. The uniform is regulation except for the use of a brass, in place of white metal, eagle on the cartridge box flap and the omission of the small grenades in the corners. This may be an example of the initial use of some French equipment by the Regiment. The shade of green and red shown is probably due to the pigmentation changing in the two centuries since it was painted rather than an exact reflection of that in use. (Contemporary illustration by 'CM' in the Anne S. K. Brown Military Collection, Brown University Library.)

17 Aristide Martinien, *Tableaux par Corps et par Batailles des Officiers Tués et Blessés Pendant les Guerres de l'Empire 1805–1815*, (Paris: Henri-Charles Lavauzelle 1899), p.692.

Granatiere of the *Guardia Reale*[18] in the new pattern of bearskin, the single cords of the new regulations but the Guardia del Presidente pattern plate – suggesting it was an old pattern bearskin which had been 'adapted'.

Fatigue caps, of the French pattern, were dark green with red piping and tassels and had a red grenade on the front.

Coat Button of the pattern used throughout the Guardia Reale. Note the design on the breast of the Eagle, *c.f.* the pouch badge below. (Private Collection, ©photo courtesy of Laurent Claudet)

Coat

The dark green habit[19] was of the same pattern as that worn by the French Army and the majority of the Italian Army, although if the French Guard is a guide it was made from a finer cloth. It had a red collar, cuffs and turnbacks, white lapels and three-pointed cuff flaps, all unpiped. The turnback device was a white grenade and the vertical pockets were piped red. The full-fringed epaulettes were red and all buttons were pewter. For campaign wear the regiment wore a dark green surtout with all details the same as the full dress coat.[20]

Breeches, Et cetera

Breeches and waistcoats were white, with pewter buttons; the over-the-knee gaiters were white for full dress and black for campaign wear, both had white metal buttons. Dark green overall trousers were also issued for campaign wear with the surtout coat and bicorne hat. The greatcoat was dark blue, double-breasted with two rows of white metal buttons and it was worn with epaulettes transferred from the coat. The senior infantry regiments of the French *Garde Impériale* were unique in wearing double-breasted greatcoats and it is not a stretch to suggest that the Italian *Guardia* received their initial issues and stock from the Depot of the French *Garde* as suggested by the blue colour. According to French regulations a greatcoat was to last a minimum of two years so coats issued in 1805 would still be in use in 1807 and it was therefore more economical to continue their manufacture in blue than replace the perfectly good coats in issue, which becomes a self-perpetuating custom. (This is the author's speculation and suggestion, nothing has come to light to confirm, or discredit, the suggestion.)

Equipment

All equipment was of the same design as that of the elite companies of the line infantry with whitened leather belting and brass buckles and fittings. Cartridge boxes were black leather with a white metal Royal Eagle[21] surmounted by the Iron Crown on the flap and a small grenade in each corner. In 1805 the flap is often shown as decorated with a simple brass grenade, presumably the older pattern from the Presidential Guard. The

Large Eagle Badge of the pattern used throughout the Royal Guard, this example is probably from the lid of a Cartridge Box. Note the design on the breast of the Eagle. (Private Collection, ©photo courtesy of Laurent Claudet)

18 Alain Pigeard (ed.), *Le Manuscrit de Weiland: Uniformes de l'Armée Français et de ses Alliés de 1806 à 1815*, (Paris: Tradition, 1998), p.28.

19 It is worth noting that Weiland's work, published in 1807, although probably compiled the previous year, shows a Grenadier of the Italian Guard still wearing what was probably a coat of the previous Presidential Guard pattern with white fringed epaulettes and red lapels piped white. Alain Pigeard (ed.), *Le Manuscrit de Weiland : Uniformes de l'Armée Français et de ses Alliés de 1806 à 1815*, (Paris: Tradition, 1998), p.28. As with all such things coats would be issued from the depot until stocks were exhausted whatever new regulations had been promulgated since they had been made.

20 The senior infantry regiments of the French *Garde Impériale* famously donned their full dress uniform before battle and there is some evidence that the *Guardia Reale* did the same.

21 The Italian Royal Eagle faced to its right while the French Imperial Eagle faced to its left.

sabre-briquet was of the usual pattern with a brass hilt and carried in a black scabbard fitted in brass, the sword-strap was white with a red knot and tassel. The bayonet was carried in a brown leather scabbard fitted in either iron or brass.

N.C.O.s

Unsurprisingly the Italian Army followed the French system of rank distinctions; the senior grades of non-commissioned officers using silver or gold thread worked through the bearskin cords and epaulette fringes. The knot of the sabre-briquet was mixed silver and red.

Rank was indicated by diagonal bars worn above the cuff, in exactly the same form as those of the French Army:

Sergente Maggiore	Two diagonal silver bars, piped with the regimental colour.
Sergente	A single bar as above
Caporale	Two white woollen bars piped with the regimental piping colour.
Caporale Furiere	As above, with the addition of a silver lace inverted chevron on the upper right sleeve.

The *aiutante-sottufficiale* wore the uniform of a *sotto tenente* with the epaulettes reversed, although without a gorget plate and with the sabre-strap as for an N.C.O.

Caporali were uniformed, armed and equipped identically to the reminder of their company, their rank indicated only by their rank stripes.

Officers

Officers' bearskins were of the same pattern as that of the other ranks but the cords were silver.[22] The plate was also often silvered.

Staff officers, the *Capo di Battaglione* and all field officers wore white plumes, company officers wore plumes of the same colour as the rank and file of their company.

As with the line infantry (see below), in undress and for campaign officers are often shown wearing the surtout with dark green waistcoats and breeches.

Officers' rank was indicated by their epaulettes, vizt:

Colonello/ Colonello Sotto	Two silver bullion-fringed epaulettes
Maggiore	As above but with gold straps
Capo Battaglione	Silver bullion fringe epaulette on the right shoulder, contre-epaulette on the left
Capitano	As above but fine fringed epaulette
Tenente	As above but with a narrow red stripe along the straps
Sotto Tenente	As above but with two red stripes

The *Aiutante*, usually a *Capitano*, wore the same uniform with the epaulettes of rank on opposite shoulders.

Musicanti

Tamburi wore the uniform of the other ranks but two variations of the coat are recorded. The first is the same cut and pattern as that of the rank and file with the addition of red and white *tamburi* lace on the collar, cuffs, lapels and pockets. The second has silver lace in place of the red and white and also has silver lace on the buttons and buttonholes. Other details of equipment, et cetera were as for the *tamburi* of the line infantry. The brass barrel of the drums was embossed with steel grenade badges and is often shown with mid-blue hoops in place of red and white hoops.

Tamburo Maggiore c. 1809: Black bicorne with white feather edging, trimmed with a silver scallop-edged lace and tassels, a tall white plume with two red and one green ostrich feathers at the base, National cockade. The coat was dark green with a dark green collar, but otherwise the same colouring as the rank and file. The collar, lapels, cuffs, cuff flaps and turnbacks were all edged with silver lace, and the buttons and buttonholes had silver lace trim. The fringed epaulettes were silver and the rank stripes were silver piped in red (the turnback badges, not visible in the illustration these details are mainly taken from, were silver). The waistcoat had silver trim to the pockets and front and lower edge. All buttons were silver. The breeches had silver spearheads on the thighs and the short black ankle-boots had silver fringing around the top. The Drum Major's baldric was red edged with silver and with a silver drumstick plate on the chest, the waist belt was the same colour, with a silver buckle plate embossed with the Imperial Eagle. The sword was an infantry officer's pattern sabre with silver hilt, sword-knot and tassel, carried in a black leather scabbard fitted in silver. The gauntlets were white with silver scallop-edge lace on the cuffs. The baton was brown wood, fitted in silver with silver cords.

Musicanti c. 1809: Similar uniform to the *Tamburo Maggiore* but with silver trefoil epaulettes in place of full-fringed ones, no shoulder belt and a plain white waist belt supporting an infantry officer's English pattern boots.

22 If the Army of Italy followed the formula of other nations (and of the British and Danish Guards even today) then officers' bearskins were made of a finer fur than that of the men. The officers' bearskins used the fur of the female bear, the rank and file's used the fur of the male.

Zappatori

The *zappatori* wore the same basic uniform as the rank and file but with the addition of a red *zappatori* badge on the upper part of both sleeves. This badge was in the form of crossed axes with a red grenade above. *Zappatori* had the usual white leather apron, and the smaller cartridge box worn on the right hip. The musket was of the same calibre as those of the rank and file but of a shorter, lighter pattern. In all Guard Regiments muskets were bound and fitted with brass. The axe had a black wooden shaft and a brass heel. All other details and equipment were as for the line regiments.

Regimental Artillery Company

Very little information survives on the dress of the regimental artillery companies of the Guard beyond a brief note by Prince Eugène of 27 April 1811 which states that they were to have a bearskin, dark green coat with dark green collar, cuffs and lapels piped red, red turnbacks and cuff flaps. The company probably had dark green breeches and a mid to dark grey greatcoat.

Eugène ordered that this uniform was also to be that of the artillery companies of the other foot regiments of the Guard, although presumably with the shako replacing the bearskin as appropriate.

Cacciatori / Carabinieri a Piedi Della Guardia

(Foot Chasseurs / Carabiniers of the Royal Guard)

History and Organisation

Originally titled as *Cacciatori*, the battalion's title was changed to *Carabinieri Della Guardia Reale* in 1810. As mentioned above the battalion was disbanded in 1813 following the 1812 campaign in Russia and the survivors were drafted into the *Granatieri*.

Service

1805	
14 October	Surrender at Ulm
2 December	Battle of Austerlitz
1806	
20 March to 2 June	Siege of Colberg
1807	
15 January to 20 August	Siege of Straslund
1808	Dalmatia
1809	
27 to 30 April	Battle of Caldiero
14 June	Battle of Raab
5 July	Battle of Wagram (349 officers and men)
1812	
7 September	Battle of Borodino
24 October	Battle of Maloyaroslavets
16 November	Battle of Krasnoi
28 November	Battle of the Beresina?

Martinien records no casualties from this battalion at any action although it is more than possible that some of its casualties are recorded under the *Granatieri* and perhaps in 1812 are recorded under the *Conscritti* (who from 1813 carried the same Regimental name).

Uniform

Until April 1806

Before it was changed by the Order of 15 April 1806 the battalion continued to wear the uniform it had been using at its raising in May 1804, and had worn as part of the *Guardia del Presidente*. This consisted of a leather helmet, similar to that worn by the Austrian Army of the period although without the crest, a red coat, with all facings in green, white waistcoat and breeches and short black gaiters. The only known illustration of this uniform by Hoffmann when the battalion was in Paris for the Imperial Coronation in 1804, he shows the red coat but with a green waistcoat and a shako.

The new uniform of 1806 appears to have come into use fairly swiftly however and no vestiges of the old uniform remain by the time the painter/compiler of 'the Otto Manuscript' made his observations in 1807.[23]

Uniform from the 1806 Regulations

Headwear

The bearskin was of the line light infantry pattern; black fur without a front plate and with a red patch decorated with either a white hunting horn or possibly a simple white cross. The full dress cords were white and the plume was dark green tipped red, above the National cockade. Fatigue caps were dark green with red piping and tassel with a red bugle horn at the front.

23 The best modern version of the manuscript is that edited by Guy Dempsey, *Napoleon's Soldiers: The Grande Armée of 1807 as Depicted in the Painting of the Otto Manuscript*, (London: Arms and Armour Press, 1994). This is an absolutely invaluable guide to the actual appearance of the *Grande Armée* as opposed to what the various regulations said it was supposed to look like.

Coat

The dark green habit coat had pointed lapels and cuffs. The lapels were white and the collar, turnbacks and cuffs red. Turnbacks were decorated with white bugle horn patches and the pockets were piped red. The epaulettes were originally yellow with a green fringe and crescent but this was swiftly altered (by 1806) to green straps with red crescents and fringes. All buttons were pewter. The surtout was the same pattern as that of the *Granatieri* but with pointed cuffs and bugle horn badges on the turnbacks.

Breeches, Et cetera

All details the same as those for the *Granatieri*. When the greatcoat was worn, as was customary the epaulettes were transferred from the coat and worn on the greatcoat.

Equipment

Of the same pattern as used by the *Granatieri* but the sword-knot was green with red tassel.

Officers & N.C.O.s

N.C.O. rank stripes were in the form of chevrons, in keeping with the pointed 'Polish' cuffs of the coats. All other details and variations were as used by the *Granatieri a Piedi Della Guardia Reale* (see above).

Musicanti

Tamburo Maggiore c.1809:[24] Black bicorne with silver lace figured with a zigzag pattern along the edge and a short white feather edging trim, and silver tassels. National cockade secured with a silver strap and button. The coat was dark green with a red collar, green (pointed) lapels, green cuffs and red cuff flaps, unusually the cuffs are not of 'Polish' pattern. The turnbacks cannot be seen but as the coat has a red lining it may be assumed that they are red with silver devices. The collar, lapels, cuffs, and turnbacks(?) are all edged with a wide silver lace, the cuff flaps with a narrow silver piping. The fringed epaulettes are silver but notably no rank stripes are shown. The waistcoat and breeches are white, without decoration. All buttons are silver. The Drum Major's baldric is red edged with wide silver lace and, outside that, a short silver fringing. A zigzag pattern of wide silver lace runs along the complete length of the baldric. The sword is the infantry officer's straight epée with a gilt hilt, but no sword-knot or tassel, and is carried in a black leather scabbard fitted gold. No waist belt is visible. The gauntlets are white and the officer wears standard pattern 'jockey boots'. The baton is brown wood, fitted in silver with silver cords.

Tamburi: of the *Carabinieri* had the same distinctions as the *Granatieri* but with the brass drum barrels embossed with bugle horns in place of the grenades of the latter.

Zappatori

Zappatore distinctions were the same as those for the *zappatori* of the *Granatieri*.

Veliti Della Guardia Reale

(Velites of the Royal Guard)

History and Organisation

The Decree which created the *Guardia Reale* specified that recruits for the *Veliti* should be at least 5ft 2in (Paris, equal to 5ft 5in Imperial or 1.65m metric), between 18 and 25, be able to read and write, and have an annual income of 200 Milanese Lira to be paid to the State for their training and maintenance. After two years service *veliti* could be transferred to the line with the rank of *sergente*.

Initially it was planned to raise three battalions of *Veliti*, one of *Veliti Granatieri* and two of *Velite Cacciatori*, each of four companies. The initial plan for there to be departmental recruiting areas was abandoned by the formal regulations of 19 August 1805, which set out the establishments as:

Regimental Staff	
1 *Colonnello*	1 *Maggiore*
3 *Capo Battaglione*	3 *Aiutanti-Maggiori*
2 *Sottoaiutanti-Maggiori*	1 *Quartiermaistro*
2 *Chirurge Maggiore*	1 *Vammastro*
1 *Tamburo Maggiore*	2 *Caporale-Tamburo*
30 *Musicanti*[25]	
2 *Maestro-Artigiani* (Master craftsmen: Boot maker and Armourer)	
Company Establishment	
1 *Capitano*	2 *Tenente*
1 *Sergente Maggiore*	4 *Sergenti*
1 *Quartiermaistro*	1 *Furriere*
8 *Caporali*	3 *Tamburi*
80 *Soldato*	

24 This description is based upon a plate that appeared in 'Le Briquet 3/88'.
25 Including a Head of Music and two Deputies.

Veliti Granatieri Della Guardia Reale, c. 1806
Although dated in the collection to '1809' it seems likely that this contemporary illustration actually dates to late 1805 or early 1806. Amusingly the indentations created by the bearskin cords are shown on the illustration but in two of the three figures the cords themselves are not shown. If this does date to 1806 then the white metal bearskin plate sometimes mentioned in uniform descriptions must be an error, and is perhaps a confusion with the senior regiments. (Contemporary illustration by 'CM' in the Anne S. K. Brown Military Collection, Brown University Library.)

In the autumn of 1806[26] a 5th *cacciatore* company was raised. Then on 10 June 1807 a 6th *cacciatore* company and a 5th *granatiere* company were added to the regiment, at the same time a *sotto tenente* was added to the establishment of each company. By 1813 the establishment was back to 5 companies per battalion with the 5th company essentially working as a depot company.

On 14 March 1808 the establishment was increased again when one sub-adjutant, one medical officer and two additional craftsmen were added to the Staff, each company formally gained two *zappatori* and the rank and file strength was increased to 97. On 16 October of the same year the rank and file was further increased to 122.

When, in 1809, the senior Regiment changed its designation from *Cacciatori* to *Carabinieri* the *Veliti* followed suit and the battalion became *Velite Carabinieri*.

From 17 January 1811 it was decided that *veliti* with five years' service and who had not yet been transferred to the line would no longer have to pay the annual fees.

Problems with recruitment meant that the 3rd Battalion was not actually raised until 9 March 1808 and even then only with an establishment of one *granatiere* and one *cacciatore* company. On 15 November 1810, however, the lack of recruits caused the 3rd Battalion to be disbanded and its personnel transferred into the two other battalions. Thereafter the Regiment constituted only two battalions throughout its existence

In 1813 the majority of the men who returned from Russia were passed into the line as N.C.O.s and the Regiment took the field as a single battalion, almost all of whom were new recruits.

During the ten years of its existence 3,679 men passed through the Regiment, a large percentage of whom actually did progress into the line as N.C.O.s.

Service

1806	
29 September	Skirmish at Cattaro (1 *Capitano* killed, 1 *Capitano* wounded)
1807	
15 January to 20 August	Siege of Straslund
1808 (Dalmatia)	1 Battalion
1808 (Spain)	1 Battalion
18 June	Skirmish at St Paul (1 *Tenente* wounded)
2 September	Skirmish at San-Roy (1 *Capitano*, 3 *Tenenti* killed)
12 October	Skirmish at St-Golgat (1 *Tenente* wounded)
1809 (Germany)	1 Battalion
16 April	Battle of Sacile (1 *Capitano* killed)
30 April	Skirmish at Illasi (1 *Capo Battaglione* killed, 1 *Tenente* died of wounds, 3 *Capitani* and 3 *Tenenti* wounded)
8 May	Battle of the Piave
14 June	Battle of Raab (1 *Tenente* wounded)

26 I have not found the exact date for this increase.

5 July	Battle of Wagram (610 officers and men)
1809 (Spain)	1 Battalion
5 May	1 Officer wounded while on advance guard duty at Caldiero
June	Siege of Gerona (610 officers and men)
8 July	Storm of Mountjoie (1 *Tenente* killed, 1 *Capo Battaglione* wounded, 1 *Tenente* died of wounds, 1 *Capitano* and 2 *Tenenti* wounded)
1810 (Spain)	1 Battalion
1811 (Spain)	1 Battalion
1812 (Spain)	1 Battalion
1812	
7 September	Battle of Borodino
24 October	Battle of Maloyaroslavetz (2 *Capo Battaglione* killed, 2 *Capitani* killed, 2 *Chirurgi* killed, 1 *Capo Battaglione* wounded, 3 *Capitani* wounded – 2 subsequently died of their wounds, 11 *Tenenti* wounded of whom 3 subsequently died of wounds)
14 November	Smolensk (1 *Tenente* wounded)
16 November	Battle of Krasnoi
28 November	Battle of the Beresina (1 *Capitano* killed, 1 *Tenente* wounded)
1813 (Spain)	1 Battalion
1813–1814	Defence of the Kingdom of Italy
1813	
8 September	Skirmish at Leybach (1 *Capitano*, 3 *Tenenti* wounded)
12 September	Skirmish at San-Marein (1 *Capitano* killed, 2 *Tenenti* wounded)
1814	
8 February	Battle of the Mincio (638 officers and men)

Uniform

Headwear

In full dress the *velite* battalions wore the *granatiere* or *cacciatore* pattern bearskin as appropriate, as used by the senior regiments, except that by at least 1808, and possibly even from 1805, the *Velite Granatiere*' plate was brass in place of white metal. On campaign the regiment often wore the infantry pattern shako with a white metal crown and Imperial Eagle plate on the front and the usual National cockade secured by a white cockade strap. The shako cords were white and plumes followed the pattern of those worn on the bearskin. The white fatigue caps had grass green piping and either the grenade or bugle horn badge as appropriate on the front.

Veliti Granatieri Della Guardia Reale, c. 1812
This illustration carries the title "Italie Velite Grenadiers". The illustration shows the brass bearskin plate mentioned in the text. (Vinkhuijzen Collection, General Research Division, New York Public Library Digital Collections. Public Domain)

Coat

The white habit coats of the 1st Battalion, the *Velite Granatieri*, had square, grass green lapels and grass green collars, cuffs[27] and three-pointed cuff flaps, all piped white. The turnbacks were grass green, unpiped, and the turnback ornaments were white grenades (changed to yellow by 1808/9). Pockets were piped in grass green. All buttons were initially pewter, but by 1808/9 had changed to brass, and full-fringed red

27 When first formed the cuffs were white piped green but these had been replaced by green piped white before the end of 1806.

epaulettes were worn. By 1811 the cuffs of the coats had been changed to white piped in grass green.

The coats of the 2nd Battalion, *Veliti Carabinieri*, had pointed lapels, Polish cuffs and bugle horn insignia but were otherwise the same as those of the 1st Battalion. Epaulettes were the same pattern as worn by the *Carabinieri della Guardia Reale*.

Breeches, Et cetera

Breeches and waistcoats were white and the over-knee gaiters were black with white metal buttons. White overall trousers were issued for campaign. The dark grey greatcoats were of the double-breasted pattern worn throughout the *Guardia Reale*, with white metal buttons and were worn with the epaulettes transferred from the coat.

Equipment

All equipment was identical to that of the appropriate *Granatieri* and *Cacciatori* companies of the senior guard regiment although the crowned eagle badge on the cartouche box lid was brass.

Officers & N.C.O.s

All distinctions and rank badges were the same as those of the *Granatieri* and *Carabinieri* except with gold differencing in place of silver. A surviving officer's coat in the collection of the Museo del Risorgimento in Bologna has gold grenades on red cloth backing on the turnbacks. The Officer's gorget was gold with silver details – either an Imperial Eagle or a crowned 'N', both are recorded.

On campaign officers frequently wore a dark green surtout with grass green collar and cuffs, piped white, white cuff flaps, grass green piping to the pockets and grass green turnbacks with the same badges as on the habit.

The Regimental *Colonnello* is shown *c.* 1810 wearing a regulation uniform with the square lapels of the 1st Battalion. His headwear is a black bicorne with silver scalloped edge lace and cords and a silver cockade strap, with no plume. He carries a straight infantry style epée with silver hilt and a gold sword-knot and tassel in a plain black scabbard. Unusually he is not shown wearing a waist belt. His boots are black, heavy cavalry pattern and his horse furniture is a dark green shabraque edged with a broad silver (outer) and a narrow silver (inner) lace, with silver grenades in the rear outer corners. The dark green double pistol holster covers are edged with two rows of wide silver lace.

Musicanti

Tamburi wore a coat of the same pattern and colour as the rank and file but with the addition of gold lace on the collar, lapels, buttonholes and cuffs. The drums had the customary brass barrel with blue hoops decorated with white grenades between the cords.

One source for 1812 gives the lace as red and white and only on the collar and cuffs and with all other details as for the senior regiments of the *Guardia Reale*.

A contemporary illustration of *tamburi* on campaign in 1812 shows exactly the same uniform as the rank and file without differencing in any way.

Tamburo Maggiore, Veliti Grenadier c. 1809: Black bicorne with white feather edging trimmed with a gold scallop-edged lace and tassels, a tall white plume with two red and one grass green ostrich feathers at the base, National cockade with a gold cockade strap. White coat with a grass green collar, lapels and turnbacks, all laced with gold and with gold lace around the buttons and buttonholes, gold fringed epaulettes, gold rank stripes and gold lace on the seams of the sleeves and back of the coat. The waistcoat had gold trim to the pockets and edge. All buttons were gold. The breeches had gold Hungarian knots and the boots were the cuffed English pattern. The baldric worn by the *Tamburo Maggiore* was red edged with gold with gold grenades and embroidery along its length and with a gold drumstick plate on the chest, the waist belt was the same colour with a gilt buckle plate. The sword was the infantry officer's sabre with gilt hilt, sword-knot and tassel, carried in a black leather scabbard fitted in gold. The gauntlets were white with gold scallop-edge lace on the cuffs. The baton was brown wood, fitted in gold with gold cords.

Musicanti, Veliti Granatieri c. 1809: The same uniform as the above but with gold trefoil epaulettes, plain waist belt with brass buckle, straight bladed epée, and plain breeches. No baldric.

Zappatori

All distinctions were the same as those in use in the *Granatieri* and *Carabinieri* battalions, although Boisselier shows the *zappatore* with a red collar.

An axe, which was sold at auction in 1916, had its head engraved 'Reggimento Veliti' and must have been from this Regiment.[28]

28 Piero Crociano, Massimo Fiorentino, and Alfred Umhey, 'À Propos de l'"Esponton" des "Dragoni Napoleone…" in *Soldats Napoleoniens: Les Troupes Françaises, Alliés et Coalisées. Hors-série No.1, Avril 2003*, (Paris: Éditions de la Revue Napoléon, 2003), pp.78–84.

Regimental Artillery Company

See the notes above for the senior regiment.

Marinai Della Guardia Reale

(Sailors[29] of the Royal Guard)

History and Organisation

Although traditionally the *Marinai Della Guardia Reale* (Sailors of the Royal Guard) date from 1806 when Venice was absorbed into the Kingdom[30] there is no firm evidence for the unit's existence prior to an Order of August 1807, and they were only formally attached to the *Guardia* by an Order of 13 June 1808.

The Order of 13 June 1808, by which the *Marinai* became a part of the *Guardia*, set out an establishment for the unit of:

1 *Comandante Tenente*	1 *Luogoenente*
1 *Primo Mastro*	1 *Secondo Mastro*
1 *Quartiermastro*	1 *Capo Timoniere*
2 *Aiutante Timonieri*	1 *Mastro Cannoniere*
2 *Cannonieri*	1 *Pilota*
40 *Marinai*	

On 14 February 1811, the establishment was increased by the addition of 14 N.C.O.s, 60 *marinai 1º classe*, 60 *marinai 2º classe* and 6 "boys", 2 of whom were listed as *tamburi* (presumably in training since European armies did not use 'drummer boys'). It is doubtful if the unit ever reached its full establishment strength.

The unit was raised mainly in the Venetian provinces and throughout its existence remained in garrison in that locality.

Service

Carmignani gives no campaign service for the *Marinai* except that they were with the *Grande Armée* in the campaigns of 1806–1807 and thus almost certainly at the Siege of Colberg (20 March to 2 June 1806) and the Siege of Straslund (15 January to 20 August 1807). In 1809 they remained in Venice, but in 1812 a detachment of 3 officers and 103 N.C.O.s and other ranks were with the *Grande Armée* in Russia. Additionally it is almost certain that the unit would have been involved in the defence of the Kingdom in 1813–1814, probably alongside larger units such as the *Reggimento Guardia Alla Città di Venezia*. Martinien records no casualties, wounded or killed, amongst the unit's handful of officers at any point.

Uniform

The unit wore two distinctly different uniforms, the earlier one is not recorded officially but illustrations (including an unpublished watercolour by the usually reliable Boisselier, regrettably, without a source given on it) show it to have essentially been a dark green version of the full dress uniform of the Sailors of the French *Garde Impériale*, with red cuffs and all piping, braid and frogging in white, and a 'top hat' as worn with the post 1810 uniform. The later, simpler version was ordered by Eugène in a letter dated 6 March 1810.

Post March 1810[31]

Headwear

Post 1810 the Regiment wore a hat that resembled a top hat with a wide, curled-up brim; the same pattern as the hat worn by the Navy. This hat had a brass lozenge plate embossed with an anchor at the front. Above the plate was the National cockade secured with a white cockade strap, the cockade was, in turn, surmounted by an elongated carrot-shaped plume; red for *1º classe marinai* and green for *2º classe marinai*. The dark green fatigue cap was piped red and almost certainly had a red anchor badge at the front, although this is not always shown on illustrations, so perhaps there was initially some use of caps from the stores of another unit of the Army

Coat

The short tailed coat was of a similar cut to the surtout and was dark green with red collar and cuffs, and dark green turnbacks piped red. The fringed epaulettes were red or dark green, following the pompom colour. All buttons were white metal.

Breeches, et cetera

The unique pattern of waistcoat was double-breasted and either red or dark green, as appropriate for *1º classe* or *2º classe marinai*, with white metal buttons. Breeches were dark green, with 'Hungarian' pattern gaiters trimmed with red or green lace and tassels as appropriate, and with white metal buttons. For campaign wear dark green overall trousers were issued with a red or dark green stripe, again as appropriate, on the outer seam. The dark green infantry pattern greatcoats had a red collar and

29 As with the French unit this is often translated as "Marines", correctly it should be sailors and indeed they were Naval personnel **not** combat marines.

30 Piero Crociano, *L'Esercito Italico 1805–1814 : Guardia Reale*, (Parma: Albertelli, 2005), p.42.

31 There is a superb study of the Sailors in this uniform in the Collection of H.M. The King and reproduced (sadly in monochrome) in Otto von Pivka (Digby Smith), *Napoleon's Italian and Neapolitan Troops*, (London: Osprey, 1979, p.15.

white metal buttons and were worn with the epaulettes transferred from the coat.

Equipment

All equipment was of the same pattern as that used by the elite companies of the line infantry, the sword-strap was white with a red tassel, and the cartridge box flap had a white metal lozenge shaped plate bearing an anchor beneath the Iron Crown.

Officers & N.C.O.s

N.C.O.'s distinctions and rank stripes were the same as those used by the rest of the infantry regiments of the *Guardia Reale*. In addition senior N.C.O.s added silver lace to the brim and edge of the crown of the hat.

Officers wore the same hat as the rank and file with any metalwork silvered and silver lace on the brim and upper edge of the crown of the hat. The carrot-shaped pompom was red over white over green but in full dress officers wore a tall red over white plume with a green ball pompom at the base. Officers' coats were of the long tailed surtout pattern, with silver epaulettes of rank in the same system as those of the *Granatieri a Piedi della Guardia Reale*. Waistcoats were red with silver lacing on the front. Breeches were dark green with silver Hungarian knots on the front of the thighs and silver piping on the outer seam, although on campaign it appears that officers wore plain dark green breeches. Boots were Hungarian pattern with silver lace and tassels. All officers carried the curved, light cavalry pattern sabre suspended from a black leather light cavalry pattern waist belt.

Tamburi

The uniform was that of the rank and file with the addition of red and white lace on the collar and cuffs. All other variations of uniforms, equipment, et cetera were the same as those of the *tamburi* of the Line Infantry regiments.

Coscritti Della Guardia Reale

(Conscripts of the Royal Guard)

Cacciatori Della Guardia Reale from 1813
(Chasseurs of the Royal Guard)

History and Organisation

The *Coscritti Della Guardia Reale* were raised in 1810 following an initiative by Eugène to increase the size of the Guard[32] along the same lines as the increase in the strength of the French *Garde Impériale* effected by the raising of the 'Young Guard' regiments from 1809.[33] Like these latter French Regiments the *Coscritti Della Guardia Reale* was to be recruited from the best of the conscripts, with a height of at least 5ft 5in.[34] The intention was, as in the French *Garde Impériale*, that suitable candidates from the regiment's rank and file would, after two years, be transferred into the line regiments as N.C.O.s.

The Regiment was raised at a strength of two battalions, each of five companies, and a regimental staff. Companies were to be of the same establishment as those of the *Veliti*.

On 4 February 1811 the Regiment was augmented with an Artillery and Support company comprising two 3pdr guns and caissons, a four horse ambulance, 4 six horse caissons for supplies, 2 caissons for ammunition of musket cartridges, a 4 horse wagon for the administrative papers, et cetera, and a field forge to be drawn by three horses.

As with the other foot regiments of the *Guardia* the 5th company of each battalion appears to have functioned as a depot company, forwarding trained personnel to the Regiment rather than serving as a field company in itself.

In the reestablishment and reorganisation of the *Guardia Reale* in 1813, a Decree from Eugène, dated 26 February, abolished the title *Conscritti* and retitled the Regiment as *Cacciatori Della Guardia Reale* (Chasseurs of the Royal Guard), traditionally in recognition of the Regiment's service in Russia. By the same Decree the Regiment was reformed as four battalions, each of five companies, with an establishment the same as before.

The Regiment's depot was, throughout its existence, at Milan.

---

32 The first mention of the raising of the unit is in a letter from Eugène to Napoleon dated 13 September 1810. Napoleon gave his approval in a reply of 4 October.

33 Piero Crociano actually refers to the Conscritti as "the Italian Young Guard." 'Napoleon's Italian Army, Part V', in *Tradition No.46*, (London: Belmont-Maitland 197?), pp.29–32.

34 This is 5ft 5in Paris, equal to 5ft 8in Imperial (1.72m metric). These would most definitely have been the tallest of the recruits.

Service

1812	
7 September	Battle of Borodino
24 October	Battle of Maloyaroslavets (1 *Colonnello* wounded, 1 *Major* wounded, 1 *Capitano* subsequently died of wounds, 4 other *Capitani* wounded, 2 *Tenenti* killed, 27 *Tenenti* wounded of whom 7 subsequently died of wounds)
1813	
6 September	Skirmish at Laybach (3 *Capitani* wounded)
12 September	Skirmish at St Marein (3 *Tenenti* killed)
13 September	Skirmish at St Marein
16 September	Skirmish at St Marein (2 *Capitani* and 5 *Tenenti* wounded)
19 September	Skirmish at Tchernütz
25 September	Skirmish at Tchernütz (4 *Capitani* wounded, 4 *Tenenti* wounded, 1 subsequently died of his wounds)
27 September	Skirmish at Tchernütz
1814	
8 February	Battle of the Mincio
16 February	Skirmish at Salo (1 *Capo Battaglione* wounded, 3 *Capitani* killed, 1 wounded, 4 *Tenenti* wounded)

Uniform

Headwear

The *Coscritti* wore the infantry pattern shako with a white upper band and a brass Italian Imperial Eagle plate. The National cockade at the front was secured with white cockade strap. Shako cords were white and the full dress plume was green with a black tip; on campaign the plume was replaced with a black over green ball pompom. Chin scales were brass. The dark green fatigue caps had white piping and tassel and a white Imperial Eagle badge at the front.

Coat

The habit was dark green with square lapels, the dark green lapels, cuffs, and turnbacks, were all piped white. The collar and three-pointed cuff flaps were red piped white, and the pockets were also piped white. The turnbacks were red piped white, with a white Imperial Eagle turnback badge. Full-fringed epaulettes were green with a red crescent (although Boisselier in his 1955 study shows green shoulder straps piped white). All buttons were white metal.

The two additional battalions raised in 1813 wore the short tailed habit-veste with square lapels but all facings and other details were as for the 1810 pattern habit. Some illustrations show green shoulder straps piped white in place of the full epaulettes, and red cuffs with white cuff flaps are also sometimes shown on this coat.

Breeches, et cetera

Breeches and waistcoats were white, with white metal buttons. Gaiters were black over-knee pattern, also with white metal buttons. On campaign white overall trousers were issued. Greatcoats were the same pattern as worn by the *Veliti* and worn with the fringed epaulettes of the coat when these were used. By 1812 the Regiment had adopted the short, below-knee pattern gaiters, as always these were black with either white metal, or black cloth covered, buttons.

Equipment

Equipment was of the same pattern as that used by the senior regiments. The sword-strap was red with white knot and tassel, or white with a red knot and tassel.

Officers & N.C.O.s.

All distinctions and rank badges were the same as those used by the *Granatieri a Piedi Della Guardia Reale* (as above). The officers' turnback devices were in silver. A print dated to 1812 shows an officer in service dress wearing a green surtout and green breeches with silver Hungarian knots on the thighs.

Musicanti

All distinctions and equipment was as used by the *Veliti*. *Musicanti* were also uniformed the same as those of the *Veliti* but with silver distinctions in place of gold.

Zappatori

All distinctions and equipment was as used by the *Veliti* but one contemporary source shows the bearskin with a brass plate, red cords and tassels and a green plume.

Regimental Artillery Company

There is little information on the regimental artillery beyond that recorded for the senior Regiment, except that the coat turnbacks had a white eagle badge and the company wore a shako with red cords, in place of the bearskin.

2 (3) *Artigliera Della Guardia Reale*

(Artillery of the Royal Guard)

Knötel Plate III / 17. *Artigliera della Guardia Real, Treno d'Artilgieria di Guardia Reale*, 1812. (Author's Collection)

History and Organisation

The Decree of 20 June 1805 that raised the *Guardia Reale* also disbanded the majority of the *Artigliera della Guardia del Presidente*, retaining only a 64 strong horse artillery company commanded by *Capitano Comandante* Raspi.

However the need for logistical support forced the raising of a *Treno Compagnia* on 30 June 1806 with an establishment of:

1 *Tenente*	1 *Sotto Tenente*
1 *Maresciallo d'Alloggio Capo*	2 *Marescialli d'Alloggio*
1 *Brigadiere Furiere*	2 *Brigadieri*
1 *Tromba*	2 *Maniscachi*
1 *Sellaio*	
21 *1ª Classe Soldati*	53 *2ª Classe Soldati*

A Decree of 1808 set out a new establishment to the Horse Artillery (although the Train establishment remained unchanged):

1 *Capitano Comandante*	1 *Capitano*
1 *1º Tenente*	2 *2º Tenenti*
1 *Veterinario*	1 *Custode d'Artiglieria*[35]
1 *Operaio*[36]	1 *Maresciallo d'Alloggio Capo*
6 *Marescialli d'Alloggio*	1 *Brigadiere Furiere*
6 *Brigadieri*	2 *Tromba*
1 *Maniscalco*	
24 *1º Classe Cannonieri*	36 *2ª Classe Cannonieri*

By a Decree of 4 February 1811 the Guard's artillery arm was strengthened again with the addition of a company of foot artillery of:

1 *Capitano Comandante*	1 *Capitano*
1 *1º Tenente*	2 *2º Tenenti*
1 *Sergente Maggiore*	4 *Sergenti*
1 *Caporale Furiere*	8 *Caporali*
6 *Artificieri*	2 *Tamburi*
40 *1º Classe Cannonieri*	60 *2º Classe Cannonieri*

a second Train company, with each company with an increased establishment of:

1 *Tenente*	1 *Sotto Tenente*
1 *Maresciallo d'Alloggio Capo*	4 *Marescialli d'Alloggio*
1 *Brigadiere Furiere*	4 *Brigadieri*
1 *Tromba*	2 *Maniscachi*
1 *Sellaio*	
40 *1º Classe Soldati*	60 *2º Classe Soldati*

and a staff for the whole artillery arm of:

1 *Capo Battaglione*	1 *Tenente Aiutante Maggiore*
1 *Sotto Aiutante Maggiore*	1 *Quartiermastro*
1 *Ufficiale di Santa*	1 *Veterinario*
1 *Guardia d'Artiglieria*	4 *Capi Operai*

35 Literally a "Warder of Artillery".

36 Literally "worker" but obviously a professional artisan.

In Moscow, on 4 October 1812, Napoleon brought together the artillery companies of the infantry regiments of the *Guardia Reale* into a second, provisional, foot artillery company and a *Capitano*, a *Brigadiere Trombettiere* and 14 *bracciante* were added to the Staff.

Artiglieria a Cavallo

(Horse Artillery)

Headwear

The uniform was modelled on, and almost identical to, that worn by the French *Artillerie à Cheval de la Garde Impériale.* The headwear was a black colpack but without a bag, but at the left side the National cockade surmounted by a red plume. A number of contemporary drawings show a red bag to the colpack but the Decree of 15 April 1806 is definite in stating 'without bag'.[37] By 1811, however, it appears that the colpack had, regulations or not, gained a red bag. Cords were red and the chin scales brass. Fatigue caps were as for the foot battery but blue.

Coat

For full dress the uniform was a dark blue hussar style dolman and pelisse with dark blue collar and cuffs, both edged red, eighteen rows of red frogging and five rows of brass buttons. The pelisse was edged with black fur. The hussar style barrel sash was red and blue.

On campaign the dolman and pelisse were replaced with a dark blue surtout, or a habit with pointed lapels, the sources are unclear and it is *possible* that the former replaced the latter at some point. The coat (whichever pattern it was) had a black collar piped red, red Polish cuffs and red turnbacks with a dark blue grenade turnback badge. A red, fringed epaulette was worn at the right shoulder and red trefoil epaulette and aiguillette on the left. All buttons were brass.

In 1811 a change of uniform colour from dark blue to dark green was projected and this *was* in use by 1813 but when the changeover was actually effected is unknown, perhaps the 1811 uniform issue or in the rebuilding of the Army after the 1812 campaign. The dark green surtout/habit coat was certainly issued and in use in 1813–14 but whether the dark green hussar style full dress uniform ever got further than the projected stage and some officers' privately purchased versions is unknown.

Breeches, et cetera

Breeches were dark blue with red Hungarian knots on the thighs and a red stripe on the outer seam, and were worn with Hungarian boots with red lace and tassel. The waistcoat worn with the surtout was dark blue with brass buttons. Greatcoats were of the cavalry pattern with red lining and red piping at the edge of the collar and cape and white metal buttons. A red and dark blue barrel sash with red cords was worn with the dolman and pelisse.

In the 'new' uniform of 1813 all of the dark blue items were replaced with green and the barrel sash became green and red.

Equipment

The basic equipment was the same as that used by the senior infantry regiments of the guard, with a brass grenade badge on the cartridge box lid. The sword-strap was white with a red knot and tassel. Additionally the sabretaches were blue edged red with a brass crossed cannon badge below an Imperial Eagle, also in brass. From 1813, after the return from Russia, the rebuilt unit adopted a green field to their sabretaches but all other details of the design were unchanged.

Officers & N.C.O.s.

The officers' and N.C.O.s' rank badges and distinctions worn on the surtout were the same as those used by the foot regiments of the *Guardia Reale*, with all lace, epaulettes, et cetera in gold or yellow.

Officers' rank badges on the hussar style dolman were in the form of chevrons above the cuffs; the first chevron trimmed the upper edge of the cuff and was 14mm wide.

Capitano Comandante	Four gold chevrons alternately 14mm and 23mm[38]
Capitano	Three gold chevrons, two of 14mm with one of 23mm in between
Tenente	Two gold 14mm chevrons
Sotto Tenente	One gold 14mm chevron

The same sequence and colouring was used for the spearheads on the breeches.

All officers' lace and braid was gold, the barrel sash was blue and gold, and belts were red leather with gold edging and fittings (at least in full dress, whether such finery was much used in the field is debatable). Sabretaches were dark blue edged gold and with a gilt design of crossed cannon surmounted by the Imperial Eagle. For the undress uniform all belts were black leather with gilt fittings.

As with the rank and file, after 1812 dark green replaced the dark blue.

37 Piero Crociano, *L'Esercito Italico 1805–14: Guardia Reale*, (Parma: Albertelli, 2005), . 95.

38 I have not seen the rank badges of the *Capitano Comandante* laid down anywhere, as the *Artiglieria a Cavallo* had a *Capitano* as second in command it is likely that the *Commandante* used the rank badges of a squadron commander in the cavalry.

Musicanti

There are two recorded variations of the *trombettieri'* uniforms, both from contemporary illustrations. Given that a new uniform might expect to be issued each year (or sometimes two years) there is no reason why both cannot have been worn at different time periods.

One version, dated to *c.* 1806, shows a white colpack with a white plume tipped sky blue, gold cords and a sky blue bag piped red and with a gold tassel. Red dolman and pelisse with sky blue collar and cuffs, both piped gold. Black fur on the pelisse. Mixed gold and sky blue frogging and aiguillette. Red and sky blue barrel sash. Sky blue breeches with red and gold lace and decorations. Hungarian boots edged red and gold. The sabretache has a sky blue face with the usual gold lace border and brass badges. Brass trumpet with mixed red and gold cords.

The second illustration repeats the white colpack but with a red bag piped dark blue, white plume and mixed red and white cords. Red dolman and pelisse with dark blue facings, white lace and frogging, and brass buttons. White fur on the pelisse. White cords for the trumpet and a red sabretache edged yellow. The trumpet is brass with red cords.

The surtout was red with black (possibly dark blue) collar piped red and red cuffs and turnbacks piped dark blue. Epaulettes and aiguillettes were mixed red and white.

Horse Furniture

Gunners' shabraques were of the same pattern as those of the line in dark blue with a wide red edge and red grenades in the rear corners. *Trombettieri'* shabraques were of reversed colours and the officers had a double gold edging with red piping at the extreme edge.

Artiglieria a Piedi

(Foot Artillery)

The 1811 Decree that ordered the raising of the *Reggimento di Artiglieria a Piedi della Guardia Reale* made no mention of a uniform for it. However there is a letter in the State Archives of Milan asking for information about the new regiment's uniform, and the same document packet contains the following answer:

> The Foot Artillery will have the same uniform as the Artillery of the Line, except for having vertical pockets [to the coat] as in the other Guard Corps. Officers and Gunners will have the bearskin of the Gendarmerie.[39]

Headwear

Overall the *Artiglieria a Piedi della Guardia Reale* had, unsurprisingly, a uniform similar to that of their French counterparts. Headwear was a black bearskin of the same model as that of the *Gendarmerie* (although a contemporary illustration shows it without the peak) with a white grenade on the red rear patch. In full dress this cap had red cords and a red plume above the National cockade; on campaign the cap's only decoration was the cockade. The fatigue caps were dark green with red piping and tassel and a red grenade badge at the front.

Coat

As laid down in the Milan Archives document mentioned above the dark green habit was of the same pattern as that of the line artillery, with black collar and lapels piped red and red cuffs, turnbacks and cuff flaps piped dark green. Turnbacks were decorated with dark green grenade badges and the vertical pockets were piped red. All buttons were white metal. All rank and file wore red full-fringed epaulettes.

In 1813 a dark green surtout was ordered for the artillery but it seems unlikely that this was issued before the fall of the Kingdom the following year.

Breeches, et cetera

Breeches and waistcoats were dark green with white metal buttons and the black over-the-knee gaiters had white metal buttons for parade dress and cloth covered buttons on campaign. The dark green greatcoats were of the Guard Infantry pattern and worn with the epaulettes from the coat.

Equipment

As with the horse artillery the equipment was of the same basic pattern as that used by senior infantry regiments of the *Guardia Reale*, with either a brass grenade badge or a brass badge of crossed cannon barrels on the cartridge box lid. The sword-strap was white with red knot and tassels.

Officers & N.C.O.s

Officers' & N.C.O.'s distinctions and rank insignia were the same as those of the rest of the foot regiments of the *Guardia Reale*. Officers' bearskins had the grenade badge in silver and silver cords for parade dress. Officers' belts were white for full dress and a more practical black leather for campaign, and all dismounted officers wore English pattern 'jockey boots', mounted officers wore the high cuffed heavy cavalry pattern boots.

39 Piero Crociano, *L'Esercito Italico 1805–1814 : Guardia Reale*, (Parma: Albertelli, 2005), p.74.

Musicanti

The *Tamburi* of the *Artiglieria a Piedi* wore the basic uniform prescribed for their company but with the addition of broad white lace trim, inside the piping, to the lapels, collar and cuffs.

Drum aprons and the drum carriage belts were white leather with brass buckles and the carriage belt was decorated with a brass drumstick plate on the upper front. The drums had brass barrels and the hoops were painted with diagonal stripes of green-white-red-white.

Treno d'Artilgieria della Guardia Reale

(Artillery Train of the Guard)

Headwear

The *Treno d'Artilgieria della Guardia Reale* wore a czapska similar, if not essentially identical, to that originally issued to the line *Artiglieria a Cavallo*. This had a black upper part, piped black at the top and red down the vertical edges. The lower part was a black fur turban with a brass lozenge plate at the front bearing a device of crowned crossed cannon barrels over a pyramid of cannonballs. The National cockade was secured with a white cockade strap and was surmounted by a light green carrot-shaped pompom.

There is one interesting and notable aspect of the czapska as it was worn throughout the Kingdom's Army: in most armies, including the French and Polish, the czapska was designed in such a way that, when worn, a corner of the flat top was central at the front. In the Army of Italy all illustrations of the czapska show it designed and manufactured in a different way, so that when worn the corners of the top were square to the front and the flat top parallel to the peak. This peculiarity is shown throughout the Army wherever the czapska was in use.

In 1811 the shako was introduced to replace the czapska, while some illustrations show this as the line artillery peakless pattern others show the more traditional style worn throughout most of the Army. The latter certainly seems the more likely of the two. It had the same plate, cockade and pompom as the czapska but, for parade dress, had light green cords and plume.

Fatigue caps were mid-grey with light green piping and tassels.

Coat

The mid-grey coat was of the surtout style with short tails. The collar, Polish cuffs and turnbacks were light green and the vertical pockets and front of the coat leading down into the turnbacks were piped in the same colour. The front of the coat had lace batons in the same form as the coats of the *Artiglieria a Cavallo della Guardia Reale* and there were two similar batons on the cuffs. The coat had light green fringed epaulettes. All buttons were white metal. In 1811 the battalion serving the foot artillery made changes to their coats (how far, if at all, these changes were reflected by the *Artiglieria a Cavallo* battalion is unknown): the epaulettes were replaced by mid-grey shoulder straps piped in light green and the cuffs were changed to the Brandenburg pattern with cuff flaps, all still in light green, with two light green batons, worn one above the other but both on the cuff, although a painting in the collection of H.M. The King shows the cuffs without these lace batons.

When the Army was reformed after the 1812 campaign the Regiment was given coats of the same cut as above but in dark green with red facings and red lace batons.

Breeches, et cetera

Waistcoats were mid-grey with white metal buttons and breeches were soft buff leather with white metal buttons on the outer seams and were worn with high, cuffed riding boots with steel spurs. Members of the regiment who were not mounted wore mid-grey breeches and black gaiters as for the infantry. Whitened leather gauntlets were worn for parade and buff gauntlets on campaign. The light grey greatcoats were of light cavalry pattern, with a light green collar and lining.

In 1813, when the regiment was reformed after the disastrous Russian campaign, the breeches and waistcoats were changed to dark green.

Equipment

The drivers wore a pouch belt and cartridge box of the line light cavalry pattern, with a brass crossed cannon badge on the cartridge box lid. The second shoulder belt supported an infantry pattern sabre-briquet in a black leather scabbard with light green sword-strap and a white knot with light green tassel. Short, dragoon pattern muskets were carried on the saddle.

Officers & N.C.O.s

Insignia was the same as that used by the light cavalry and *brigadiere* were equipped as for the drivers. Senior N.C.O.s and all officers carried the light cavalry sabre worn from a waist belt, and on campaign both favoured the bicorne hat with silver lace and tassels, although the official headwear after 1811 was the shako the same as the troop. An illustration by Brandani shows an officer *c.* 1811 with a shako with a silver upper band and a triple inverted chevron of silver lace at the sides, the point of the outer chevron just touching the upper band.[40] After 1813 officers' uniforms followed the pattern of the officers of

40 Piero Crociani, *L'Esercito Italico 1805–14: Guardia Reale*, (Parma: Albertelli, 2005), p.75. Neither author nor artist give the source for this but with Crociani's reputation I am loathe to discount it.

the *Artiglieria a Cavallo*. Greatcoats were dark grey with a light green collar.

Musicanti

The regiment's *trombettieri* were uniformed as for the rank and file with the addition of white lace to the edges of the collar and cuffs and red cords and plume worn on both the czapska and shako. *Trombettieri* carried the light cavalry sabre with a red sword-strap and tassel. Trumpets were brass with green or red cords.

Tamburi had the same distinctions as the *trombettieri* but wore mid-grey breeches and black gaiters and all equipment was as for the *tamburi* of the line infantry.

Horse Furniture

All draught horse harness was plain mid-brown leather with brass buckles and fittings. The outriders' saddles were brown leather with a plain grey saddle blanket and a round mid-grey valise, piped light green at the ends.

Sergenti and other senior N.C.O.s were mounted, and used a mid-grey version of the 1805 pattern dragoon shabraque, with wide light green lace at the edge, piped mid-grey. The pistol holsters were light green laced white and piped light green.

In 1811 the half shabraque was introduced; the cloth was the same colouring as the 1805 pattern and the dogtooth edging to the white sheepskin was light green. The valise was changed to a square pattern and was mid-grey with light green lace on the ends.

Trombettieri' shabraques were mid-grey (possibly green from 1813) with red trim, the sheepskin was black with a red dogtooth edging.

Officers' shabraques were of the 1805 dragoon officer's pattern in mid-grey with silver lace decorations and grenades, the silver lace was piped with light green. This pattern continued in use by officers after the half shabraque was introduced for other ranks.

All ordnance, halter collars, et cetera were painted dark green (NB this was not the olive green of the French artillery but a true dark green).

3
Cavalleria di Linea (Cavalry of the Line)

Organisation

When the Kingdom of Italy was created in 1805 the new Kingdom's mounted arm comprised only two regiments of *Dragoni*, (Dragoons, converted from the two regiments of hussars of the former Cisalpine Republic by an Order of 5 February 1805) and a single regiment of *Cacciatori a Cavallo* ('Chasseurs a Cheval' / Light Horse[1]). Subsequently a further three Regiments of *Cacciatori a Cavallo* were raised in 1806, 1810 and 1811 and numbered consecutively as the *2°*, *3°* and *4° regimmenti.*

The internal organisation of all cavalry regiments, both heavy and light, was broadly similar. A regiment consisted of a regimental staff, four field squadrons and a depot. A squadron comprised of two companies and, as with much of the Kingdom's Army, was organised along the lines of the French cavalry regiments.

Regimental Staff:	
1 *Colonnello*	2 *Colonnello Sotto*
1 *Maggiore*	2 *Capo Squadrone*
2 *Aiutante*	1 *Quartiermaistro*
1 *Chirurge Maggiore*	2 *Chirurgo-Sotto*
8 *Aiutante Sottoufficiale*	1 *Aquile-Alfiori*
1 *Tromba-Maggiori*	1 *Veterinario*[2]
1 Furieri	
5 *Maestro-artigiani*	(Master Craftsmen: boot maker, tailor, breeches maker, armourer, saddler)
Company Establishment	
1 *Capitano*	1 *Tenente*
2 *Sotto Tenente*	1 *Sergente Maggiore*
2 *Sergente*	1 *Caporale furiere*
4 *Caporali*	1 *Maniscalo*
2 *Tromba*	1 *Tamburo*[3]
75 Soldati	

Additionally all regiments had a 9th, depot, company with a permanent establishment of officers and N.C.O.s but varying numbers of rank and file as they came in, were trained, and were forwarded to the Regiment.

Reggimenti de Dragoni

(Regiments of Dragoons)

Service

1° Reggimento 'Regina'

1805 Italy	
November	'Venice Observation Corps'
1806 Naples	Conquest of the Kingdom of Naples
1809 Austria	
July 5–6	Battle of Wagram (*Capo Squadrone* Charpentier wounded)
1812 Russia	
November 3	Battle of Wiasma (4 Officers killed)
November 16	Battle of Krasnoi (1 Officer killed)
November 28	Battle of the Beresina (4 Officers mortally wounded. *Capitano* Pessina was killed near the Beresina the following day)
December 10	Skirmish at Wilna (1 Officer killed)
1813 Germany	
September 16	1 *Capitano* killed on reconnaissance near Laibach
1814	
February 8	Battle of Mincio (7 Officers wounded, including *Colonello* Narboni and *Colonello Sotto* Charpentier)

2° Reggimento 'Napoleone'

1805 Italy	
November	'Venice Observation Corps'
1806 Naples	Conquest of the Kingdom of Naples
1808 Spain	
October	One *Tenente* wounded "escorting a courier to the frontier."

1 The term *Cacciatori a Cavallo* in Italian or *Chasseurs à Cheval* in French is, literally, "hunters on horseback" and it is found in the military of many European Nations of the era. Light Horse is the nearest English-language equivalent, although not quite conveying the same 'feel'.

2 A second *veterinario* was added to the wartime establishment of the Regiment by an Order of 11 April 1812.

3 Only in the dragoon regiments.

December 6	'Skirmish in Catalonia' (1 Officer wounded)
1809 Italy/Austria	
April 18	Battle of Sacile (2 Officers wounded)
June 14	Battle of Raab (2 Officers wounded)
November 5	Skirmish at Brixen in the Tyrol (1 Officer wounded)
1810 Spain	
February 28	Skirmish in Catalonia (1 Officer killed, 1 wounded)
December 30	Skirmish at Boria-Blancas, Catalonia (1 Officer killed, 6 wounded)[4]
1811 Spain	
January 3	Two officers wounded while 'on a reconnaissance'.
September 29	Skirmish at Tarrés (1 Officer wounded)
October 25	Battle of Sagunto (Strength of 466 Officers and men, 1 Officer wounded)
1812 Spain	
August 11	Skirmish at Guadarrama (1 Officer wounded)
1813 Spain	
March 24	Skirmish at Castro-Cordiala (1 Officer killed, 6 wounded) Germany
May 2	Battle of Lützen (3 Officers wounded)
May 21	Battle of Würschen (1 Officer wounded)
May 27	1 Officer killed, 10 wounded (one mortally) 'on reconnaissance near Goldberg'.
August 26	Battle of Dresden (1 Officer wounded)
September 12	Skirmish at Weissenfeld (1 Officer wounded)
October 16–18	Battle of Leipzig (3 Officers killed, 9 wounded)
October 30	Battle of Hanau (1 Officer wounded)

1813 Italy	
November 9	Skirmish at Roveredo (1 Officer wounded)
(On 23 December 1813 the Regiment mustered only 10 officers and 111 men with a total of 82 horses at its depot in Milan)	

Button of the Army of the Kingdom of Italy
The form of the crown is unusual in not showing the 'Iron Crown' but an 'Imperial Crown', there are a number of buttons with this anomaly recorded. If this is indeed from the Army of the Kingdom then it may be from 2º *Regimentto de Dragoni, Napoleone*. (Author's collection)

Uniform

Headwear

The Italian dragoon regiments wore the French pattern of heavy cavalry helmet, brass with a high brass comb crest and a black horsehair tail and houpette. The front of the crest was embossed with a stylised head of Medusa at the top directly below the houpette. The helmet was trimmed with a turban of black-brown fur, except in the 1st Squadron of the *Regina* Regiment where the turban was leopard skin, the upper and lower edges of the turban appear as being trimmed with a narrow line of brass, although actually this was a part of the helmet and the turban sat between these two lines of brass. The peak was of shiny black leather trimmed with brass. From 1808 the Regiment *Napoleone* wore a brass metal crowned 'N' at the front of the fur turban.[5] The chin scales were brass. In

4 To date, I have been unable to identify this village or location.

5 This 'N' is sometimes shown as being white metal, although this seems unlikely and is probably no more than an error of observation.

full dress the small brass socket at the left side above the chin-scale boss held a tall, dark green plume with a facing colour tip or plain dark green in the 1st Squadron of the *Regina*. A variation of a facing colour plume with a green tip is shown by André Jouineau for the *Regina* in 1812.[6]

Fatigue caps were of the same pattern as used by the infantry but from about 1811 the cavalry regiments began to use the *Pokalem* style cap, a round cloth cap with soft top. Both patterns of cap were dark green with facing colour piping.

Following the form of French dragoon regiments (indeed, all French Line and Light Mounted regiments[7]), the first company of the first squadron was designated as an elite company and wore the bearskin in place of the helmet, again in the same manner as the French dragoons (and the grenadier companies of the infantry). The bearskin was of black-brown fur, with a red cloth patch at the rear with a white cross, from around 1808–09 the cross was replaced with a white grenade. Two patterns of bearskin were in use, the first was of the infantry style without front plate and the other, apparently more common and of an older pattern, had a black leather peak bound in brass and a brass front plate embossed with a grenade. Given the extreme longevity of bearskins it is unlikely that the older pattern totally disappeared until perhaps 1810 or even 1812/1813. The cords on the bearskin were either white (1st Regiment) or red (2nd Regiment) and the plume, worn at the left side of the bearskin, was red with a National cockade at its base. There is some evidence that from *c.* 1809 the elite companies replaced

Dragoons of the Kingdom of Italy c. 1812. Drawings by René North from various contemporary sources. 'North's Paint Your Own Cards' set 106. (Author's Collection)

6 F. G. Hourtoulle, *Borodino The Moskova : The Battle for the Redoubts*, (Paris: Histoire & Collections, 2000), p.91.

7 The French Army designated the regiments of *Chasseurs à Cheval* and *Hussards* as 'Light', the regiments of *Dragons* (and later the *Chevau-Léger-Lanciers*) as 'Line', and the *Carabinier* and *Cuirassier* regiments as 'Heavy'.

Set 106 Italian Dragoons 1812

No 3. Trooper 1st. Regiment

Set 106 Italian Dragoons 1812

No.5 Elite Coy.

Set 106 Italian Dragoons 1812

No. 4. Drummer 2nd. Regt.

Set 106 Italian Dragoons 1812

No.6. Trooper 2nd. Regt.

their bearskin on campaign with the dragoon helmet with either a red, or a dark green tipped red, plume.

Coat

The dark green habit had the collar,[8] lapels, turnbacks and cuffs in the regimental facing colour, and dark green three-pointed cuff flaps piped in the regimental facing colour. The vertical pockets were piped with the regimental facing colour. The turnbacks had dark green grenade badges. The elite company wore red fringed epaulettes with brass scaled straps; the centre companies had dark green shoulder straps piped in the facing colour. All buttons were of white metal and two designs are known, both have a crowned 'N' but the crown could be either the Iron Crown or the French style Imperial Crown.[9]

Facing Colours	
1° Reggimento Regina	Pink
2° Reggimento Napoleone	Crimson (red from 1812?)

Given the state of dyes in the early nineteenth century there may have been little actual difference between 'crimson' and 'red', and any such 'change' could possibly have been no more than a change in dye batch or the interpretation of the individual observer.

In 1813 the dragoons adopted the 'Spencer' habit-veste with short tails and lapels closed to the waist, the same cut as that adopted by the French Army under the so-called *Bardin Regulations*.[10] With the new coat the facing colours remained unchanged, as did their placement on the coat. On this new coat pattern however, the regulations gave the elite companies' standard cloth shoulder straps although the previous fringed epaulettes may well have been retained at the discretion of the Colonnello – certainly such things were usual in most contemporary armies. It should perhaps be noted that given the stocks of coats held in the depots it is possible that the new coat may not have actually been evident in the Army until late 1813, or even 1814 (something that applies throughout the Army).

During the campaign in Spain the exigencies of war, and the problems of supply, forced the *Reggimento Napoleone* to have coats made in the locally available dark brown, or mid red-brown, cloth. These coats were nonetheless made to the regulation cut and retained their original facings although of a colour nearer claret than the original crimson, buttons were transferred from the original coats, as were elite company epaulettes.

An unusual button is traditionally from the *2° Reggimento Napoleone* and is embossed with a cursive 'N' below an Imperial or Royal

Knötel Plate VI/42, The Two Regiment of Dragoons of the Kingdom of Italy, 1812. (Author's Collection)

8 A contemporary painting in Castel St Angelo in Rome is recorded by René North in the notes to his 'Paint Your Own Cards, set 106' as showing the 2nd with green collar and cuffs. All other sources however record these as of the facing colour, an option that I would favour.

9 My feeling, and I would stress that it is no more than that, is that the latter are French 'stocks' perhaps sent to Italy to cover for a shortage for whatever reason.

10 More correctly these should be, *Manuel de l'Administration et de la Vérification des Masses d'Habillement et de Harnachement et Ferrage*, par le Goupil (Paris: Libraire pour l'Art Militaire, 1812) – perhaps 'Bardin Regulations' is easier…

Crown (not the Iron Crown). It is possible that this pattern of button was the first used by the dragoon regiments. Given the longevity of such items, these buttons could have remained in use in many cases throughout the life of the regiments.

Breeches, et cetera

Breeches were white and the regiments wore the high cuffed heavy cavalry boots with steel spurs. On campaign the breeches were replaced with, or worn underneath, grey overall trousers with cloth covered buttons at the outer seam (these were also made in the local brown cloth when the regiments were in Spain). Waistcoats were white with white metal buttons. White leather gauntlets were worn for parade, replaced by gauntlets of buff leather on campaign. In Spain there is some evidence of the use of brown trousers in place of grey.

Greatcoats were very light grey, almost white, with a lining of the regimental facing colour, and with a light grey shoulder length cape. The front of the greatcoats and the capes were closed with large, cloth covered buttons, and they had deep, turned-back cuffs.

Equipment

The whitened leather pouch belt was worn over the left shoulder and supported a black leather cartridge box against the right hip; the belt had a large, open, brass buckle behind the shoulder. The cartridge box lid was decorated with a brass grenade for the elite company, but was plain for all other companies. The waist belt was white with a closed brass buckle and supported the straight heavy cavalry sword on double slings. On campaign the belt was often worn over the right shoulder, and with the pouch belt it thus gave the appearance of cross belts. Swords had a brass three bar hilt and the scabbards were black leather with brass fittings. The sword-knot was red in the elite company and all white for the centre companies.

The musket was a shorter version of the same weapon as that carried by the infantry, and was of the same calibre, thus it was a true musket and not a cavalry carbine. Like the infantry musket it was bound and fitted in steel and had a whitened leather sling with a brass buckle. When mounted, dragoons carried their muskets in a bucket, butt downward, on the right side of the saddle.

Officers and N.C.O.s

As might be expected, the N.C.O.s' insignia and rank badges were the same as those of the infantry, in silver or white and with a narrow regimental facing colour piping along the edge. Senior N.C.O.s of the elite companies had mixed silver and red fringes on their epaulettes and mixed silver and red cords on the bearskin. The sword-knots were mixed silver and company colour, or mixed silver and red in the elite company.

Officers' helmets were gilded brass with gilded brass chin scales and leopard skin turbans. Field Officers' helmets had the leopard skin extended down to cover the peak. On campaign, and when not in action, many officers wore the bicorne with silver lace trim to the upper edges and National cockade with silver lace cockade strap. Field Officers used white plumes while those of the company officers were white with a tip of the regimental facing colour. Officers of the elite company wore the bearskin with silver cords, white plumes tipped red and the grenade on the rear patch was in silver.

Officers' coats were of the same cut as those of the rank and file but of a finer cloth, all buttons were silver-plated,

2° *Dragoni Napoleone*, 1811/1812
Left: *Colonello*. The absence of turnback badges could be a personal affectation but may be no more than an error on Boisselier's part.
Centre: Officer. Note that there is (probably) a small error on the illustration and that the epaulette on the right shoulder should be fringed
Right: *Dragone*
(Watercolour by Henri Boisselier, Author's Collection)

2° *Dragoni Napoleone*, *Tamburo* and *Trombettiere* 1810/1812
The *trombettiere* is from the Regiment's elite company, as indicated by the white fringed epaulettes, note his sword hooked directly to the waist belt for ease of movement while dismounted – a practice common throughout the Army (and other armies of the period). The red mane on the *tamburo*' helmet is otherwise unrecorded in sources I have seen. (Watercolour by Henri Boisselier, Author's Collection)

and the turnback badges were silver. The epaulettes of rank, which followed the same sequence as the infantry, were silver. On campaign officers customarily wore a dark green surtout coat with collar, cuffs, turnbacks and piping as on the habit.

Breeches and waistcoats were white, gauntlets were whitened leather and spurs were usually silvered. Greatcoats were dark green and of the same pattern as those of the troopers with white metal, sometimes silvered, buttons.

Officers' pouch-belts and waist belts were white leather for parade and black leather for campaign, all buckles and fittings were silvered. Swords were of essentially the same pattern as those of the other ranks but had gilded hilts, and were carried in a black leather scabbard with gilt fittings and silver sword-knot and tassel.

Musicanti

The *trombettieri* of dragoons wore the same pattern of helmet as the other ranks with a white horsehair tail and houpette and a facing colour plume with dark green tip. The coat was of reversed colours, that is either pink or crimson, with dark green facings. The *trombettieri* of the elite companies had white full-fringed epaulettes. The collar, cuffs and lapels were trimmed with either plain white or mixed white and facing colour lace. Trumpets were brass and had either green or mixed green and facing colour cords.

The *tamburo* wore the same uniform as the *trombettieri* but with black gaiters instead of the riding boots of his mounted colleague. The drummer's apron and drum carriage belt were whitened leather with brass buckles, the carriage belt was decorated with a brass drumstick plate on the breast. The drums had brass barrels and the hoops were painted with diagonal stripes of green-white-red-white. Sword-knots and tassels were of the regimental facing colour.

The *Tromba-Maggiori* wore the same uniform as the rest of the *musicanti* with the addition of the usual rank insignia and the silver, or mixed silver and facing colour lace to the collar, cuffs, and lapels. The bicorne had silver lace edging silver tassels and the plume was of the regimental facing colour tipped green.

1° Reggimentto

Trombettiere, 1806–1807: A sky blue coat of the same cut as that worn by the light horse Regiments with white lace batons on the breast, a crimson collar and crimson Polish cuffs, both edged with a wide white lace. White fringed epaulettes with brass scaled straps and crescents. Usual dragoon pattern helmet with white mane and houpette. Light grey overalls with crimson lace to the seams and pockets. Black leather sword scabbard fitted with brass.

Trombettiere, Elite Company, 1810–1812: Pink habit with pink collar and dark green lapels, both edged with wide white lace. White fringed epaulettes with brass scaled straps and crescents. White gauntlets. Black peaked bearskin with brass chin scales, peak binding and plate embossed with a grenade badge, white plume tipped pink. Dark green early pattern shabraque with white laced edging, edged again with a narrow pink lace, and a white grenade badge in the rear corners, dark green double-holster covers with the same lace as the shabraque and a dark green square portmanteau again with the same lace. Plain white trumpet cords.

2° Reggimentto

Trombettiere, 1810: Crimson habit coat with dark green collar, lapels and turnbacks, all edged with wide white lace. White fringed epaulettes with brass scaled straps and crescents. Usual dragoon pattern helmet with brown fur turban, white houpette and white plume tipped crimson, and white mane. Buff gauntlets with white cuffs. Dark green half shabraque with white lace edging piped dark green and a white grenade badge in the rear corners, brown sheepskin with crimson dogtooth edging. Plain white trumpet cords.

Tamburo, 1810: Coat as above but with crimson collar, laced white, crimson Brandenburg cuffs piped dark green and plain green cuff flaps. Plain white fringed epaulettes. Dragoon pattern helmet with black fur turban with brass crowned 'N' on the front, black houpette, crimson mane, white plume tipped crimson. Black gaiters. Brass drum with the hoops diagonally striped in red / white / green / white / red / et cetera. Brown wooden drumsticks and brass drumstick plate on the cross belt.

Zappatori

Two regimental *zappatori* were attached to the elite company and wore the regulation uniform of that company with the addition of the usual *zappatore* insignia and equipment. The buff leather apron was slightly shorter than that of the infantry sappers and when mounted the apron was rolled up and held at the waist by a wide waist belt with brass buckle plate, embossed with a grenade. The *zappatori* may have carried the lance after the fashion of the French dragoon *sapeurs*, possibly with a facing colour over white pennon – this is shown in some modern illustrations (e.g. those of Lucien Rousselot) but no contemporary sources are given.

In the Museum der Bundeswehr in Dresden is a halberd identified as being from the *2° Reggimentto 'Napoleone'* and taken at the Battle of Dresden on 27 August 1813. Dr Gerhard Bauer has suggested that this is from the Eagle Guard of the Regiment. The head is similar in style and size to that of the *zappatore* axe but on a shaft approximately six feet eleven inches in length. To my mind this seems an incredibly impractical weapon to carry on horseback and, assuming that the head hasn't been remounted onto a longer shaft (for which there is no evidence), it may simply be a parade item.[11]

Horse Furniture

In 1805 the shabraque used by the dragoon regiments was dark green with squared rear corners and a brown leather saddle with black leather rubbing patches. The shabraque and pistol covers had a wide white band around the outer edge and white grenades decorated the rear corners of the shabraque. The dark green valise was square and dark green with white edging at the ends. When not worn the cloak was folded with the facing colour lining on the outside and strapped on top of the valise.

Trombettieri' shabraques were of the same pattern with white trim and were of the regimental facing colour.

Officers' shabraques were of a similar pattern; dark green but with triple holster covers and a double silver stripe, the outer stripe twice the width of the inner, in place of the white. The rear corners of the shabraque were devoid of the grenade decoration.

In 1808 the dragoon troopers and *trombettieri* adopted the French style half shabraque with white sheepskin saddle cover edged with a dark green dogtooth cloth. The dark green cloth was decorated the same as the 1805 pattern. As in the French Army the officers continued to use the 1805 pattern shabraque.

Cacciatori a Cavallo

(Light Horse Regiments)

Service

1° Reggimento, Reale Italiano (Royal Italian)

1805 Italy	
November / December	Venice Observation and then Blockade Corps
1807 Germany	
June 5	Engagement on the Passarge (7 Officers killed, including *Colonnello* Zapetti, and six more wounded)
June 7	Storm of Guttstadt. After this engagement the Regiment left the Army to return to Italy.
1808 Spain	No engagements of note although one officer was wounded in June (location and exact date unrecorded)
1809 Austria	
July 6	Battle of Wagram (1 Officer wounded)
1809 Spain	
December 3	Skirmish at Girona (1 Officer wounded)
1810 Spain	
April 10	Skirmish at Mora (*Colonnello* Villeta wounded)
December 10	One officer wounded on patrol in Catalonia

11 For a full discussion of this item see Dr Berhard Bauer, 'Comme Les Licteurs Romains,' in *Soldats Napoleoniens: Les Troupes Françaises, Alliés et Coalisées. Hors-série No.1, Avril 2003*, (Paris: Éditions de la Revue Napoléon, 2003), pp.60–62.

1811 Spain	
January 4	Action near Lerida (1 Officer mortally wounded)
October 26	Combat at Daroca (1 Officer killed, 2 wounded)
1812 Spain	No memorable actions recorded
1813 Germany	
August 26	Battle of Dresden (2 Officers wounded)
August 29	Battle of Culm (11 Officers wounded, 1 mortally)
October 3	One Officer wounded on patrol in Saxony
October 30	Battle of Hanau (1 Officer wounded)

1° Reggimento di Cacciatori a Cavallo, Reale Italiano, Senior Officer, full dress *c.* 1810
The full dress leopard skin shabraque is recorded as being used by the officers of the elite company of both the *1°* and the *4° Reggimenti*. The white plume is indicative of an officer on the regimental staff, officers of the elite company wore either the yellow plume with a green tip, as for the rest of the regiment or, possibly, a red plume. (Watercolour by Henri Boisselier, Author's Collection)

1° Reggimento di Cacciatori a Cavallo, Reale Italiano, Capitano c. 1810
This is the regulation full dress uniform after the issue of the shako *c.* 1808. Note the use of hussar style chevrons of rank on the cuffs even though he is not wearing an hussar style uniform. (Watercolour by Henri Boisselier, Author's Collection)

1814 Italy	
March 3	Battle of Parma (7 Officers wounded)
March 6	Battle of the St-Maurice Bridge (1 Officer wounded)

2° Reggimento, Reale Prince (Royal Prince)

1808 Spain	
November 8	Skirmish at Sana (1 Officer wounded)
1809 Austria	
June 6	Skirmish at Klagenfurt (1 Officer wounded)
1812 Russia	
July 22	Skirmish at Rechenkevitchi (3 Officers wounded)

July 29	Skirmish at Welissa (3 Officers killed, 7 wounded – 1 mortally)
August 9	Skirmish at Janoyotschi (1 Officer wounded)
September 7	Battle of Borodino (1 Officer killed, 2 wounded)
September 22	One officer wounded on outpost duty "near Moscow"
October 24	Battle of Maloyaroslavets (1 Officer wounded)
November 3	Skirmish at Wiasna (*Colonnello* killed, 2 other Officers wounded)
December 10	Skirmish before Wilna (3 Officers missing, 2 wounded)
December 13/14	Skirmishing at Kowno (2 officers wounded, 1 mortally)
1813 Germany	
March 4	One Officer wounded during the retreat from Berlin
August 26 / 27	Battle of Dresden (3 Officers wounded) Two further Officers were killed and 10 wounded, 1 mortally, during the defence of Dresden up to 13 October
1813 Italy	
November 15	Battle of Caldiero (1 Officer wounded)
1814 Italy	
February 8	Battle of the Mincio (1 Officer killed, 1 wounded)

3º Reggimento

1812 Russia	
September 7	Battle of Borodino (1 Officer killed, 2 wounded)
October 7	1 Officer killed in a nameless skirmish "near Moscow"
October 24	Battle of Maloyaroslavets (1 Officer killed, 2 wounded)
November 3	Skirmish at Wiasna (1 Officer killed, 5 wounded – 2 mortally)
November 9	One officer killed in a minor skirmish near Smolensk
1813 Germany	
March 4	One Officer wounded in a skirmish "near Berlin".
April 5	Skirmish on the Elbe (1 Officer wounded)

1813 Italy	
September 3	One officer killed while on reconnaissance "in Italy".
October 21	Skirmish at Ceneda (1 Officer killed)
October 22	One officer wounded while on outpost duty near Ceneda
December 3	Battle of Rovige (10 Officers wounded, including *Colonnello* Ramboure)
1814 Italy	
February 8	Battle of the Mincio (6 Officers wounded)
February 23	Skirmish near Mantua (1 Officer wounded)
March 3	Battle of Parma (1 Officer wounded)

1º Reggimento di Cacciatori a Cavallo, Reale Italiano, Colonello and *cacciatori c. 1810*
Uniformed according to the regulations except for the unusual aspect of the lack of thigh decorations for the *Colonello* and the left-hand *cacciatore*, and the Hungarian Knots in place of spearheads on the right-hand *cacciatore*. All are recorded variations however but the overall simplicity of the uniform of the *Colonello* suggests perhaps campaign dress. Note the inverted 'V' leather reinforcements on the right-hand *cacciatore'* shako, this style seems to have been common throughout the Kingdom's Army and may have more to do with the manufacturer's methods rather than any deliberate variation of the usual French shako style of a simple 'V'. (Watercolour by Henri Boisselier, Author's Collection)

March 11	Skirmish near Guestalla (1 Officer wounded)
March 31	One officer wounded on reconnaissance near Milan

4º Reggimento

1813 Germany	(began the campaign with a strength of 433 Officers and men)
February 22	Skirmish at Münchberg (9 Officers wounded)
May 20	Battle of Bautzen (2 Officers wounded)
August 26	Skirmish of Liegnitz (2 Officers wounded)
October 13	1 Officer wounded while on outpost duty near Leipzig
1813 Italy	
November 10	1 Officer wounded while on patrol "in Italy"
November 13	Skirmish at Caldiero (1 Officer wounded)
1814 Italy	
February 8	Battle of the Mincio (strength of 261 officers and men, 12 Officers wounded in the battle)
March 10	Skirmish at Roverbella (1 Officer wounded)

1º Reggimento di Cacciatori a Cavallo, Reale Principale, Trompettiere and *Cacciatori*, c. 1810
Notable is the unusual shape of the thigh decoration lace – a hybrid of a true Hungarian Knot and the plainer spearhead style. The lack of a shako plate on all three figures is also unusual but may reflect a temporary shortage? The left-hand figure gives a good, and rarely shown, rear view of the carbine and cartouche box belts. (Watercolour by Henri Boisselier, Author's Collection)

Uniform

Headwear

Although the regiment was formed in 1805 the new regulation uniforms were not issued to the *1º Reggimento* until the following year and until then the regiment continued with its earlier uniform from the Cisalpine Republic.[12] Even with the 1806 issue, although the regiment should then have been equipped with the shako it seems that the older Polish style czapska remained in use. The box of the cap was black, trimmed at the edges with black cord and with a black fur turban. The National cockade with white cockade strap was worn at the front left upper edge and was surmounted by a dark green over yellow plume or ball pompom. The peak was black leather with brass edging and the chin scales were also brass. Some companies of the regiment may have continued wearing the czapska until as late as 1808 or 1809 (this could simply have been because such things take a decade to wear out and replacement was thus not a priority).

The *2º Reggimento may* also have been issued with the czapska but it is more likely that it received the shako of black felt with black leather reinforcement to the upper and lower edges and a white metal lozenge plate embossed with regimental number within a bugle horn. The shako had white metal chin scales and a National cockade, with white cockade strap, surmounted by a green ball pompom or plume. By 1810 both the *1º* and *2º Reggimenti* were

12 This may be for no other reason than that there was already supply still in stores. A similar delay happens in any change of uniform, military prudence always dictates that whatever is in store is used first, thus contemporary illustrations often show a mix of old and new patterns of equipment. Even after the disaster of 1812 modern research has shown that much of the new Grande Armée of 1813 were issued with the older style of coat, so great was the number of coats in store. Records for the French Army indicate that the depot may have held enough coats at the end of any year to re-equip the whole regiment. It is likely that the Kingdom's Army had similar provision.

definitely wearing the shako and the *3º* and *4º Reggimenti* were issued the shako from their raising in 1811 (see below for notes on the headwear of the *3º Reggimento* however). For parades the centre companies wore white shako cords and a dark green plume with a pompom of regimental colour at the base and a tip of the same colour.

A variation to the above known to have been worn by the *1º Reggimento* was that the shako had a large National cockade with long white cockade strap at the front in place of the lozenge plate. Knötel shows this shako with a white inverted 'V' of lace at the sides.

The elite companies[13] of all regiments wore the black fur hussar style colpack with facing colour bag piped white for the *1º Reggimento*, dark green for the *2º* and *4º Reggimenti*, and probably also for the *3º*. Cords were white for the *1º Reggimento* and red for the *2º*, *3º* and *4º Reggimenti*, with red pompoms or plumes in all four regiments.

It has been suggested that all companies of the *3º Reggimento* initially wore the black fur colpack without the customary bag, with white metal chin scales, white cords and regimental colour pompom, or plume as above. However in his article on the *3º Reggimento*[14] Ricardo Papi presented definitive arguments that this is simply a

1º Reggimento di Cacciatori a Cavallo, Reale Italiano, 1812
Regulation trooper's uniform although the shako should have a plate or the 'long cockade strap' as discussed in the text. The illustration appears as though the plate has been painted out but the cockade strap never added.
(Vinkhuijzen Collection, General Research Division, New York Public Library Digital Collections. Public Domain)

2º Reggimento di Cacciatori a Cavallo, Reale Principale, Cacciatore, campaign dress, Russia 1812
Based on contemporary eyewitness descriptions and illustrations, this figure shows how far, in many instances, what should have been worn was adapted in the field. Note the unadorned colpack, apparently even without its bag, but also the use of a cloth shabraque in place of the regulation sheepskin in the elite company. This *cacciatore* also appears to have dispensed with the carbine belt but probably kept the carbine itself, perhaps attached to the shabraque or the saddle as was the custom in many French light cavalry regiments.
(Watercolour by Henri Boisselier, Author's Collection)

13 As in the dragoon regiments the 1st Company of the 1st Squadron was designated as the elite company.

14 Ricardo Papi, 'Le 3e Régiment de Chasseurs à Cheval Italiens,' in *Soldats Napoleoniens : Les Troupes Françaises, Alliés et Coalisées. No.26, Juin 2010.*, (Paris: Éditions de la Revue Napoléon, 2010), pp.58–63.

misinterpretation of the sources and the centre companies *3º* wore the shako, with the colpack reserved for the elite company, the same as the other three regiments.

In 1814 the regiments officially adopted the cylindrical shako as regulated for the French light cavalry in the 'Bardin Regulations'. This was of black felt with the National cockade at the front upper edge, white cords and the upper edge trimmed with yellow. Chin scales were white metal and the peak and rear cuff of black leather. Whether this was ever issued in any quantity before the dissolution of the Kingdom at the end of 1814 is subject to a great deal of conjecture.

The fatigue caps of the *Cacciatori a Cavallo* were dark green with facing colour piping and tassel and may, in some cases, have been decorated with the bugle horn insignia at the front of the headband.

Coat

The first coat pattern of the *1º* and *2º Reggimenti* was a dark green surtout with the collar, pointed cuffs and turnbacks of the regimental colour and the vertical pockets piped in the regimental facing colour. The coat was closed with a single row of eight white metal buttons and each button and buttonhole had a broad white lace baton with pointed end. Each side of the collar was decorated with a similar baton of white lace and there were two similar batons on the lower sleeves, one above and one below the cuff edge. The *3º* were initially issued with the same pattern of coat as the *1º* and *2º Reggimenti.*

The *4º Reggimento* wore a *à la kinski* pattern coat, which was similar in cut to the surtout but with short tails (with vertical pockets?), all other details as for the first three regiments although this coat did not have the lace batons. This pattern of coat was adopted by the other three regiments in 1812 apparently before the Russian campaign.

For service dress all regiments wore the surtout or *habit-a-kinski*. In most respects this appeared the same as the full dress coat but was without the lace batons on the breast or cuffs.

The regimental facing colours were:

1º Reggimento Reale Italiano	yellow
2º Reggimento Real Principale	red
3º Reggimento (untitled)	orange
4º Reggimento (untitled)	crimson

Before 1810 the centre companies of the *1º* and *2º Reggimenti* wore facing colour contre-epaulettes with white metal scales on the straps, the elite companies

2º Regimentto di Cacciatori a Cavallo, Reale Prince, c. 1806/6
These paintings by Henri Boisselier are undated and unusually the mounted trooper is also without his sources on either the front or the back, although the source may well be the same as that of the two dismounted. Nonetheless the depiction of a czapska in place of a shako and the use of a full cloth saddlecloth confirms that these are from the earliest part of the Regiment's history. Boisselier's depiction of the way of wearing the czapska MAY be an error. (Watercolours by Henri Boisselier in the Author's Collection)

wore full-fringed versions of the same epaulettes with white fringes. From 1810 dark green bastion ended shoulder straps with facing colour piping were adopted by the centre companies; the elite companies continued the fringed epaulettes of the previous pattern but these now with red crescents and fringes; NB this pattern may never have been taken into use in the *1º Reggimento* the sources are somewhat contradictory.

The *3º Reggimento*, although wearing the *à la kinski* pattern coat as above for campaign wear, is recorded as having equipped its elite company with an hussar style full dress uniform. The hussar style dolman and pelisse were dark green with white lace trim to the edge, white lace 'trees' on the rear seam and orange collar and pointed cuffs edged with white lace. The pelisse was trimmed with black fur. Braiding on both dolman and pelisse was white and all buttons on both dolman and pelisse were white metal.

By 1814, shortly before the dissolution of the Kingdom, the *1º Reggimento*, and possibly the *2º Reggimento* as well, also appear to have adopted the full hussar style uniform for their elite companies with sixteen rows of white braid on the breast of the pelisse and dolman and three rows of small white metal buttons, the collar and cuffs were of facing colour and the barrel sash was red and white for all regiments.

Breeches, et cetera

Breeches and waistcoats were dark green, the former having facing colour spearheads on the thighs and a wide facing colour stripe (white in the *2º Reggimento*) on the outer seam.

Boots were of the Hungarian pattern with shaped tops and white, red for the elite companies, lace trim and tassel.

Dark green or grey overall trousers with black leather inserts and cuffs were issued for campaign wear in 1811. These had a wide facing colour stripe on the outer seam, a double stripe in the *3º Reggimento*, and a single row of either white metal or cloth covered buttons.

Greatcoats were dark green and of the same pattern as those of the dragoons, with facing colour lining and collar as on the coat, all buttons were white metal.

On full dress parades all ranks wore white wrist gloves but these were replaced by white leather gauntlets on campaign.

Equipment

The pouch belt was whitened leather and the cartridge box was black leather with a plain lid in the centre companies but with a brass bugle horn badge for the elite companies. The narrow white waist belt fastened with a brass 'S' clasp/buckle, all other fittings were also brass.

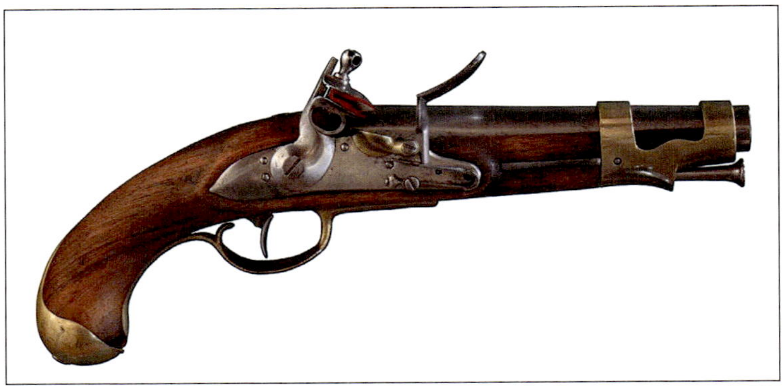

French *An IX* Pattern pistol
(Rama, CC BY-SA 3.0 fr, https://commons.wikimedia.org/w/index.php?curid=11581719)

The sabre was of the curved light cavalry pattern, with brass hilt (both single-bar and triple-bar hilt variants were in use[15]) and a white sword-knot and tassel, or red in the elite companies. The sabre was carried in a black leather scabbard, fitted in brass, suspended from twin white leather slings.

Pistols, carried in holsters at the front of the saddle and hidden beneath the shabraque, were copies of the French Year IX light cavalry model, but made within the Kingdom not in France.

In 1809 the French light cavalry carbine of Year IX pattern, fitted in brass, was issued to all regiments. This was suspended from a whitened leather carbine bandolier fitted with brass, with a steel carbine clip, and worn over the pouch belt. Although of French pattern the carbine was again actually manufactured in arsenals within the Kingdom.

The *3º Reggimento* wore a facing colour sabretache suspended from the waist belt on white slings. The face of the sabretache had a white edging and bore the regimental number in white at its centre.

Officers & N.C.O.s

The N.C.O.s had the same basic distinctions as the infantry with the sleeve insignia in the form of lace chevrons above each cuff. *Sergenti* and senior N.C.O.s did not carry the carbine.

Officers' headwear followed the pattern worn by the regiment and was trimmed with the normal silver lace and had silvered cords. The sword-knots were silver. Plumes were white for Field and Staff officers and white with a tip of the facing colour for company officers.

As with so much in the Kingdom's Army many officers imitated their French counterparts and, even

15 I have not found confirmation as to whether the two variants were issued differently to different regiments, different companies within the same regiments, or even entirely randomly as stocks were available.

4° *Regimentto di Cacciatori a Cavallo*, *cacciatore*, campaign dress, Russia 1812 (left); *Colonello*, full dress 1813–1814 (centre); *cacciatore*, full dress 1813 (right).
(Watercolour by Henri Boisselier in the Author's Collection)

Officer's Belt Buckle, 3° *Cacciatori a Cavallo*. Date unknown. (Private Collection, ©photo courtesy of Laurent Claudet)

when serving in the centre companies, wore the black fur colpack. Elite company officers and senior field and company officers are also sometimes recorded wearing variants of the hussar style uniform with facings of the regimental colour, silver braid and black or white fur on the pelisse. Many of these 'fantasies' were quite individual, particularly for the field officers.

The officers' surtouts and kinski coats had silver lace batons, and breeches were decorated with silver lace Hungarian knots or spearheads on the thighs and silver stripes on the outside seams. Boots had silver lace and tassels and, at least on parade, silver-plated spurs were worn. Silver epaulettes were worn on the surtout and kinski coat and followed the same rank epaulette sequence as that of the dragoon regiments.

Officers' rank badges on the hussar style dolman were in the form of chevrons above the cuffs; the first chevron trimmed the upper edge of the cuff and was 14mm wide.

Colonello	Five silver chevrons, three of 14mm alternating with two of 23mm
Maggiore	As for the *Colonello* but with the centre 14mm chevron in gold
Capo di Squadrone	Four silver chevrons alternately 14mm and 23mm
Capitano	Three silver chevrons, two of 14mm with one of 23mm in between
Tenente	Two silver 14mm chevrons
Sotto Tenente	One silver 14mm chevron

2° *Regimentto di Cacciatori a Cavallo*, *Reale Prince*, c. 1810. The uniforms shown follow that laid down in the regulations and the absence of a shako plate is confirmed from many other sources. Similarly the hussar pattern boots without lace and tassel as worn by the right-hand figure is not unusual. (Watercolour by Henri Boisselier in the Author's Collection)

2° *Regimentto di Cacciatori a Cavallo, Reale Prince*, c. 1813
Cacciatore in field dress (left) and full dress elite company (right). Following regulations although the left-hand trooper's 'round' shako is not normally commented on but it logically follows the style in use in the French Army. The facing colour 'patch' on the collar in place of a full facing colour collar is again unusual. (Watercolour by Henri Boisselier in the Author's Collection)

The same sequence and colouring was used for the spearhead-shaped lace on front of the breeches.

A plate by Guglielmo Aimaretti for Luca Cristini's study of the Army[16] shows an officer, dated 1813, wearing the cylindrical shako that was introduced into the French Army by the 'Bardin Regulations'. The shako is scarlet with a black leather peak, upper and lower leather bands. The upper band has a silver 'chain effect' braid and below the band is a wide band of silver lace. The plume is a white feather 'falling' style. The same plate shows the officer wearing a green pelisse with silver braid and brown fur and scarlet lancer style trousers with a broad silver stripe down the seam. He is armed with a heavily curved Mameluke style sword in place of the normal sabre (this was also a highly-fashionable affectation in French and British Armies as well as the Italian).

Musicanti

Trombettieri generally wore the same pattern coat as the troop but in reversed colours, i.e. facing colour coat with green facings, but with white lace as for the regiment. The fringed epaulettes were white, and trumpet cords either white or mixed white and facing colour. Headwear was as for the rest of the troop with a facing colour plume, tipped white. Swords, et cetera were the same as for

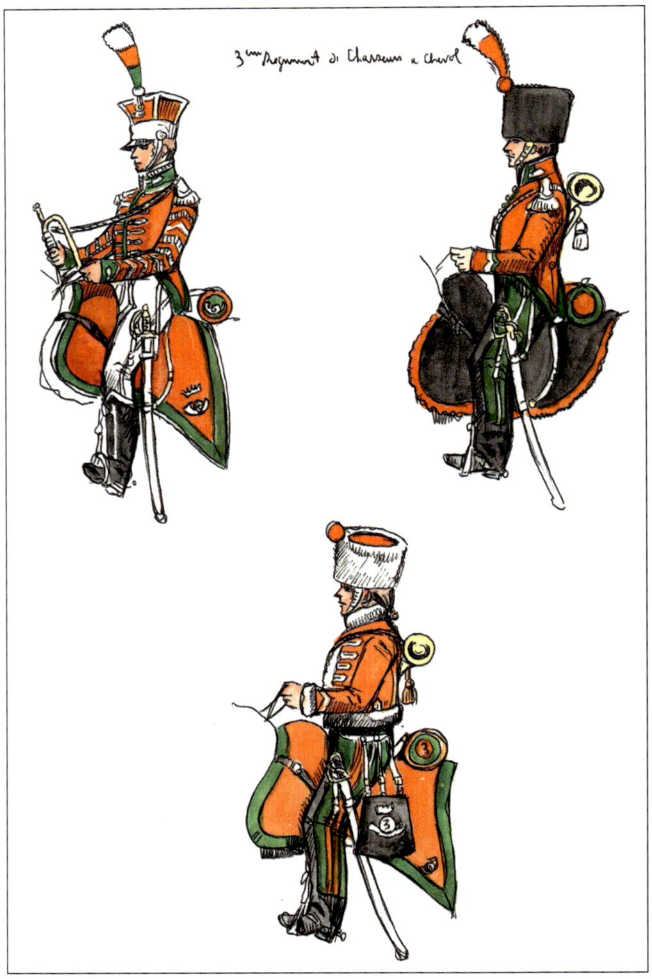

3° *Regimentto di Cacciatori a Cavallo, Trombettieri*
Top Left: full dress, c. 1806. Top right: campaign dress, c. 1810. Bottom: campaign dress, c. 1813. *Trombettieri'* uniforms could vary almost year to year as each issue could change with the whim of the Colonel or the availability, and cost, of any particular item. The white breeches with white decorations on the 1806 *trombettiere* are particularly striking. As mentioned in the text the *trombettiere* of 1813 may be wearing a dolman beneath his pelisse, although this is by no means a certainty. (Watercolour by Henri Boisselier in the Author's Collection)

16 Luca Stefano Cristini and Guglielmo Aimaretti, *L'Esercito Del Regno Italico 1805–1814. Volume 2: La Cavalleria*, (Lodigliano: Soldiershop, 2011), plate A.

3º Regimentto di Cacciatori a Cavallo, Elite Company 1811/1812

Trombettiere and trooper of the Regiment's elite company in 1811. There is evidence that the elite company wore hussar dress, see the plate below, in full dress so these two figures probably represent service dress. Note the collar patch lace recorded in some sources. It is unlikely that the colpack's use survived beyond the 1812 campaign. (Watercolour by Henri Boisselier in the Author's Collection)

the troop although *trombettieri* were not issued with carbines, although they did receive pistols and thus wore the cartouche box of the same pattern as the troop.

1º Reggimento

Trombettiere, Elite Company, *c.* 1811: yellow hussar style dolman and pelisse with white braid and yellow collar and cuffs, both trimmed with white lace. A black colpack with yellow bag, laced white with a white tassel, and a green plume with yellow tip. The Breeches were green with white lace and a red sabretache edged white with a central white wreath encircling a white 'R'. Saddlery was a white sheepskin with yellow dogtooth edging.

NB Boisselier illustrates an almost identically dressed Trumpeter under the date of 1805. The only noticeable difference is that the colpack is more noticeably brown-black, the thigh decorations on the breeches are Hungarian knots, and, unusually, the trumpet cords are mixed red and yellow.[17]

Trombettiere, 1812: a yellow coat of the same pattern as in use by the rank and file, with green collar and cuffs, both trimmed with white lace. Plain black shako with National cockade but no plate, brass chin scales and a white over yellow plume. Green breeches with white Hungarian knots and lace to the outer seam. Green cloth covered cartridge box belt trimmed with white lace. Mixed green and yellow trumpet cords.

Trombettiere, 1813: a sky blue uniform as for the rank and file, with yellow collar, cuff flaps and turnbacks, white lace and blue cuffs piped yellow. Red epaulettes with brass scaled straps. Breeches were sky blue with yellow Hungarian knots and stripes. A white colpack with red bag piped yellow, cords and plume. Black sheepskin shabraque with yellow dogtooth edging. Mixed green and yellow trumpet cords.

2º Reggimento

Trombettiere, 1812: red coat of the same pattern as the rank and file with green collar and cuffs, both trimmed with white lace, white lace batons on the breast collar and cuffs and a wide piping of green down the front seam of the coat continuing into the green turnbacks. White full-fringed epaulettes. Plain black shako with National cockade but no plate, brass chin scales and a white over red plume above a white over red ball. Green breeches with white lace and Hungarian knots. Black Hungarian boots trimmed silver. Plain white trumpet cords.

Boisselier shows a (undated) variant of this uniform with red decorations on the breeches and a plain red ball at the base of the plume.

Trombettiere, 1812–13: white colpack with red plume and red bag piped white, white tassel. Sky blue coat with red collar, turnbacks and Polish cuffs all piped white. White breast lace and white metal buttons. Brass covering on the epaulette straps with white crescents and fringes. Buff yellow gauntlets. Grey overalls fitted and cuffed in black leather and with a broad red stripe at the outer seam. Black sheepskin shabraque with red dogtooth edging. Dark green portmanteau with red lace and a red '2' on the ends. Brass trumpet with red cords.

3º Reggimento

Tromba-Maggiori, 1810: Orange coat of the same cut as the rank and file, with green facings, white epaulettes with mixed orange and white fringes, white lace and six white lace chevrons on each sleeve. Buff breeches with orange stripe and spearheads and an orange czapska with white fur turban, piping and cordon, with tricolour plume, red, over white, over green surmounting a white pompom. Orange cloth shabraque with a wide dark green lace piped orange and with a white horn below the Iron Crown in the rear corners. Green portmanteau with

17 Plate 5 by Henri Boisselier in *Le Sabretache*, (Paris: SCFH, 1957).

orange lace at the ends and a white horn badge. White cords on the brass trumpet.

Trombettiere, Elite Company, 1810: Orange coat of the same cut as the rank and file, with green facings edged with white lace, epaulettes with green straps and white fringing. Dark green breeches with orange stripe on the outer seam. Black colpack, with white cords and a white over orange plume. Trumpet and shabraque as above except for the omission of the badge on the shabraque and portmanteau.

Trombettiere, Elite Company, 1810: Orange surtout coat with orange collar and Polish cuffs and plain green turnbacks. Both the collar and cuffs had a wide white lace edge, itself in turn trimmed with a wide dark green lace. The collar had a single dark green bastion tipped baton from the front edge. White fringed epaulettes. Black colpack without a bag, brass chin scales, and a white over orange plume above a white over orange ball. Dark green overalls with orange lace trim. Black sheepskin shabraque trimmed orange, orange portmanteau with green lace. Brass trumpet with white cords.

Trombettiere, Elite Company, 1813: Orange pelisse[18] with white lace batons, as worn on the rank and file's coats, and white fur trim, orange cuffs laced white, and white lace at the rear seams. White colpack with orange bag and a red ball pompom. Dark green overalls with a

3° Regimentto di Cacciatori a Cavallo, Elite Company 1811 & 1813
The left-hand figure is the full dress hussar style recorded for the Regiment's elite company from its raising and from the red shako probably dates to 1813. The right-hand figure, is the campaign dress for the elite company with the simpler coat *à la kinski* and dates to *c.* 1811. It is unlikely that the colpack's use survived beyond the 1812 campaign. (Watercolour by Henri Boisselier in the Author's Collection)

3° Regimentto di Cacciatori a Cavallo, *zappatore* and *cacciatore*, campaign dress, 1812.
Notable is the plain surtout coat of the *cacciatore* and the retention of the baton-laced coat of the *zappatore*, although otherwise he is uniformed closely to the *cacciatore*. The lance was commonly carried by *zappatori* of mounted regiments although the small National flag pennon is unusual and definitely not regulation. Also notable is the lack of a bag on the *zappatore*' colpack which had a red patch with a green cross, suggesting that the bag has not just been removed for campaign wear but did not form a part of the cap even in full dress. (Watercolour by Henri Boisselier in the Author's Collection)

18 The *trombettiere* is illustrated wearing the pelisse, presumably over the dolman but this is speculation.

double orange stripe. Orange cloth shabraque with green lace edge and a white horn badge in the rear corners. Orange portmanteau, laced green and with white '3' on the ends. The black leather sabretache is plain except for a large white horn badge below a white Iron Crown. Brass trumpet with white cords.

4º Reggimento

1811–1812: Crimson coat of the same pattern and style as the rank and file with dark green collar and Polish cuffs, both trimmed in wide white lace, itself trimmed with wide dark green lace and a wide dark green piping down the front of the coat, dark green turnbacks piped crimson. White fringed epaulettes with mixed white and crimson fringes. Plain shako with National cockade but no plate and a white over crimson plume with a crimson ball pompom base. Dark green breeches with crimson Hungarian knots and lace. White sheepskin with crimson dog's tooth edging. Dark green portmanteau with the ends laced in the appearance of a cockade of crimson (outer) then white then dark green. Brass trumpet with white cords.

Zappatori

The two *zappatori* attached to the regiment's elite company wore the uniform of the company with red epaulettes and white crossed axe badges on the sleeves of the coat, but they did not wear the traditional *zappatore* apron. They wore the hussar style colpack of the same pattern as the regiment's elite company.

1º Reggimento, 1807: *Cacciatori* style infantry bearskin with white cords and red plume.[19] Dark green hussar style dolman with white lace and braid and white crossed axe badges on the sleeves. The *Zappatori* of the *1º* had worn this uniform at least as early as 1801 and it is recorded again in 1807.

3º Reggimento, 1807: Essentially the same uniform as that described for the *1º* but with the colpack of their regiment with white cords, red plume and a yellow patch with a green cross, similar to that on the bearskins of the infantry *granatiere*, in place of the more usual bag.

3º Reggimento, 1812: Coat of the same cut as the rank and file but with a dark green collar with an orange 'patch' at the front edge, at the rear of which is a single white button, and the sapper's crossed axes badge in white on the upper arms. Red epaulettes with brass scaled straps. Black colpack without bag but with an orange patch in the manner of the bearskin, with a green cross; and a red ball pompom. Green overalls with orange stripe and white buttons. Buff gauntlets with black leather cuffs. White sheepskin shabraque with orange dog's tooth edging, dark green portmanteau with white lace ends, trimmed orange, and a white '3' at the centre.

Horse Furniture

The full dress shabraque was dark green with rounded front and pointed rear corners and trimmed with a wide white band piped at the outer edge with the regimental distinctive colour. The rear corners may have been decorated with a white bugle horn in some regiments. The rubbing patch, girth strap and all leatherwork were of black leather. On campaign the above was replaced with a plain white sheepskin saddle cover with dogtooth edging of the regimental facing colour. From 1811 this shabraque replaced the cloth version described above for all orders of dress. The round portmanteau was dark green with a broad white band, piped in the facing colour, around each end.

Trombettieri' cloth shabraques were of the same pattern as the rank and file but of facing colour edged and piped green. On campaign, like the men, they used white sheepskin shabraques with facing colour dog's tooth edging. However, the sheepskins of *Trombettieri* of the *2º Reggimento* were black.

Officers' shabraques were as for the men with silver lace trim and piping and a silver bugle horn badge in the rear corner. Officers used the full cloth shabraque for campaign as well as for parades, although officers of the elite companies of the both the *1º* and *4º Reggimenti* are recorded using a leopard skin shabraque trimmed yellow and crimson respectively, of the same pattern as the rank and file's sheepskins, although these were almost certainly for parade use only.

Gendarmerie Legione

(Gendarme Legion)

The *Gendarmerie* was originally raised in 1806 as a single legion,[20] but by 1808 it had increased to three legions; each with a strength of two mounted squadrons and two foot companies. The squadrons were of two company strength, each with the normal cavalry establishment. The companies of dismounted *Gendarmerie* had a similar establishment to the line infantry but with only 100 rank and file.

The *Gendarmerie Legione* were charged with policing the borders of the Kingdom as well as apprehending deserters and 'draft dodgers' and although not designated as a part of the field army certainly experienced combat in the fighting within the Kingdom in 1813 and 1814.

19 Around 1803–1804 this had a yellow rear patch with a green cross.

20 The term 'Legion' for a military unit had re-emerged during the Eighteenth Century to designate a unit which was composed of both horse and foot – and sometimes artillery.

Knötel Plate II / 45, Mounted Chasseurs, *Gendarmerie*, et cetera of the Army of the Kingdom of Italy, 1812
(Author's Collection)

Headwear

The *Gendarmerie* wore the black felt bicorne trimmed with white lace at the upper edge and with white tassels at the outer tips. The bicorne had the National cockade with a white cockade strap and white metal buttons and a tall red plume for parades, this latter replaced by a carrot-shaped pompom for all other orders of dress. Fatigue caps were dark green with crimson piping and tassel.

Coat

The coat was the regulation pattern habit in dark green with crimson collar, cuffs, turnbacks and lapels, and dark green three-pointed cuff flaps and pockets piped crimson. The turnbacks were decorated with white grenade badges and all buttons were white metal. A white, fringed epaulette was worn on the right shoulder and a white trefoil epaulette and aiguillette on the left.

Breeches, Et cetera

For the mounted companies, breeches were initially of buff leather, later replaced with cloth, with white waistcoats and buff leather gauntlets. The boots were of the same heavy cavalry pattern as worn by the dragoons. Greatcoats were light grey with crimson lining and collar.

In the foot companies the breeches and waistcoats were white, gaiters were black over-the-knee pattern with white metal buttons and from 1810 white overall trousers were issued for everyday wear. Greatcoats were again as issued to the line infantry.

Equipment

The equipment of the mounted companies was of the same pattern as that used by the *dragoni* regiments but with the light cavalry waist belt and sabre with a white sword-knot and tassel.

The dismounted companies used equipment of the same pattern as that issued to the elite companies of the *Fanteria di Linea*, although the flap of the cartridge box was undecorated. The sabre-briquet had a white sword-knot and tassel.

Officers & N.C.O.s

N.C.O.'s rank distinctions were as for the *dragoni* and the *fanteria di linea*, senior N.C.O.s had silver trim on the bicorne.

Officers had white plumes and silver trim to the bicorne and plume. Buttons and turnback badges were silvered. Rank epaulettes were the same as those worn in the *fanteria di linea* and *dragoni*. All belts were of buff leather edged with silver and the light cavalry sabre had a silver sword-strap and tassel.

Musicanti

Trombettieri and *tamburi* were uniformed essentially the same as the *Gendarmerie* but with the addition of red and white lace on collars and cuffs. *Trombettieri* had crimson plumes and are shown, as sometimes are the *tamburi*, with mixed red and white fringing on the epaulette.

Trumpets were brass with mixed crimson and white cords. Drums were of the same pattern as used by the *fanteria di linea*. *Trombettieri*' and *tamburi*' equipment was the same as that of the *dragoni* and the *fanteria di linea* respectively.

Tamburo, 1812–1814:[21] Black bicorne trimmed with white scalloped lace, pink plume with a green tip above the National cockade. Pink coat with green collar, lapels, and cuffs all trimmed white, green turnbacks, green epaulettes with white fringes. Breeches, gaiters, equipment, et cetera as above. Brass drum with red / white / green / white, diagonally striped hoops.

Musicante, 1812–1814: The same plate shows a musician in a uniform differing only in the sabre-briquet being worn on a waist belt.

Zappatori

The same source as mentioned above shows a *Zappatore* of the *Legione* in a regulation coat with crimson crossed axes on the upper arms. Black bearskin, without plate, with white cords and a red plume, and the usual *zappatore* equipment of apron, axe, et cetera

Horse Furniture

The *Gendarmerie* used the 1805 pattern of horse furniture described for the dragoon regiments. The shabraque had white trim and grenades badge, or silver for officers.

21 Unpublished watercolour by Henri Boisselier

4
Fanteria di Linea (The Infantry of the Line)

Knötel Plate III / 25, Infantry of the Army of Italy
From Left: *Bersaglieri di Brescia, Compagnie Dipartmentali di Riserva, fuciliere* and *volteggiatore* of the *fanteria di linea, fanteria di linea granatiere, Fanteria Leggera*. (Author's Collection)

Fanteria di Linea

(Infantry of the Line)

History and Organisation

When the Kingdom of Italy was created in 1805, it had five regiments of *fanteria di linea,* inherited from the dissolved Cisalpine Republic. A sixth regiment was raised in July 1806, and in June 1808 a seventh regiment was created from troops of the disbanded Papal Army.[1] Napoleon had entrusted Eugène, as Viceroy, with the organisation of the Army, and he had planned an eventual establishment of twelve *fanteria di linea* regiments, however the continuing recruitment difficulties for even the existing seven regiments meant that there was never an expansion beyond these seven.

In 1805 the regimental establishment was two battalions, each with an establishment of seven *fuciliere* (fusilier or centre companies) and two elite companies, one *granatiere* (grenadier) company and one *volteggiatore* (voltigeur/light) company. In 1808, in line with the changes to the French establishment, the battalions were reorganised as four centre and two elite companies. At the same time a third battalion was authorised for each regiment and the disbanded companies were used as the cadre for this battalion – by 1809 all regiments had raised the third battalion. In 1811 the strength of the infantry regiments was further increased to four field battalions, a regimental artillery company (again in line with the French establishment) and a depot battalion of four fusilier companies only. The establishment of a regiment was identical to that of the French *Infanterie de Ligne* and conformed to the Order of 18 February 1808:

Regimental Staff	
1 *Colonnello*	1 *Colonnello Sotto*
1 *Maggiore*	3 *Capo Battaglione*
5 *Aiutanti*	10 *Aiutanti-Sottufficiale*
2 *Quartiermaistro*	1 *Chirurge Maggiore*
4 *Chirurgo-Sotto*	1 *Aquile-Alfiori*[2]
1 *Tamburo Maggiore*	1 *Caporale-Tamburo*
8 *Musicanti*	
4 *Maestro-artigiani* (master craftsmen : Boot maker, Tailor, Breeches maker, Armourer)	

Additionally, from June 1808, 2 *Sergente Porta Aquila* (*Secondo Portatore d'Aquila* and *Terzo Portatore*

1 At first this Regiment continued to wear the uniforms of its constituent units but by the beginning of 1809 the records indicate that it had been re-uniformed and re-equipped in line with the rest of the Kingdom's infantry regiments.

2 Initially a *sergente* or a *sergente maggiore* from a Decree of 27 June 1808 he was to be a *tenente* or *sotto tenente* and was termed *Primo Portatore d'Aquila.*

d'Aquila)[3] were added to the staff. They carried the rank of *sergente* but were paid as a *sergente maggiore* – as with so much of the Kingdom's Army this is a direct reflection of the French Army's practice.

Company Establishment	
1 *Capitano*	1 *Tenente*
1 *Sotto Tenente*	1 *Sergente Maggiore*
4 *Sergenti*	1 *Caporale furiere*
8 *Caporali*	2 *Tamburi / Cornette*
121 *Soldato*	
Regimental Artillery Company Establishment	
1 *Capitano*	1 *Tenente*
1 *Sotto Tenente*	4 *Sergenti*
4 *Caporali*	1 *Tamburo*
58 *Soldato*	

The artillery company was armed with two 4-pdr guns. This company was also responsible for the transportation of the regimental baggage and supplies.

Service

(NB if no location is given for a Regiment/Battalion it was in the Kingdom)

1º Reggimento

1807 Germany	
February 17	Skirmish at Neugarten (4 Officers wounded)
mid-March to July 2	Siege of Colberg (5 Officers killed, all on 18 May, and 14 Officers wounded)
1809 Italy / Austria	
April 16	Battle of Sacile (2 Officers killed, 15 wounded)

1º Fanteria di Linea, Porta Aquila and Escort, 1811–1813
The *Porta Aquila* is uniformed in the regulation dress of a company Officer, he would usually be a *tenente* but the epaulette straps are not shown so this cannot be confirmed. The white plume shows that the officer is attached to the Regimental Staff and the only change to the regulation uniform is the red colour belt.
The 2º *Porta Aquila*, apparently introduced onto the establishments in 1808, is dressed like the *granatieri* of the regiment with the addition of a shoulder belt supporting a holster with two pistols, he is additionally armed with a halberd. All are in direct imitation of the 2ᵉ and 3ᵉ *Porte-Aigles* of the French Army. The most unusual aspect of this figure is the green coat when the rest of the regiment was wearing white. Whether this eccentricity was repeated in the other *reggimenti di fanteria di linea* I am unable to say. The fact that Boisselier shows the figure in a green coat and the other two figures in white, suggests that this is a deliberate choice and not any sort of error.
The fusilier at right is again dressed following the regulations except for the white over red plume. I have been unable to find confirmation of the size of this guard but other indications suggest eight men, perhaps including a *caporale* to command it. (Watercolour by Henri Boisselier in the Author's Collection)

3 These were added to the regiments by a Decree of 27 June 1808 to guard the Regimental Eagle. At the same time that the Battalion Eagles were withdrawn to be replaced with a single Regimental Eagle – as so often, this is a reflection of the changes in the French Army.

April 30	Battle of Castel-Cerino (4 Officers wounded)
May 8	Battle of the Piave
May 21	Battle of Pressburg
June 13	2 Officers wounded on outpost duty near Raab
June 14	Battle of Raab (4 Officers wounded)
November 4	Skirmish at Nieder-Basen, Tyrol (1 Officer wounded)
1810 Spain	No actions of note
1811 Spain	
October 7	One officer wounded at an unknown location
October 25	Battle of Sagunto (1 Officer killed, 7 wounded)
October	Siege of Sagunto (2 Officers killed, 2 wounded)
November 7	Battle near Valencia (2 Officers killed, 7 wounded)
December 25 1812[4] to 9 January 1813	Siege of Valencia (1 Officer killed, 2 wounded)

2º Reggimento

1805 Italy	
October 30	Battle of Caldiero (3 Officers wounded)
November / December	Venice Observation and Blockade Corps
1806 Naples	
February 26 to July 18	Siege of Gaeta (2 officers wounded. Strength of 533 men at the start of the Siege)
July 25	Storm of Capua (1 Officer wounded)
1809 Italy / Austria	
April 16	Battle of Sacile (1 Officer wounded)
May 8	Battle of the Piave (1 Officer wounded)
May 21	Battle of Pressburg
June 14	Battle of Raab
October	One *Capitano* was killed at an undated and unnamed Engagement in Croatia
1810 Ionian Islands	
April	One Officer was killed and another wounded in the defence of the islands against a British raid.
1812 Russia	
October 24	Battle of Maloyaroslavets (*Capo Battaglione* Zampa and 6 other officers killed, 19 officers wounded including the *Colonello*, 4 of whom subsequently died of their wounds)
November 30	*Capitano* Reugeot wounded in skirmishing near Borisov
1813 Germany	
February 27	*Tenente* Vigaud wounded on the roads between Magdeburg and Berlin
September 7	Battle of Lippa (3 Officers killed and 4 wounded, one mortally)
September 15	Skirmish near Lippa (2 Officer killed and 11 Officers wounded)
1813 Italy	
November 7/8	4 Officers wounded in skirmishes in North Italy
November 9	Skirmish near Goriza (1 Capitano mortally wounded)
1814 Italy	
January	Siege of Ancona, 2nd Battalion was part of the Garrison

3º Reggimento

1805 Italy	
November	Venice Observation Corps
1806 Naples	
February 26 to July 18	Siege of Gaeta (strength of 531 men at the start of the Siege)

4º Reggimento

1805, Italy	
November / December	Venice Observation and Blockade Corps
1808,	(1st Battalion), Spain
	(2nd & 4th Battalions), Germany
	(3rd Battalion), Italy
1809, Spain	

4 The date of the opening of the siege is variously recorded from as early as 3 November.

1810, Spain	
1811, Spain	
1812,	(1st & 3rd Battalions), Germany
	(2nd Battalion), Spain
1813,	(2nd Battalion), Germany
	Returned to Italy to join the other battalions of the Regiment during the Armistice (2nd June to 10 August)
1814, Italy	
February 8	Battle of the Mincio

5º Reggimento

1805, Italy	November / December Venice Observation and Blockade Corps
1807,	(1st Battalion), Spain
1808,	(1st & 2nd Battalions), Spain
	(3rd & 4th Battalions), Germany
1809,	(1st & 2nd Battalions), Spain
1810,	(1st & 2nd Battalions), Spain
1811,	(1st & 2nd Battalions), Spain
1812,	(1st Battalion), Germany
	(2nd Battalion), Spain
1813,	(2nd Battalion), Germany
	Returned to Italy to join the other battalions of the Regiment during the Armistice (2nd June to 10 August)
1814 Italy	
February 8	Battle of the Mincio

6º Reggimento

1805,	(1st Battalion), Spain
1806,	(1st & 2nd Battalions), Spain
1807,	(1st & 2nd Battalions), Spain
1808,	(1st, 2nd & 3rd Battalions), Spain
	(4th Battalion), Germany
1809,	(1st, 2nd & 3rd Battalions), Spain
1810,	(2nd Battalion), Spain
	(3rd Battalion), Germany
1811,	(2nd Battalion), Spain
	(3rd Battalion), Germany

7º Reggimento

1805,	(1st Battalion), Spain
1806,	(1st Battalion), Spain
1807,	(1st Battalion), Spain
1808, Spain	
1809 Italy / Austria	
May 8	Battle of the Piave
June 14	Battle of Raab
July 8	Skirmish at Pressburg (503 men present, 2 Officers wounded)
1810, Italy	
January 2	A *Capitano* was mortally wounded at an otherwise unrecorded skirmish or action "near Mantua" (he died on the 7th)
1811, Spain	
October 17	Fight at Ayerbe during the Siege of Sagunto (3 Officers killed, 4 wounded)
1812, Spain	
January 6	*Capo Battaglione* Ruse wounded while on patrol
February 8	2 Officers killed, 3 wounded in an unnamed action
May 5	*Capo Battaglione* Ruse wounded in an action against guerrillas
May 26	Battle of Molino Del Rey (2 Officers wounded)
1813, Germany	
May 19	Battle of Königswartha (*Capo Battaglione* Ventura and 5 other officers killed, 8 wounded)
August 18	Assault on Lahn (1 Officer killed)
September 6	Battle of Jutterboek (1 Officer killed, 12 wounded)
October 16	Battle of Leipzig (1 Officer wounded)
1813, Spain	
June 7	Defence of Tarragona (1 Officer wounded)
1814, Italy	(probably only one battalion or perhaps a provisional battalion)
February 8	Battle of the Mincio (1 Officer wounded)
March 2	Attack on Parma (1 Officer wounded)
March 6	Skirmish near Reggio (3 Officers wounded)

1° *Fanteria di Linea c.* 1806. Undated but it is likely that this illustration dates to *c.* 1806 There is no indication of the piping that should have shown on the facings (see text) and this may be no more than an error on the artist's part. A similar omission is present (can an omission be present?) on the other plates of the *Fanteria di Linea*. As with other pieces by the artist his exact hues of red and green have changed over two centuries and the blue-green hue should not be taken as necessarily a correct hue. (Contemporary illustration by "CM' in the Anne S.K. Brown Military Collection, Brown University Library, reproduced with thanks)

2° *Fanteria di Linea c.* 1806. The series includes only *Reggimenti* 1 to 5 and thus probably dates to before the 6° *Reggimento* was added to the Army in July 1806. There is no indication of the piping that should have shown on the facings (see text) and this may be no more than an error on the artist's part. A similar omission is present (can an omission be present?) on the artist's other plates of the *Fanteria di Linea*. As with other pieces by the artist his exact hues of red and green have changed over two centuries. (Contemporary illustration by 'CM' in the Anne S.K. Brown Military Collection, Brown University Library, reproduced with thanks)

3° *Fanteria di Linea* c. 1806. As with all of this series the exact hue of green is unusual, probably from the ageing of the artist's pigments (NB it is always possible that the blue-green hue is correct...). For general notes see the illustration notes to the illustration of 1° *Fanteria di Linea* above. (Contemporary illustration by 'CM' in the Anne S.K. Brown Military Collection, Brown University Library, reproduced with thanks)

4° *Fanteria di Linea* c. 1806. The 'blue-green' collar is almost certainly a problem of the artist's pigments after two centuries, exemplified by the cockade appearing to be red/white/blue instead of red/white/green. The black gaiters are 'field order' although the officer would normally be wearing boots in field order. (Contemporary illustration by 'CM' in the Anne S.K. Brown Military Collection, Brown University Library, reproduced with thanks)

5° *Fanteria di Linea* c. 1806. For general notes on these illustration see above. (Contemporary illustration by 'CM' in the Anne S.K. Brown Military Collection, Brown University Library, reproduced with thanks)

Uniform

Headwear

In 1805 all companies were supposed to wear the black felt bicorn, with the National cockade of (from the outside) white, red and green at the upper left, held in place by a white cockade strap, fastened with a white metal button. The regulations laid down that the bicorne was to have a carrot-shaped pompom above the cockade; green over white for the *fucilieri*, red for the *granatieri* and green for the *volteggiatori*. Interestingly however, a series of contemporary illustrations of the *1° to 5° Fanteria di Linea* in the Anne S K Brown Collection show the *fucilieri* of all five regiments with white disc pompoms edged red. The same illustrations also show the *granatiere* companies to have been wearing black bearskins with red cords and plume and a brass plate embossed with a grenade device. My sense is that these illustrations are probably correct as to what the grenadier companies were actually wearing, even in 1805, despite the regulations…

NB Even after the introduction of the shako, all companies continued to wear the bicorne in undress uniform and on the march.

By 1808 the *fuciliere* and *volteggiatore* companies should have received the French style shako,[5] of black felt with black leather peak and top, reinforcing trim at the upper and lower edges, and a wide 'V' of reinforcing leather at the sides; this is certainly what the regulations of July 1807 set out. The front of the shako was decorated with a white metal lozenge shaped plate (brass in some regiments until at least 1809/10) embossed with the regimental number surmounted by the 'Iron Crown of Lombardy'. The National cockade, as above, was worn above the plate and fastened with a white cockade strap and white metal button. The chin scales were of white metal with plain round bosses.

A surviving plate of the *2° Reggimento* from c. 1808 sold by Bertrand Malvaux of Paris in 2020 is of the regulation lozenge pattern showing a hunting horn with '2' in the loop of the horn and with the Iron Crown above. The horn would suggest that it is almost certainly from the *volteggiatore* company. Interestingly, however, the plate is brass and not the regulation white metal. A similar brass

5 The contemporary illustrations of the Italian Army in the Anne S K Brown Collection painted by CM have been dated to 'c1809' and show the bicorne still in use by all regiments of *Fanteria di Linea*. It is probable that the date ascribed to these paintings is incorrect, although to complicate matters the coat depicted is white and it may simply be that the shako had yet to be delivered to many regiments (the lack of marching order items precludes the illustrations showing that Order of Dress).

plate of regulation pattern is recorded which carries the '1' of the *1º Reggimento*, one in the author's collection has the '5' of the *5º Reggimento* (see photographs below) and yet another is recorded with the '6' of the *6º Reggimento* strongly suggesting that brass plates were worn in all of the *reggimenti di linea*, at least initially. It is possible, perhaps even probable, that these were brass French Army 'blanks' in use until the Army of Italy acquired its own white metal pattern, although given the life of such items some would have remained in use throughout the Kingdom's existence.

Capitano and *Granatiere*, *1º di Linea*, c. 1807
See text for discussion of these uniforms. The *capitano*' boots are an 'interpretation' of the English, jockey boots style. The colouring of the *granatiere* coat is almost certainly a result of discolouration of the paint pigment - green dyes fade to blue with exposure to sunlight, so it is possible that the individual's coat in 1806 had changed colour. (Contemporary illustration from 'The Otto Manuscript' in the Anne S.K. Brown Military Collection, Brown University Library, reproduced with thanks)

Capitano and *Granatiere*, *1º di Linea*, c. 1807
See text for a more general discussion of these uniforms. As with the companion plate above, the *capitano*' boots are an 'interpretation' of the English, jockey boots style. The fact that the officer's epaulettes are gold, rather than the prescribed silver, is notable and unexplained. His shako's lace decoration is a superb example of the sort of personal latitude of dress that officers were allowed. As Guy C Dempsey notes it is unclear whether the buff colour was originally yellow.[79] (Contemporary illustration from 'The Otto Manuscript' in the Anne S.K. Brown Military Collection, Brown University Library, reproduced with thanks)

Front and back of brass shako plate of 5º *Reggimento*, c. 1807. Note the damage to the right-hand fastening where it has been broken from the shako. (Author's Collection)

6 Guy C. Dempsey, *Napoleon's Soldiers: The Grande Armeé of 1807, as Depicted in the Paintings of the Otto Manuscript*, (London: Arms & Armour Press, 1994), pp 238–239.

The *granatiere* companies wore bearskins of the same pattern as the French elite companies with a brass plate at the front embossed with the traditional flaming grenade motif, again as used in the French Army.[7] The red cloth patch at the back of the bearskin bore a white cross, later probably replaced with a white grenade.[8] On campaign, *granatieri* sometimes wore a shako of the same pattern as those of the *fucilieri*, with a lozenge shaped plate embossed with a grenade above the regimental number. In 1811 the bearskins were formally withdrawn from all line regiments, although as in the French infantry, the evidence suggests that this Order was widely ignored.

Fatigue caps were of the French *bonnet-de-police* pattern and were white (green prior to 1808) with piping and tassel of the regimental facing colour and the front of the headband decorated with the regimental number for the *fuciliere*, and a grenade or bugle horn for the *granatiere* and *volteggiatore* companies, respectively. When not worn the cap was rolled and strapped beneath the cartridge pouch, with the tassel hanging to the soldier's right-hand side.

During inclement weather both the shako and the bearskin could be fitted with a black, oiled cloth or oilskin cover with a neck-flap at the rear. These covers often had the regimental number painted in white on the front. Contemporary illustrations also show white cloth covers in use on the shako with the regimental number stencilled in black on the front.

Coat

In 1805 the coat was a dark green habit, of the same pattern as used in the French Army, with either white piped red or red piped white tails and white square-cut lapels piped white. The upright red collar, sometimes shown with white piping, was open in a 'V' at the throat to expose the black stock. The coat's red piped white 'Brandenburg' pattern cuff had a dark green three button cuff flap piped white, both square and three-pointed variants of flap are recorded (although it is possible that square cuff flaps are simply poor observation by the artists). Suhr shows a fusilier of the *1° Reggimento c.* 1807, in a green coat without cuff flaps but with three buttons, in a vertical row, on the cuff, in a style reminiscent of the French '1791 pattern' cuff. The lapels were fastened each side with six white metal buttons plus a further button at each shoulder point. The red piped vertical pockets had three white metal buttons.

Coat Buttons of the 1° and 6° *Fanteria di Linea*
Although the example from the 6° *Fanteria di Linea* is fairly crude I have seen examples that are quite delicately made. (Author's Collection)

On 1 July 1807 Eugène accepted new dress regulations for the Army and thus from 1808 the green coats were replaced with almost identical coats of white with regimental facings whose colour and placement varied from regiment to regiment (see below). As with all such things with the level of stock of coats at regimental depots it no doubt took some time for this change to work through the army.[9] A painting of the *2° Reggimento* by Johann Georg Paul Fischer, dated 1808, shows green coats for the *granatiere* and the *Colonello*, although the NCO of *granatiere* is in a white coat as are the *zappatori*.[10]

Some modern writers have stated that in 1812 infantry regiments which formed part of the Grande Armée for the invasion of Russia were partially re-uniformed with the new style habit-veste or 'Spencer' coat, with lapels closed to the waist and short tails. However I have not found a contemporary source for this assertion, or a contemporary illustration of it, and very few of these coats were ever issued to the Italian line regiments, and at best they were probably worn only by small numbers of the elite companies, certainly the great majority of the Kingdom's infantry continued to wear the habit until the fall of the Kingdom in 1814. There is no doubt, however, that the 'project of 1812' intended the Army of the Kingdom to be re-uniformed along the lines of the French 1812 'Bardin Regulations'.

---

7 René Forthoffer's series of plates show the bearskin for all *fanteria di linea* regiments to have had peaks but no other source confirms this and no contemporary illustration shows it. Unusually, this seems to be an error on Forthoffer's part but it nonetheless deserves to be noted.

8 The *Guardia* changed in about 1809/10 and it would seem safe to assume that the *linea* changed around the same time.

9 In the French Army many regiments were still issuing the pre-1812 pattern coat as late as 1814.

10 The painting was sold at Sothebys in November 2000. Despite the 1808 it was actually a work made in 1815 although apparently from earlier notes. A set of Fischer painted engravings is in the Royal Collection and another is in the British Museum, only one of the series shows the Army of the Kingdom of Italy.

Regimental Facings 1808–1814[11]					
Number	**Lapels**	**Collar**	**Cuffs**	**Cuff Flaps**	**Turnbacks & Pockets**
1[12]	White piped Green	Green	White piped Green	Red	White piped Green
2	Red piped White	White piped Red	White piped Red	Green	White piped Red
3	Green	Red piped Green	Green	Red	White piped Green
4	White piped Red	Red	White piped Red	Green	White piped Red
5	Red piped Green	Green	Red piped Green	Green	White piped Green
6	Green piped Red	Green piped Red	White piped Red	Red	White piped Red
7	Red piped Green	Red piped Green	Green	Green	White piped Green

1º *Fanteria di Linea*, *Colonello* and *Fuciliere* c. 1811–1812
Uniformed according to regulations and note the lack of turnback badges, although on the back of the painting Boisselier has noted that a green, crowned 'N' is a possibility. Note also the *Colonello*' heavy cavalry pattern boots, which would have made service on foot highly difficult if not near impossible and may have been replaced on campaign with the more practical English 'jockey boots' (even a colonel can lose his horse in action). (Watercolour by Henri Boisselier, Author's Collection)

11 A series of manuscript drawings of the Army of the Kingdom of Italy by 'CM' in the Anne S K Brown Collection, dated to *c.* 1809 but probably slightly earlier, agrees with the colours in this table but appears to show no piping on collar, lapels or cuffs for any of the regiments.

12 The Otto Manuscript's illustration of a grenadier of the *1º Reggimento c.* 1807/08 shows a green coat with red collar and cuffs, both piped white. Suhr shows the same colourings for the green coat.

2º *Fanteria di Linea*, full dress 1808–1810. Left to right: *granatiere* (rear view), *granatiere* (front view) *zappatore*, *tamburo* of the *granatiere* company.
All figures are uniformed following regulations, although note that the *granatieri*' sword-knots are shown white on the rear view and red on the front view – this seems an odd error for an artist to make so may represent an actual variation present in the source. (Watercolour by Henri Boisselier, Author's Collection)

Fucilieri Distinctions

The pompom worn on the shakos of the *fucilieri* was of the ball pattern with a tufted top; usually coloured green over white with a green tuft. Several versions of the pompom are noted however, giving distinctions between the companies of *fucilieri* either by the white lower half of the pompom being coloured for the 2nd, 3rd and 4th companies or decorated with a coloured ring; the distinctive colours appear to have followed the French system of green for the 1st company, sky blue for the 2nd, orange for the 3rd and violet for the 4th. The regulations of 14 January 1809 replaced this pompom with a flat disc pompom of green, red and white, the white centre having the company number in black. Faber du Faur shows shakos without pompoms of either type, albeit that he shows the regiments in the field. For full parade dress, white shako cords and flounders were worn. The coat was as described above with bastion tipped shoulder straps of coat colour piped with the lapel colour or lapel piping colour. Turnbacks are recorded both as plain and with a badge of a green star, although Henri Boisselier shows a crowned red 'N' and the *2º* as using a silver crown on a green patch, but unusually does not give his sources.[13]

13 Unpublished watercolours in the author's collection.

3º Reggimento Fanteria di Linea c.1812
In the style of the illustrations by 'CM' (see above) but showing the uniform at a later period. (Vinkhuijzen Collection, General Research Division, New York Public Library Digital Collections. Public Domain)

Granatieri Distinctions

In full dress both the bearskin and the shako had red cords and plume, the Otto Manuscript shows both the Line and Light *granatiere* to have had double cords falling on the right side rather than the more usual left.[14] On campaign the bearskin was worn without decorations, the shako without cords and with the plume replaced with a red carrot-shaped pompom. The habit had red full-fringed epaulettes, or red with white crescents, and the turnback badges were red grenades, although one of Suhr's illustrations shows the turnbacks to be undecorated.

Volteggiatore Distinctions

The full dress plume could have been of any of several green/yellow colour combinations; plain green or yellow, green tipped yellow or the reverse and the carrot-shaped pompom worn on campaign could be either green or yellow. Shako cords were green, yellow or a mixture of both and the coat had epaulettes of all green, green with yellow crescents and fringes or the reverse. In all of these there could even be variations in the combinations between battalions of the same Regiment although the *1º di Linea* is known to have used green epaulettes with a yellow crescent across all of its battalions. The turnbacks were decorated with green bugle horn badges.

Breeches, Etc

Breeches and waistcoat were white for all regiments, and for parade dress white cloth, over-the-knee gaiters with white metal buttons were worn; on campaign these were replaced by black gaiters with cloth covered buttons. After 1810, shorter knee length gaiters were issued with overall trousers of white, grey or brown worn on campaign – the colour apparently dependent on no more than what cloth was available at the 'right price'. Albrecht Adam shows Italian infantry, both officers and men, of Pino's Division in Russia in 1812 wearing linen trousers over their

14 Guy C. Dempsey Jr *Napoleon's Soldiers : The Grande Armée of 1807 as Depicted in the Paintings of the Otto Manuscript*, (London: Arms & Armour, 1994), various plates.

breeches, which was the practice in the French Army and obviously copied in the Italian.

Greatcoats were of French pattern, single-breasted and either grey or brown. The front was closed with six or eight white metal buttons, presumably depending on the height of the wearer.[15] The coat came down to the mid-calf and had an upright collar and deep, tuned back cuffs. The greatcoats of the elite companies were decorated with the epaulettes from the tunic. When not in use the greatcoat was folded and strapped on top of the pack.

Equipment

The equipment of the Italian *fanteria di linea* was of the same pattern, usually with the same variations, as that used by the French Army. *Fucilieri* wore a single, whitened leather shoulder belt with white metal buckles and fittings, over the left shoulder to support the black leather cartridge pouch. The lid of the pouch was usually plain but on campaign was often covered with a white, or very occasionally black, cloth cover; sometimes with the regimental, battalion and company number, painted on it, e.g.:-

.... Rgt di Fanteria
.... Battalione
.... Compagnia

or sometimes simply the regimental number. Use of such a cover was not in any regulations and, again as in the French Army, was simply a company or battalion convention.

The bayonet scabbard was black leather with brass heel and fittings and was carried in a frog attached to the lower front of the pouch belt.

The elite companies wore twin shoulder belts, the first supporting the cartridge pouch identical to that of the *fucilieri* but with a brass grenade or bugle horn badge on the lid as appropriate. The second belt supported the French pattern sabre-briquet in a double frog with the bayonet. The sabre-briquet had a brass hilt and its black leather scabbard had brass fittings; sword-straps and knots were red for the *granatieri* and green, green with a yellow knot, or white with green knot and tassels for the *volteggiatori*.

Packs were of brown hide with white leather straps and brass buckles and fittings.

Muskets were Italian-made copies of the French Year IX pattern with iron fittings and whitened leather sling. The *volteggiatore* companies were initially armed with the shorter dragoon pattern musket, however, these appear to have been almost entirely replaced with the normal infantry pattern musket by the end of 1811. I have found no mention of rifles in use by the *volteggiatori* of the Italian *fanteria di linea*, even though they were in use by French *voltigeurs* during the early Empire.

N.C.O.s

The Italian Army adopted the French system of rank distinctions and the senior grades of non-commissioned officers had silver or gold thread worked through the shako cords and epaulette fringes. N.C.O.s in the elite companies had silver epaulette crescents. The *fusiliere* N.C.O.s wore the shoulder straps of the company rank and file but had the twin shoulder belts of the elite companies. The knot of the sabre-briquet was mixed silver and white for the *fusiliere* and mixed silver and company colour in the elite companies.

Diagonal bars worn above the cuff, as in the French Army, indicated rank

Sergente Maggiore	Two diagonal silver bars, piped with the regimental colour.
Sergente	A single bar as above
Caporale	Two white woollen bars piped with the regimental piping colour.

French *An IX* (1777) Pattern musket
Although this example is of French manufacture the Italian version was identical, except perhaps for some minor details of examples carried by the *Fanteria Leggera* (see below) (Rama - Own work, CC BY-SA 3.0 fr, via https://commons.wikimedia.org/w/index.php?curid=59730666)

15 A similar variation in the number of buttons depending on the wearer's height was regulation in the uniform coat of the Austrian Army of this period.

Caporale Furiere	As above, with the addition of a silver lace inverted chevron on the upper right sleeve.
The *Sergente Maggiore* also had silver lace trim to the upper edge of the shako.	

The *aiutante-sottufficiale* wore the uniform of a *Sotto Tenente* with the epaulettes reversed, although without a gorget plate and with the sabre-strap as for an N.C.O. Additionally, like the *Sergente Maggiore*, he had silver lace trim to the upper edge of the shako.

Caporali were uniformed, armed and equipped identically to the remainder of their company, their rank indicated only by their rank stripes.

Officers

Officers' shakos were of the same pattern as that of the other ranks but with all metalwork silvered and silver shako cords and tassels. The upper edge of the shako, and often the 'V' reinforcing at the sides, was decorated with silver lace, frequently embroidered with stars, oak-leaves or similar fanciful patterns; this lace was of varying widths indicating the rank of the wearer (see below). The lace at the sides of the shako of the senior field officers sometimes formed a solid 'wedge' shape.

After 1810 a prescribed pattern of lace was laid down for the officers of the French Army and this appears to have been adopted by the Italian Army, although a number of more 'individual' patterns continued to be used, probably not least because any replacement of existing items was expensive.

Colonello / Colonello Sotto	Gold band of 35mm above a second 15mm gold band
Maggiore	Silver band of 35mm above a 15mm gold band
Capo Battaglione	Silver band of 35mm
Capitano	Silver band of 30mm
Tenente	Silver band of 25mm
Sotto Tenente	Silver band of 20mm

Field officers and *Capo di Battaglioni* wore white plumes. Company officers' plumes followed those of the rank and file in the elite companies, or white tipped green in the centre companies, however, fusilier officers often wore only the pompom without the plume.

On campaign in place of the shako many officers preferred the bicorne with a silver lace trim to the upper edges, National cockade, silver lace cockade strap and company colour pompom.

Officers' full dress coats were the same cut and colour as the other ranks but the cloth was of a finer quality and all buttons were silver-plated. The silver epaulettes of rank followed the French system and the silver-plated gorget, worn when on duty, was embossed with a gilt Imperial Eagle.

The turnback badges on company officers' coats were the same as those of their men but in silver. Field officers often had Imperial Eagle badges on their turnbacks.

The Musée de l'Armée in Paris has an early period officer's coat of *Capitano* Consonni of *3º Reggimento* (at the time of writing this is not on display), it currently carries the epaulettes of a *aiutante* but it is not known if this is the original placement, or whether at some point these have been reversed. The coat follows the regulation placement and colouring of facings in all respects except one – there is no evidence of piping on the collar, although this is evident on the turnbacks and pockets. The piping of the turnbacks continues up and joins the lower edge of the lapels. The silver turnback badges are those of the *granatiere* company. The coat, and its associated waistcoat, is an extremely pale cream colour rather than pure white; this is almost certainly due to ageing of the coat. The lining throughout, including the tails is a light 'biscuit' colour, distinctly darker than the coat itself. The buttons, epaulettes and turnback badges are all now somewhat 'tarnished' and appear with an almost 'gold-coloured' hue, it is worth noting that buttons of the rank and file in the author's collection also show a distinct bronze-like colouring.

(NB Another coat that the author has seen appears to be either a Saxon or Westphalian infantry coat with its buttons replaced by those of Army of Italy pattern, perhaps to increase its value. The coat pattern and cut was, of course, exactly the same although the colour distribution of the facings does not accord to any Army of Italy infantry Regiment in any way.)

For undress and on campaign officers often wore the single-breasted nine-button 'surtout' with long tails and square cuffs, usually without cuff flaps. The collar, turnbacks, and piping were either the same as on the habit coat or were of the colour of the coat. These coats could be either dark green or white and were customarily worn with epaulettes of rank.

Colonello / Colonello Sotto	Two silver bullion-fringed epaulettes
Maggiore	As above but with gold straps.
Capo Battaglione	Silver bullion fringe epaulette on the right shoulder, contre-epaulette on the left.
Capitano	As above but fine fringed epaulette
Tenente	As above but with a narrow red stripe along the straps
Sotto Tenente	As above but with two red stripes

The *Aiutante*, who was usually a *Capitano*, wore the epaulettes of rank of a *Capitano* but on opposite shoulders.

Officers' breeches were white and normally worn with boots of the 'English pattern' (also known as jockey pattern) with turned-over tops exposing the buff lining. However, officers of *volteggiatori* often wore boots of the 'Hungarian', or hussar, style with shaped tops and silver lace and tassels. On campaign officers wore either green breeches or white overall trousers similar to those of their men. The paintings of 'CM' in the Anne S K Brown Collection show officers in parade dress wearing white or black gaiters as for the men, thus following the custom in the French Army of the period, where the regulations

4° Fanteria di Linea c. 1808–1813
'Sketch' watercolour by Boisselier of various examples of the Regiment's dress. Again, as in the example of 2° *Reggimento* mentioned above there appears to be use of brass shako ornaments. It is also notable that there are variations from the regulations on some figures even though Boisselier was aware of those regulations. (Author's Collection)

Belt Buckle, probably from an officer of the *Fanteria de Linea.* (Private Collection, ©photo courtesy of Laurent Claudet)

called for company officers to wear gaiters, and not boots, for full dress parades.

Waist belts were whitened leather for parade and black leather for campaign, both had a large brass buckle plate embossed with either the Imperial Eagle[16] or, in the elite companies, the company badge. The photograph of a surviving example shows that other designs were in use and, as with many items, a degree of personal choice may have been allowed for such items. On campaign the belt was often worn over the right shoulder in emulation of a baldric. Officers of *fusiliere* and *granatiere* companies carried the straight bladed epée and those of the *volteggiatore* company the curved sabre. Scabbards were of black leather with brass heel and fittings, sword hilts were brass and the sword-straps were silver for parade and white leather edged silver on campaign. The gorget, worn when on duty, was silver with a gilt badge.

2° Fanteria di Linea, Russia 1812
Taken from contemporary illustrations of the campaign these three figures show typical rather than regulation dress. The figure designated *fusilier* by Boisselier is notable in having the twin cross belts and sabre-briquet of the elite companies. Centre companies in the French Army are sometimes recorded as carrying the sabre-briquet but I have not otherwise seen this in the Kingdom's Army. Although this may well reflect actual practice in the 2° *Fanteria*, as opposed to the Regulations, it is also possible that this is actually a *granatiere* who has replaced his epaulettes on campaign.
The two officers confirm the use of dark blue surtouts in place of green but the half-cape of the right-hand officer is not shown elsewhere and is probably no more than a personal affectation. (Watercolour by Henri Boisselier in the Author's Collection)

16 The fact that the Iron Crown doesn't appear suggests that such buckles were perhaps imported from France, although there are a few exceptions (see photograph).

2° *Fanteria di Linea*, 1813
Redrawn by Boisselier from contemporary illustrations in the Musée de l'Armée in Paris these figures are dated *vers 1810, 1812* but the rare example of the use of Imperial Lace by the drummer suggests a date of 1812 or 1813. All shako plates are shown as brass, which echoes the surviving examples discussed in the text for various regiments, and is perhaps an indication that the early issued items lasted through to the end of the Kingdom. (Watercolour by Henri Boisselier in the Author's Collection)

Officers

1º Reggimento, c. 1807. The Otto Manuscript[17] illustrates an officer of the *granatiere* company of the *1º Reggimento* wearing a green surtout with collar cuffs and cuff flaps all in red, piped white, a bearskin with gold bearskin cords, and gold epaulettes of rank, in place of the expected silver.

Another plate in the same manuscript depicts an officer of *volteggiatori* of the same *Reggimento* wearing a shako which has at the side a 'V' of silver lace, with a third vertical strip of the same running from the point of the 'V' at the sides, and both the upper and lower bands of the shako laced silver, the shako plate is a very large lozenge embossed with a '1' below the Iron Crown. The surtout is the same as for the *granatiere* officer but again the epaulettes and gorget are gold in place of silver.

The Fischer illustration referred to above and carrying the date 1808, shows the *Capitano* of *granatieri* of the *2º Reggimento* in a green regulation green coat, as for the rank and file, wearing bearskin with the double cords recorded for some *granatieri* of the Kingdom's Army in gold with a tall red plume. The *capitano* is actually depicted with the epaulettes reversed but, given that the figure is wearing a bearskin this is probably an error on the artist's part. He is carrying a curved sabre with a brass hilt in a black leather scabbard, fitted brass, suspended from a baldric. Interestingly the *capitano* is wearing the *Légion d'Honneur.*

The mounted field officers' shabraques were dark green with squared front and rear corners. The outer edge of the shabraque was piped in silver, inside which was a wide silver lace, separated from the piping by a welt of dark green. The knee-patches were black leather. The pistol holster covers were dark green with wide silver lace trim. The girth strap and the horse harness were black with brass buckles and fittings.

Musicanti

The *tamburi* of the *fusiliere* and *granatiere* companies and the *cornetti* of the *volteggiatori* companies wore the uniform prescribed for their company with the addition of broad lace trim to the lapels, collar and cuffs, and sometimes to the cuff flaps, of the coat. This lace was most commonly either red and white diagonal stripes or red and white triangles, although a variation is recorded with the lace having 'stripes', running along its length, of white/green/white/red/white/green/white, all of equal width, of course there may have been other variations depending on the whim of the *Colonello.* After 1809, the *tamburi* of the *fusiliere* companies are often shown with 'swallows-nests' of red with the above musicians' lace. The *tamburi* and *cornetti* of the elite companies wore the epaulettes of the company.

Tamburi' aprons and drum carriage belts were whitened leather with brass buckles, the carriage belt was decorated with a brass drumstick plate on the breast. The drums themselves had brass barrels, and the hoops were painted with diagonal stripes of green-white-red-white or, occasionally simply red and white. Leliepvre records an interesting variation of the colouring of the hoops, which I have not seen recorded elsewhere but am loathe to discount from an authority such as Leliepvre. He records the hoops as being painted in a series of dog's tooth pattern in red/white/green/white/red/et cetera with the white triangles always having their base against the barrel edge of the hoop. The barrels of the drums for the *granatiere* companies were sometimes embossed with the grenade motif.

The *cornetti* of *volteggiatori* had brass bugle horns with green or mixed green/red/white cords.

The *tamburo maggiori* of the infantry regiments were dressed, as with many such things, according to the taste and whim of the regimental Colonel, however the Italian Army developed a greater degree of uniformity than in many other armies of the era (or perhaps simply didn't exist long enough for there to be a greater divergence?). Headwear was normally the black bicorne with silver lace trim to the upper edges and a silver cockade strap surmounted by a feather plume of white, red and white, or red, white and green. The coat was identical to that worn by the regiment with the addition of silver lace trim to the collar, cuffs, cuff flaps, turnbacks, lapels, pockets, the seams of the sleeves and the seams at the rear of the coat. The buttonholes were also often decorated with silver lace batons and the coat had heavy silver epaulettes. The *tamburo maggiore* wore the rank insignia of the *sergente maggiore* on both sleeves. *Tamburo maggiore* shoulder belts (sometimes referred to as sashes) were red, often embroidered with a zigzag pattern, and with a heavy silver fringing at the outer edges. The front of the belt carried a silver drumstick plate. The white breeches were normally worn with 'Hungarian' style boots of either black or red leather with silver lace trim and tassels. A Boisselier study of the *Tamburo maggiore* of the *4º Fanteria* shows him with a wide gold lace along the outer seam of his breeches and gold lace trim and tassels on his boots.[18] Waist belts were the same pattern as worn by officers, and supported the straight epée with an N.C.O.'s sword-strap.

Musicanti wore a similar uniform, again with silver lace to the collar and cuffs and trefle-knot epaulettes in place of fringed epaulettes. The bicorne was as worn by the *tamburo maggiore* but without the silver trim and

17 The best published version of the manuscript is Guy C Dempsey Jr (ed.), *Napoleon's Soldiers: The Grande Armée of 1807 as Depicted in the Paintings of the Otto Manuscript*, (London: Arms & Armour, 1994). Dempsey's text is first class! The manuscript is in the Anne S. K. Brown Military Collection at Providence, Rhode Island.

18 Private collection.

1º Fanteria di Linea c. 1806, *Tamburo Maggiori* 1808
Of particular note is the mixture of silver lace on the coat and on the cane contrasting with gold lace on the breeches and boots. Although not visible I would suggest that the front of the breeches had gold knots on the thighs. The continued use of white powdered hair and a queue is unusual at this date, although famously the regiments of the French 'Old Guard' also continued its use, this may be no more than a personal affectation.
(Watercolour by Henri Boisselier in the Author's Collection)

the boots were 'English style' jockey boots. *Musicanti*, in common with company *tamburi* and *cornetti*, wore a single shoulder belt supporting the sabre-briquet with a white sabre-strap. *Musicanti* are also sometimes shown wearing a single-breasted coat, similar to the officers' surtout, with regimental facings.

1º Reggimento

Tamburo Maggiore, 1807:[19] A figure, identified as a *Tamburo Maggiore* of this regiment appears in the 'Zimmerman manuscript' but from the shape of the lapels and the yellow waistcoat and piping is more likely from the *1º Fanteria Leggera* and is described under that section below. Its superficial similarity to the 1809 uniform described below may be the source of the confusion.

Tamburo Maggiore, 1809:[20] Brown colpack with a green bag piped in silver and with a white plume with a green and a red ostrich feather at the base. Green coat, of the same cut as the rank and file, with white lapels, green collar, and red cuffs, all piped silver and silver lace on the buttonholes, the silver lace on the collar is piped red at the outer edge and the cuff flaps are plain white. Silver rank stripes and two silver long-service stripes, all piped red, on the left arm and silver bullion-fringed epaulettes. The waistcoat is red with silver lace on the pockets and edges. All buttons are silver for both coat and waistcoat. The breeches are green with silver spearhead lace on the thighs and silver stripes on the outer seams. Boots are hussar style edged and tasselled silver. The baldric is red edged in silver lace, a silver lace zigzag pattern along its length, with silver fringe along the edges, and with a silver drumstick plate. Light cavalry pattern sabre with silver hilt in a black scabbard fitted silver, carried from a red shoulder belt edged with wide silver lace. Brown mace with silver head and silver cords plaited along its length.

A similar unpublished Boisselier watercolour shows the 1808 uniform to be identical except that he wears, in place of the colpack, a black bicorne with a silver lace edging and tassels and three white feathers.

Musicanti, 1809:[21] Black bicorne with silver scalloped lace and tassels and white plume. The National cockade has a silver strap. Green surtout style coat with collar as for the *Tamburo Maggiore*, red Polish cuffs laced silver, plain white turnbacks, silver piped vertical pockets, wide silver lace on the front buttonholes, and silver trefoil epaulettes. All buttons silver. Waistcoat, breeches and boots as for the *Tamburo Maggiore*.

Tamburo of *Fucilieri*, *c*. 1807:[22] Black bicorne as for the rest of the Regiment. Dark green coat with red collar and cuffs, and dark green cuff flaps without piping, white lapels piped red. The cuffs are edged with gold braid and the red swallows' nests on the shoulder have three narrow lines of gold piping around the edges, the red cloth of the wings is clearly visible between the two inner lines. All buttons are white metal and the drum plate on the shoulder belt is brass. The drum itself is brass with red

19 This figure appears in the Zimmerman manuscript which carries the title 'Costume des Troupes Francaises et de celles de l'Alliance Du Rhin qui ont é a Berlin depuis le 24ième Octobre 1806 Desfiné par Zimmerman.' As the *1º Reggimento* did not arrive in Germany until 1807, this illustration must date to 1807 or possible early 1808.

20 Unpublished plate by Boisselier in the author's collection, based on a contemporary illustration.

21 Unpublished plate by Boisselier in the author's collection.

22 Illustration in the Suhr 'Bourgeois de Hambourg' collection.

and white diagonally striped hoops. All other details are as for the rank and file with white gaiters, even though the *fuciliere* shown alongside the *tamburo* wears black.

Tamburo, c. 1807:[23] Shako with a white upper edge, a dark green plume tipped white above a disc pompom of National colours, itself above a National cockade. Mixed red and white cords and racquets. Dark blue coat with red collar and cuffs edged with red and white lace (NB no cuff flaps are apparent but, if present, they would probably have been dark blue with red and white lace), and white lapels with plain red lace, red swallows' nest epaulettes with red and white lace. Brass drum with diagonally striped red/white/blue hoops. All other details as above.

Cornette of *Volteggiatori, c.* 1807: Bicorne with a National cockade topped by a green tipped yellow carrot-shaped pompom. Dark blue coat with red cuffs, yellow collar and cuff flaps, all edged with red and white lace, and white lapels with plain red lace. Fringed epaulettes of green with yellow crescents. Brass horn with green cords. All other details as above.

2º Reggimento, *Tamburi* and *Musicante(?)*, 1808: The Fischer painting shows, at the extreme right, three *tamburi* and either a *musicante* or a *pipero* (fifer). A number of French *Régiments de Ligne* are recorded as replacing one of the drummers in the grenadier company with a fifer and it is possible that this is what is depicted here, although he may be from the *volteggiatori* (see below) and not a *musicante*. Nonetheless all four figures are shown in the same uniform, note: all three drummers are shown as negro, the *musicante/pipero* is not.

Black bicorne with National cockade and a short, carrot-shaped, red plume. Dark green habit coat with red lapels, collar, turnbacks and cuffs with a white cuff-flap. The collar and cuffs are edged with a broad white lace, including along the lower edge of the collar. The coat sleeves are decorated with eight inverted chevrons of white lace. The drummers have full-fringed epaulettes with white straps and mixed red and white fringes and crescents, the pipero appears to have mixed green and white fringes and crescent, so may be from the *volteggiatore* company. All buttons are white metal. All four figures are wearing white breeches and over-the-knee black gaiters with white metal buttons, and all are carrying a brass-hilted sabre-briquet in a black, brass-fitted, scabbard suspended from a white shoulder belt. The drums have a brass barrel and the hoops appear to be (they are unclear) horizontally striped red/white/ green. All four figures are carrying packs slung at the right rear, against their buttocks in the manner that the drummers of the Austrian Army did at the period. NB the waistcoats are not visible but were almost certainly white.

4º Reggimento

Tamburo Maggiore, 1809:[24] Black bicorne with silver scallop-edged lace, tassels and cockade strap and a white feather fringing along the edge, no plume. White coat, of the same cut as the rank and file, with white lapels and red collar, all piped silver and silver lace on the buttonholes, the silver lace on the lapels and collar is piped green at the outer edge. White turnbacks piped green. The cuffs and cuff flaps are hidden under white gauntlets. Silver bullion-fringed epaulettes, although no rank badges are in evidence. All buttons are silver for both coat and waistcoat. Waistcoat and breeches plain white. Boots are English pattern. The shoulder belt is red edged in silver lace, and with a silver zigzag of lace along its length, no drumstick badge. Light cavalry pattern sabre with silver hilt in a black scabbard fitted silver. Brown mace with silver head and without cords.

Tamburo, c1807:[25] Shako with white cords, a silver lozenge plate and red over white over green carrot-shaped pompom and usual National cockade. White coat with red collar and white cuffs edged with silver lace. White lapels and cuff flaps, both piped green, as is the outer edge of the collar lace. White shoulder straps piped green with red swallows' nests laced silver. All buttons silver. Drumstick plate in brass and brass drum with green hoops.

5º Reggimento

Tamburo Maggiore, c. 1809:[26] Black bicorne with wide gold lace, gold tassels and cockade strap, white plume with a red and a green falling ostrich feathers at the base. Red coat, of the same cut as the rank and file, with red cuffs and dark green lapels, collar and cuff flaps. The lapels, collar, buttonholes, cuffs and cuff flaps have a wide gold lace edge and the collar has a single baton of gold lace at the front. White turnbacks with the same wide gold lace as the rest of the coat. White wrist gloves. Mixed dark green and gold, fringed epaulettes. Gold rank stripes on the lower sleeve, possibly piped dark green. All buttons are gilt for both coat and waistcoat. Waistcoat and breeches white, the latter with a broad gold lace trim to the outer seam and a deep gold 'V' of lace on the thighs. Hussar pattern boots with gold lace and tassel. The sash is dark green with a wide gold lace along the edge and gilt drumstick badge. The sword pattern is indiscernible but is worn in a brass scabbard. Brown mace with gilt head and tip and with gold cords twisted along its length.

---

23 For the source for both the *tamburo* and the *cornetto* see Luca Stefano Cristini and Guglielmo Aimaretti, *L'Esercito Del Regno Italico 1805–1814. Volume 1*, (Lodigliano: Soldiershop, 2010).

24 Unpublished plate by Boisselier in the author's collection.

25 Unpublished plate by Boisselier in the author's collection.

26 Unpublished plate by Boisselier, private collection.

Tamburo of Granatieri, 1813:[27] Shako with white cords, a brass lozenge plate and rd pompom with a green tuft and usual National cockade. White coat with red lapels and cuffs and dark green collar and cuff flaps, white turnbacks. The lapels and turnbacks are edged with dark green lace and the collar and cuffs with red and white lace. Red, fringed epaulettes. All buttons gilt. Drumstick plate in brass and brass drum with green / white / red hoops.

Negro *Musicante*, 1811:[28] A white turban with a brass crescent fastening at the front around a short conical mid-green flat-topped cap with a gold scalloped edge lace around the edge. White short-sleeve coat with red lapels and turnbacks(?) and a dark green collar, all edged with a broad gold lace and the buttonholes are also gold laced. Gold, fringed epaulettes. The coat sleeves end above the elbow to show the waistcoat sleeves below. The waistcoat was dark green with plain red cuffs and gilt buttons, it had broad gold lace along the cuffs, edges and down the front and gold lace batons at each button, the ends of which are covered by the coat's lapels. The red trousers were of the baggy 'Turkish style', with gold spearhead design lace on the thighs and gold lace on the outer seam. The trousers ended above the ankle to show dark green 'socks' worn with yellow 'Turkish slippers'.

6° Reggimento

Tamburo Maggiore, 1810:[29] Black bicorn with gold lace trim and tassels and a white plume with a green, a white and a red ostrich feathers at the base. White coat, of the same cut as the rank and file, with green lapels, collar, turnbacks, cuffs and cuff flaps, all edged with a double gold lace. Gold rank stripes piped green, gold bullion-fringed epaulettes. All buttons are gold for both coat and the plain white waistcoat. Plain white breeches and English pattern boots. Green drum major's sash, edged with a broad gold lace and with a brass drumstick badge. The sword is unclear but appears to be a light cavalry pattern sabre with brass hilt and a brass scabbard. Brown mace with silver head and silver cords plaited along its length.

6° Fanteria di Linea, Tamburo Maggiori 1810.
The uniform does not fit exactly to that of any of the Regiments although the green lapels suggest either the 3°, in which case the collar should be red, or the 6°, when the cuffs should be white. There is, of course, no reason why a *Tamburo Maggiori* would have followed precisely the uniform of the rest of his regiment – indeed it was common not to. Eugene Leliepvre believed the uniform to be that of the *Tamburo Maggiori* of the 6°, and I have followed that identification. (Watercolour by Henri Boisselier in the Author's Collection)

Zappatori

The *zappatori* of the *fanteria de linea* wore the uniform of the *granatiere* companies and, as was the tradition in most armies of the period, all *zappatori* wore a full beard. The bearskin cap had white cords and a red plume, NB the bearskin had no front plate. A red crossed axe badge was worn on both upper sleeves, sometimes surmounted by a red grenade, similarly the crossed axe badge also appeared on the turnbacks of the coat. The traditional sappers' apron was covered at the waist by a broad white leather belt, fastened with a square brass buckle plate embossed with either a grenade or a crossed axe motif. Aprons were usually whitened leather, although they are sometimes shown as natural tan-brown colour.

27 Unpublished plate by Boisselier, private collection.
28 Unpublished plate by Louis de Beaufort "after Boisselier", private collection.
29 Study by Boisselier after a contemporary illustration. The figure is positively identified as of a Regiment of Line Infantry even though the overall pattern suggests the Velites of the Royal Guard.

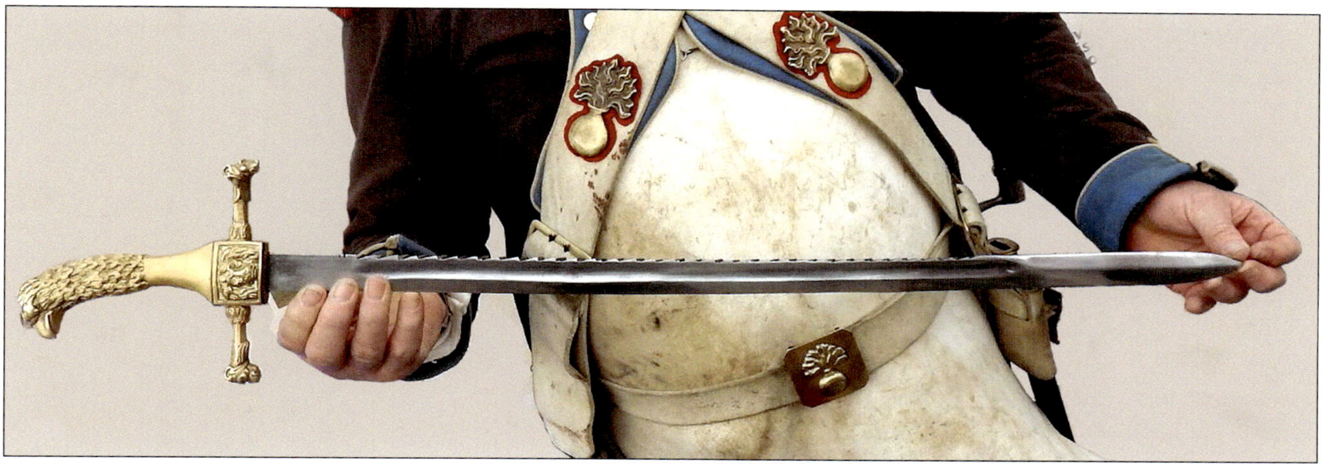

Zappatore Sword. Modern high quality, re-enactment reproduction. Here carried by a *sapeur* of the French *d'Infanterie de Ligne*. (Author's Photograph)

Pouch-belts were the same as those of the grenadiers with the addition of a brass grenade or crossed axe badge (or both) on the front. The second belt officially supported either the sabre-briquet or, more often the long sappers' sword, both had a red sabre-strap and knot, and the bayonet. The sabre-briquet or sappers' sword (which was the same pattern as carried by the *sergente* – see below) was worn in a black scabbard, the bayonet in a brown scabbard, both were fitted in brass. A wide, whitened leather shoulder belt was worn over the pouch belt to support the axe in a black leather case with a small pouch on the outside to hold the sapper's sharpening tools. Sappers carried muskets of the short dragoon pattern and of infantry calibre, with whitened leather slings. From surviving examples the exact design of the axe seems to have varied from regiment to regiment. An axe that was sold at auction in 1916 had its head engraved with the number '7' surmounted by the Iron Crown of Lombardy and thus must have been from the *7° di Linea*[30].

The sergente zappatore wore the same uniform, with the normal rank distinctions but did not carry the axe, and always carried the long heavy sappers' sword with a brass cocks-head pommel and a broad blade with serrated back edge. The sword was carried in a black scabbard fitted in brass.

Zappatore, 1° di Linea, c. 1807
See text below for discussion of this illustration
(Contemporary illustration from 'The Otto Manuscript' in the Anne S. K. Brown Military Collection, Brown University Library, reproduced with thanks)

30 Piero Crociano, Massimo Fiorentino, and Alfred Umhey, 'À Propos de l'"Esponton" des Dragoni Napoleone…' in *Soldats Napoleoniens: Les Troupes Françaises, Alliés et Coalisées. Hors-série No.1, Avril 2003*, (Paris: Éditions de la Revue Napoléon,

1º Reggimento

Zappatore, c. 1807: A contemporary illustration in the Otto Manuscript, dated to *c.* 1807, shows a *zappatore* of the *1º di Linea*[31] wearing a tall white colpack with a red bag on the right and double cords and racquets also on the right; on the left is a tall red plume above a National cockade. The coat is white with white lapels and collar but no evidence of piping, red crossed axe badges on the upper arms and red, fringed epaulettes. The waistcoat is white with white metal buttons. The long, almost ankle-length, apron is natural-coloured buff leather, and the gauntlets are a similar colour. The black cartridge box is worn at the centre front on a black waist belt. The musket is fitted in brass and the sword appears to be longer than a sabre-briquet so is probably of the heavy *zappatore* pattern as carried by *sergenti*. All belts have brass fittings.

Zappatore Sergente, c. 1807: Suhr[32] shows the *sergente zappatore* in essentially the same uniform as above but with a red collar on the coat, gold rank stripes piped red on the sleeves and red piping to the edge of the buff leather apron (which extends upwards over the lapels). The cuffs are white piped red and the cuff flaps red piped white. The left shoulder belt has a brass grenade on a red base at the front.

Zappatore, c. 1808:[33] Regulation black-brown bearskin cap without plate, with white cords and red plume. The bearskin patch is not visible but was presumably red with a white grenade badge. The coat is white with white lapels and a green collar but again with no evidence of piping, red crossed axe badges on the upper arms and red fringed epaulettes, the cuffs and cuff flaps are hidden by the white gauntlets. White apron and standard black gaiters.

2º Reggimento

Zappatore, c. 1808: The Fischer illustration shows a group of the eight *zappatori* of the *2º Reggimento*. These *zappatori* are depicted wearing a tall white colpack with a red bag with red tassel on the right (similar to that shown in the Otto Manuscript for the *1º Reggimento* – see above) with a single red cord looped up at the centre front and the centre back, there is no plume depicted and if the National cockade is present it is not visible. The coat is white with red lapels and collar with no evidence of piping. The cuffs are covered by the white leather gauntlets but just visible is the edge of a white cuff-flap piped red. The figures are depicted from the right-hand side but no badges are visible on the arm, although the nearest figure has three

6º Fanteria di Linea, Zappatore, 1812.
The uniform does not quite conform to the regulations for the rank and file of the regiment but the white collar piped red confirms that this *zappatore* is from the *6º Reggimento*. The apron would normally be worn to cover the waistcoat but worn as shown here with the top folded down over the waist belt is shown in a number of contemporary examples in many armies. Note the sapper crossed axe badge being worn only on the left arm and the white straps on the epaulettes. (Vinkhuijzen Collection, General Research Division, New York Public Library Digital Collections. Public Domain)

2003), pp.78–84.

31 Guy C. Dempsey Jr, *Napoleon's Soldiers : The Grande Armée of 1807 as Depicted in the Paintings of the Otto Manuscript*, (London: Arms & Armour, 1994), pp.234–235.

32 Illustration in the 'Bourgeois de Hambourg' collection. The illustrations are by Christian Suhr (1771–1842), although the actual engraving was the work of his younger brothers, Cornelius (1781–1857) and Pierre (1788–1857). The work shows the units that passed through Hamburg between 1806 and 1815 and is known variously as either "Suhr" or the "Bourgeois de Hambourg". I have used the term "Suhr" throughout.

33 A. Joineau, 'L'Infanterie de la Ligne Italienne 1804–1808' in *Figurines No.20, Mars 1988*, (Paris: Tradition, 1988), p.26.

inverted red chevrons on his upper arm. All *zappatori* have red, full-fringed epaulettes and all buttons are white metal. The apron is white and covers the waistcoat and the *zappatori* are wearing white trousers over white gaiters. The black cartridge box is worn at the centre front on a white waist belt that is over worn over the twin cross belts. None of the *zappatori* are carrying muskets, The sword is carried from a shoulder belt at the left-hand side, it has a brass hilt and the scabbard is black leather fitted in brass. There is a second belt worn over the right shoulder which presumably supports the usual black leather axe case. The axe has a black haft, steel head and a brass ferrule. One

1º *Fanteria de Linea*, 1809–1812. 'Sketch' watercolour by Henry Boisselier. (Author's Collection)

2° Reggimento Fanteria Leggera *c.* 1808. Contemporary painting by Johann Georg Paul Fischer (1876-1876). See text for details of this painting. (Reproduced with the help and kind permission of The Armoury of St James, Piccadilly, London. www.armoury.co.uk)

zappatore is depicted facing away from the viewer and is wearing a brown 'goatskin' pack seemingly from a single shoulder belt, as those of drummers are often shown, rather than the usual twin straps.

5° Reggimento

Zappatore, c. 1809: Bearskin without plate and with white cords and a red plume with the National cockade at its base. White coat with red lapels and collar, both without piping, the cuffs are hidden by white gauntlets. Red fringed epaulettes but no rank badges or *zappatore* badges are shown on the sleeve. All buttons are brass. Plain white breeches and *zappatore* apron.

Regimental Artillery Companies

The artillery companies attached to each regiment of *fanteria de linea* from 1811 had an establishment of 24 *artiglieri*, 32 *autisti* and two *maniscalos* who wore the same uniform as the *artiglieri*, with the addition of the appropriate rank badges.

Artiglieri wore the infantry shako with brass lozenge plate embossed with the crossed cannon motif and crown. The cords and the carrot-shaped pompom were red, and the chin scales were brass. Coats were of the usual infantry pattern in dark green with white metal buttons, and all facings were red piped dark green. The horizontal pockets were piped red and had a single button at each point, the turnbacks were decorated with dark green grenade badges. Waistcoat and breeches were dark green and the gaiters were black with white metal buttons. Equipment was as for the regiment's elite companies with a brass grenade badge on the pouch lid and red strap and tassel on the sabre-briquet. The musket was of the short dragoon pattern.

Drivers wore a shako as above with green pompom and cords but their coats were the single-breasted *habit à la kinski* style; a short tailed tunic with double turnbacks of dark green with red facings on the collar, plain round cuffs and plain shoulder straps – all piped dark green. The front of the coat was piped red, extending around the base of the coat and the dark green turnbacks. Breeches were buff leather and worn with high cuffed riding boots with steel spurs. *Autisti* and *maniscalos* were armed only with the sabre-briquet, carried on a single shoulder belt. The sabre-strap was white with a green knot.

The *sergente maggiore* of the company wore the usual rank distinctions plus black riding boots and was armed with the heavy cavalry pattern sword carried in a black leather scabbard with brass heel and fittings.

All officers were mounted and officers' distinctions were as used in the *fanteria de linea*.

Shabraques were as for the infantry officers although that of the *sergente maggiore* had white lace and grenade badges in place of silver.

Reggimento Coloniale

(Colonial Regiment)

History and Organisation

The *Reggimento Coloniale* was originally raised in 1803 as the *Legione Italiana* from vagrants, 'suspect foreigners', and beggars fit for work; in 1805 it was renamed as the *Battaglione Coloniale*. The *Battaglione* was essentially a penal unit, even if not actually titled as such, and was recruited from prisons and the 'draft dodgers' brought in by the *Gendarmeria*. In 1808 the single Battalion was expanded to a *Reggimento* of two *battaglioni*, each with an establishment of six centre companies, not surprisingly there were no elite companies as was usual with similar units. The *Battaglione* and, after 1808 the *Reggimento*, was stationed on the Island of Elba in order to deter desertion (although legally Elba was actually part of France not Italy). In 1811 the unit was absorbed into the *6º Fanteria di Linea*. Rawkins, who is usually very reliable, states that in 1813 a new *Reggimento Coloniale* of two battalions was raised but I have been unable to confirm this from any other source,[34] and Carmigniani and Boué[35] have no entry for the *Reggimento* after 1808.

Service

Although some elements of the *Reggimento* certainly served in Spain I have found nothing to confirm a formed battalion and it seems likely that they served only as separate and independent companies. The evidence is that they actually proved quite reliable despite their origins.

Uniform

Headwear

Shako of the same pattern as that worn by the *fanteria leggera* with a brass lozenge shaped plate, embossed with a crown above an 'RC' cipher, and with brass chin scales. The carrot-shaped pompom was light green. No source mentions the wearing of shako cords, again perhaps not surprising for what was essentially a 'penal regiment'. Fatigue caps were steel-grey with light green tassel and piping.

Coat

The coat was the short tailed habit-veste as worn by the *fanteria leggera reggimenti* and was steel-grey with light green collar and cuffs. The lapels, turnbacks, cuff flaps, shoulder straps and pockets were all steel-grey piped in light green. All buttons were white metal.

Breeches, et cetera

Breeches and waistcoats were steel-grey and the short gaiters were black with white metal buttons. The dark grey greatcoats were standard infantry pattern.

Equipment

All equipment was as for the *fuciliere* companies of *fanteria de linea*.

Officers & N.C.O.s

All rank distinctions were as for the *fanteria de linea*. N.C.O.s wore the twin shoulder belts of the *fanteria* elite companies.

Officers wore surtouts of steel-grey with all belts of black leather. They were armed with the straight epée, carried in a black leather scabbard fitted in steel or brass. The shabraques of the field officers were steel-grey with silver lace.

Tamburi

As for the rank and file of the regiment and with the usual distinctions.

Zappatori

The regiment did not have *zappatori*.

Reggimento Guardia Alla Città di Venezia

(City of Venice Guard Regiment)

History and Organisation

The regiment was originally raised on 17 January 1808 as a single battalion with the title *Guardia Sedentaria di Venezia*, for local defence duties in the City of Venice and surrounding districts. In November 1810 the battalion was expanded to a two battalion regiment and took the title *Reggimento Guardia Alla Città di Venezia*. Each battalion had the usual infantry establishment of four centre and two elite companies and was presumably of the regulation establishment. In 1811 a regimental artillery company was added.

Service

The regiment did not see active service until the 1813–14 campaign in the Po Valley against the British and

34 W. J. Rawkins, *The Italian Army, 1805–1814*, (Aylsham: Anschluss Publishing ND), no pagination.

35 Juan Carlos Carmigniani and Gilles Boué (Marie-France Renwick trans.), *Napoleon and Italy : A Military History of Napoleonic Italy, 1805–1815*, (Paris: Histoire & Collections 2016), p.242.

Austrian forces, when it is recorded as being amongst the army's most reliable units.

Uniform

Headwear

All companies wore the *fanteria de linea* pattern shako with the National cockade at the front and with a white metal lozenge plate embossed with the cipher 'GV'. Company distinctions were the same as those used in the *fanteria di linea*: white cords with green and white pompoms for *fucileri*, red cords and plumes for the *granatieri*, and yellow cords and plumes for the *volteggiatori*. Chin scales were white metal. The fatigue caps were dark green with red piping and tassels.

Coat

The *Guardia* wore dark green coats of the same cut as those worn by the *fanteria de linea*, but with a red collar, red cuffs and red turnbacks, and all buttons of white metal. The lapels, three-pointed cuff flaps and shoulder straps of the *fuciliere* companies were dark green piped red, the horizontal pockets were also piped in red. The elite companies wore full-fringed epaulettes of red for the *granatieri* and yellow and green for the *volteggiatori* (yellow straps and green fringes, although I have also seen the reverse). It should be noted that the facing colour of this regiment was a dull red rather than the bright red of the *fanteria de linea*.

Breeches, et cetera

Breeches and waistcoats were white and the gaiters were black over-the-knee pattern with white metal buttons. In 1811 the regiment adopted the shorter, below the knee, pattern of gaiters, again black but with black cloth covered buttons. Greatcoats were dark grey and of the regulation pattern of the *fanteria de linea*.

Equipment

All equipment was the same as that used by the *fanteria de linea*.

Officers & N.C.O.s

Officers and N.C.O.s used the same badges of rank and distinctions as in the *fanteria de linea reggimenti*. Officers' greatcoats were dark green with white metal buttons.

Battaglione Guardia Alla Città di Milano c. 1812. (Vinkhuijzen Collection, General Research Division, New York Public Library Digital Collections. Public Domain)

Musicanti

Tamburi' distinctions were the same as those used in the *fanteria de linea reggimenti.*

A Boisselier study of two *musicanti* of the *Guardia* c1812[36] show them in a black bicorne with silver lace, tassels and cockade strap (securing the National cockade), and a white over green over red plume. The coat is red with sky blue 'plastron style' lapels, collar, Polish cuffs, lining and turnbacks; all edged with wide silver lace – the collar is laced along both the upper and lower edges and there is a diamond of silver lace at the junction of the turnbacks at the back. The buttonholes of the coat have fringed silver batons and the shoulder ornaments are silver full-fringed epaulettes, the turnbacks are plain and there are no pockets visible, or at least none that are laced or piped. All buttons are silver. The breeches are white and the hussar pattern boots have silver lace and tassels.

Zappatori

Zappatori do not appear in the regiment until 1810; thereafter they were uniformed the same as the *granatieri* but with the addition of the usual *zappatore* uniform distinctions and equipment as used by the *zappatori* of the *fanteria de linea reggimenti.*

Regimental Artillery Company

The regimental artillery company had the same establishment as that of the *fanteria de linea* and was uniformed as the rest of the regiment but with all facings dark green piped red and the addition of artillery distinctions as used by the *fanteria de linea* artillery companies.

Battaglione Guardia Alla Città di Milano

(The City of Milan Guard Battalion)

History and Organisation

The original battalion was formed from the *Guardia Nazionale di Milano* (Milan National Guard) of the old Cisalpine Republic and although certainly in existence at the beginning of 1807 when it is recorded as being in Germany, at this point its history becomes rather vague and the unit would seem to have been disbanded, or at least put into some sort of abeyance. shortly afterwards. The *Battaglione* was, however, reformed as the garrison and police force of the Kingdom's capital by an Order of 10 December 1811.

The *Battaglione Guardia* was organised as a standard infantry battalion of six companies, four centre and two elite, with presumably the standard battalion strength and organisation – although I have found no contemporary confirmation of this. Only one officer and seventy-two other ranks from the battalion returned from the 1813 campaign in Germany[37] but the *Battaglione* was reformed during the winter of 1813/14 incorporating reinforcements drafted from the *Pompieri Della Città di Milano*, although given the low establishment of that unit (see below) it may have been that the whole unit was absorbed.

Service

Although the *Battaglione* is recorded as being in Germany in 1807, it saw no recorded action until 1813 when, as Napoleon scoured the Empire and its satellites to reform the *Grande Armée* after the disaster of the Russian campaign, the battalion was called up as part of the Italian contingent. It left Milan under the command of *Capo Battaglione* Varesi (or Varesio) with a strength 787 men and served in the *15e* Division of Bertrand's IV Corps.

1813, Germany	
May 2	Battle of Lützen
May 19	Ambush at Königswartha
May 20	Battle of Bautzen
August 23	Gross-Beeren
September 6	Battle of Dennewitz
October 3	Battle of Wartenburg
October 16–18	Battle of Leipzig
October 30	Battle of Hanau.
November ?	Returned to Italy
1814, Italy	
March 10	Battle of Pescheira (as part of Palombini's Division in the Po Valley)

Uniform

Headwear

The black felt, infantry pattern shako had a brass lozenge plate embossed with either 'G M' or, possibly the Imperial Eagle,[38] surmounted by the National cockade and a carrot-shaped pompom of red over white over green. The chin scales were brass and the black leather peak was trimmed with brass. The fatigue caps were sky blue and piped red.

36 Unpublished watercolour in the Author's collection.

37 This seems to be an incredibly low strength but is that given in Italian sources and it may be that some officers and men had been drafted into other Italian units during, or towards the end of, the campaign..

38 Since both are cited by different sources my suggestion would be that the 'GM' plate was the earlier and the reformed 1813 unit used the Imperial Eagle.

5º *Fanteria de Linea*, 1809–1812. 'Sketch' watercolour by Henry Boisselier. (Author's Collection)

Volteggiatore, 1º di Linea and *Carabiniere, 2º Fanteria Leggera, c.* 1807
See text for discussion of this uniform. There are differences in the uniform of the *volteggiatore* from what would be expected and he is 'still' wearing a bicorne so may simply not yet have received a shako. Note the bright blue on the greatcoat on the right-hand figure, this could be a lining or a protective cover but either way is highly unusual. See elsewhere for my comments of the colpack shape and once again note the buff colour for yellow on both figures. (Contemporary illustration from 'The Otto Manuscript' in the Anne S.K. Brown Military Collection, Brown University Library, reproduced with thanks)

Coat

The coat was a sky blue habit of the pattern worn by the line infantry with squared lapels, three-pointed horizontal pockets, and Brandenburg cuffs with plain cuff flaps. The collar and cuffs were red; the lapels, cuff flaps and shoulder straps were sky blue piped red (based on an illustration in the collection of H. M. The King at Windsor Castle, dated to *c.* 1807). Another source, however, records the cuffs as sky blue piped red and a yet a third shows both the collar *and* cuffs as sky blue piped red. It seems likely that all sources may be correct and the variations are simply variations in different issues. The turnbacks were white, piped red, with red grenade badges. All buttons were white metal.

Breeches, Et cetera

Breeches and waistcoats were white and the gaiters were black with white metal buttons.

Equipment

All equipment was the same as that for the *fucilieri* of the *fanteria de linea reggimenti*, although the above mentioned illustration at Windsor shows the bayonet being worn at the left of the pouch rather than with the sabre-briquet. This arrangement is unknown apart from this watercolour but is also recorded as being used by the *Pompieri Della Città di Milano* (see below) and thus may well simply be a variation manufactured in the City.

Officers & N.C.O.s

All details of uniform variation, rank insignia, etc are as for the *fanteria de linea*. An illustration, copied from a contemporary source, in the New York Public Library's Vinkhuizen Collection shows an officer in sky blue breeches and English pattern 'jockey boots'.

Musicanti

Tamburi had red epaulettes but all other details and variations are as given above for *tamburi* of the line infantry.

The NYPL illustration referred to above shows a *tamburo* with four, double-width, red batons across the chest of his coat

Fanteria Leggera

(Light Infantry)

History and Organisation

In 1805 when the organisation of the Army of the new Kingdom was formally established there were to be two Regiments of *Fanteria Leggera*; a third regiment, with the honorary title of *Real Bresciano*, was raised in 1806 and a fourth Regiment in 1811.

The battalion and company establishments of the *fanteria leggera* were identical to those of the *fanteria di linea* except that the title *fuciliere* was replaced by *cacciatore* and that of *granatiere* by *carabiniere*.[39] These were, however, simply a change in titles reflecting those in the French *infanterie légère* on which the Italian *fanteria leggera* was modelled; it had no influence on the tactical deployment of the companies. The post 1805 changes in the internal organisation of the *fanteria di linea* were reflected change for change in the *fanteria leggera*. Similarly the 1808 changes that changed the status of the *Aquile-Alfiori* and added the two *Sergente-Aquile* were repeated in the *fanteria leggera*. There is fairly strong evidence that the *fanteria leggera* had three *battaglione* from their initial creation, although I have not found a ***firm*** confirmation of this.

Regulations formally setting out the uniform of the *fanteria leggera* were not issued until 25 January 1811 when the *4º Reggimento* was raised. Prior to this date although the basic colouring was fairly standard across all three regiments the details of the uniforms were subject to a number of regimental variations. The uniform regulations laid down in 1811 were based on dress of the *1º Reggimento* at that time.

Service

1º Reggimento

1806,	Germany (end of year)
1807,	(1st Battalion) Germany
	(2nd Battalion) Spain
1808,	(1st & 2nd Battalions, perhaps also the 3rd Battalion) Spain
1809,	(1st & 2nd Battalions) Spain
	(3rd & 4th Battalions) Germany
1810,	(1st & 2nd Battalions) Spain
1811,	(1st & 2nd Battalions) Spain
1812,	(1st Battalion) Spain
	(2nd & 3rd Battalions) Germany
1813,	(1st Battalion) Spain. Probably returned to Italy by the Summer of 1813

2º Reggimento

1806,	Germany (end of year)
1807,	(1st Battalion) Germany
	(2nd Battalion) Spain
1808,	(1st & 2nd Battalions) Spain
1809,	(1st & 2nd Battalions, and possibly the 3rd) Spain
	(4th Battalion) Germany?
1810,	(1st & 2nd Battalions) Spain
1811,	(1st & 2nd Battalions) Spain
1812,	(1st Battalion) Spain
	(2nd Battalion) Germany
1813,	(1st Battalion) Spain. Probably returned to Italy in the Summer of 1813

3º Reggimento

1812,	(1st, 2nd and probably 3rd Battalions) Russia

4ᵉ Reggimento

No recorded deployments outside of the Kingdom

Uniform

Pre-January 1811

These details are taken almost entirely from contemporary illustrations since, as stated above, there were no complete regulations (there were some regulations in an Order of 1 July 1807) and it is almost certain that many of the recorded variations would have continued throughout 1811 and 1812. It should be noted that any dated statement is really only 'good' for the year of the illustration – we have no way of knowing whether it holds true for any prior or later period.

Headwear

In 1809 the *cacciatori* and *volteggiatori* companies were wearing the low early pattern of shako that did not have the reinforcing 'V' of leather at the sides and had less of a bell shape than later patterns. The shako had a white metal lozenge plate at the front embossed with the regimental number, and a National cockade at the side surmounted by green ball pompom for the *cacciatori* or a green plume for the *volteggiatori*. Both had white cords but the 'CM paintings' in the Anne S K Brown Collection show these cords as only at the back of the shako although still with the flounders at the right side.

39 Again, as with so many things concerning the Army of the Kingdom, this is a reflection of the titles used in the French *Régiments Légère* where the centre companies were 'chasseurs' and the elite companies 'carabiniers' and 'voltigeurs'.

The *carabinieri* wore the *fanteria leggera* pattern bearskin without front plate and with red cords and a red plume at the left side above the National cockade, but again the CM paintings of *c.* 1809 show the cords only at the back of the bearskin although with the usual flounders.

A contemporary illustration of *c.* March 1806 shows a *cacciatore*, of *3° Bataglione 1° Reggimento* in the usual uniform but wearing a black czapska with a brass lozenge shaped plate, surmounted by a National cockade held in place by a white strap. The czapska has a tall mid-green plume and white cords looped from the cockade to the rear corner, where the racquettes land. NB this czapska is worn, as with those of *Cacciatori a Cavallo*,

1° Fanteria Leggera, Germany 1806/1807
Taken from the 'Otto Manuscript' these uniforms show interesting variations in detail from what might be expected, *e.g.* the *carabiniere* with a yellow plume. However as the illustrations are based on eyewitness illustrations they are probably as accurate as anything else that we have. Comparing these to the illustrations of the 'provisional uniform' seems to confirm that the latter was indeed only worn by some battalions, and perhaps not those that joined the *Grande Armée* in Germany. (Watercolour by Henri Boisselier, Author's collection)

Cacciatore, 3° Battaglione, 1° Reggimento c. 1806 wearing a czapska of the Kingdom of Italy pattern. (Illustration by René Forthoffer from *Soldats du Temps Jadis, Fiches Documentaires No.242/243: Italie, 'Infanterie Légère (1) 1801–1808*. Reproduced by kind permission of Jean-Yves Forthoffer and 'l'Association Soldats du Temps Jadis Roger Forthoffer 1920'1982' http://forthoffer.free.fr)

3º Reggimento Fanteria Leggera
The uniform conforms to the description in the text although the officer's hussar pattern boots without tassels are unusual, as is the lack of lace and tassel on the *fanteria leggera* pattern gaiters. These may represent a genuine variation or simply an error in the original source. (Watercolour by Henri Boisselier in the Author's Collection)

with the front 'flat' rather than as in the Polish style, with a corner at the front. As with many of the early uniform 'variations' the use of a czapska may be simply a reflection of an initial shortage of uniform items.

There is no evidence for the fatigue caps of the light infantry although, since they were almost certainly issued, my speculation is that these would have been dark green, piped with the regimental colour and decorated with the company insignia as in the line infantry.

In 1807/08 the *carabinieri* of the *1º Reggimento* are shown wearing a black colpack with a red bag, piped yellow at the right side, a red falling plume (falling towards the front) and red cords. The same source shows *volteggiatori* of the *1º Reggimento* with a yellow over green falling plume and mixed green and yellow cords, the shako had a brass lozenge plate with a hunting horn badge and the regimental number in the loop of the horn.[40] Weiland shows a similar colpack for the *carabinieri* in 1806 but

40 Guy C. Dempsey Jr (ed.), *Napoleon's Soldiers: The Grande Armée of 1807 as Depicted in the Paintings of the Otto Manuscript*, (London: Arms & Armour, 1994).

it lacks a bag and the tassels and racquets hang on the right-hand side.[41]

Coat

The coat was similar to that of the line infantry but with pointed lapels and pointed 'Polish' cuffs. Coats were dark green with green lapels and turnbacks and regimental facing colour collar and cuffs. The 'CM paintings' show these without piping but other sources indicate that the lapels and turnbacks were piped in the regimental facing colour as were the vertical pockets. All buttons were white metal. There are no turnback decorations shown for any companies on the 'CM paintings'.

Regimental facing colours :-

1° Reggimento	Yellow
2° Reggimento	Red then Sky Blue[42]
3° Reggimento	White[43]

In 1809 all companies of the three regiments are shown wearing fringed epaulettes – green for the *cacciatori* and *volteggiatori* and red for the *carabinieri*. The wearing of fringed epaulettes by *cacciatori* companies is another conceit apparently taken from the French Army where the *chasseur* companies of the *infanterie légère* habitually did so.

In 1807 the *1° Reggimento* is depicted with red, square 'Brandenburg' cuffs with red cuff flaps, both piped yellow.

Weiland portrays a *carabiniere c.* 1806 wearing the above uniform, with a sky blue waistcoat, but with sky blue 'Brandenburg' cuffs and cuff flaps, both piped red and with red piping on the sky blue coat collar. The gaiters also have a red lace and tassel instead of facing colour. The bearskin has the traditional form of cords but in white. It seems likely that these variations were those of the *carabiniere* company alone, although perhaps the gaiters were also worn by other companies. The painting is titled *Troisieme Régiment des Chasseurs Italienne* but the sky blue points to this being a *carabiniere* of the *2° Reggimento*, not of the *3°*.

Waistcoats were in the Regimental facing colour with white metal buttons.

Breeches, et cetera

Breeches were dark green and worn with black under knee gaiters. These were of the light infantry pattern, which imitated the hussar pattern boots having piping around the top edge and a tassel at a 'v' cut at the front. In 1809 the *1° Reggimento* is shown without the lace and tassel whereas the *2°* and *3° Reggimenti* had lace and tassel in the facing colour. *Carabinieri* may have had red lace and tassel in all regiments. The buttons were of white metal, although some illustrations show them as black, but these may originally have been silver whose pigment has 'tarnished' with age. Greatcoats were almost certainly of the same pattern as worn by the *fanteria di linea*.

Carabiniere, 1° Reggimento, c. 1806 in the 'provisional' blue uniform. (Illustration by René Forthoffer from *Soldats du Temps Jadis, Fiches Documentaires No.242/243: Italie, 'Infanterie Légère (1) 1801–1808*. Reproduced by kind permission of Jean-Yves Forthoffer and 'l'Association Soldats du Temps Jadis Roger Forthoffer 1920'1982' http://forthoffer.free.fr)

41 Alain Pegeard (ed,), *Le Manuscrit de Weiland : Uniformes de l'Armée Français et de ses Alliés de 1806 à 1815*, (Paris: Tradition, 1998), p.28.

42 In 1805 the Regiment had red facings and this is usually cited in most modern works but by 1806/7 the Regiment was already using sky blue and when the uniforms were regulated by an Order of 1 July 1807 the sky blue was confirmed, although there is some evidence that red may have been restored in 1811.

43 In the 1811 regulations the 3° were given orange as their facing colour but in 1809 they are shown still using white

Equipment

Equipment was of the same pattern as that carried by the *fanteria di linea* except that all companies carried the sabre-briquet, with a green knot and tassel for the *cacciatori* and *volteggiatori* and red for the *carabinieri.* There is no evidence of any decoration on the cartridge box lid for any companies.

Officers & N.C.O.s

All rank distinctions were as for the *fanteria di linea* with rank lace silver or white. Officers of all companies carried the curved sabre with silver sabre-strap either on a whitened leather shoulder strap or from a whitened leather waist belt.[44] Officers habitually wore hussar pattern boots with silver lace and tassel. 'CM' shows an officer of the *1º Reggimento* in 1806 wearing laced and tasselled hussar boots even though the rank and file aren't shown wearing laced gaiters.

The Weiland manuscript[45] shows a *Capitano* of the *1º Reggimento, c.* 1806/07 in a regulation pattern uniform

Carabiniere, 2º Reggimento, c. 1805 in the 'provisional' blue uniform. Note the unusual green collar piped red and the, to be expected, red cuffs but piped in green. Forthoffer's illustration appears to show a hunting horn device on the shako plate, which combined with the figure wearing shako rather than a bearskin may suggest that the figure was misidentified in Forthoffer's source and is actually a *volteggiatori*. (Illustration by René Forthoffer from *Soldats du Temps Jadis, Fiches Documentaires No.242/243: Italie, 'Infanterie Légère (1) 1801–1808.* Reproduced by kind permission of Jean-Yves Forthoffer and 'l'Association Soldats du Temps Jadis Roger Forthoffer 1920'1982' http://forthoffer.free.fr)

Cacciatore, 1º Reggimento 1805, in the 'provisional' blue uniform, see text. Forthoffer dates this illustration to 6 July 1805. Note the unusual green cuffs, piped yellow and the red collar piped green. (Illustration by René Forthoffer from *Soldats du Temps Jadis, Fiches Documentaires No.242/243: Italie, 'Infanterie Légère (1) 1801–1808.* Reproduced by kind permission of Jean-Yves Forthoffer and 'l'Association Soldats du Temps Jadis Roger Forthoffer 1920'1982' http://forthoffer.free.fr)

44 Suhr shows a *Capitano* of the *1º Reggimento* in the regulation uniform, but with his sword supported from a white waist belt with silver buckle

45 Alain Pigeard (ed.), *Le Manuscrit de Weiland: Uniformes de l'Armée Français et de ses Alliés de 1806 à 1815*, (Paris: Tradition, 1998).

(with hussar boots, laced and tasselled silver) but with a triple inverted chevron of wide silver lace at the sides of the shako, the point of the outermost chevron resting against the black leather band.

Provisional Uniform 1805/1806

In 1805/1806 when the *fanteria leggera* were being organised a 'provisional uniform' is recorded in use by the junior battalions and depot companies of both the *1°* and *2° Regimmenti*. The uniform seems to have made use either of uniforms that were already in depots, or of cloth already purchased – although the colour is unusual. There is no evidence that this uniform survived beyond the 1806 issue.

This uniform was of the same cut and pattern as later uniform with the yellow facings for the *1° Reggimento* and the 1805/1806 red facings for the *2° Reggimento*, turnbacks were white, with appropriate colour piping (see illustrations).

Study by Henri Boisselier of a *Capitano* (left) and front and rear view of a *cacciatore* of the *1° Reggimento* in the 'provisional' blue uniform, *c*. 1806. Note the unusual cords on the shakos – Boisellier was aware enough of the 'regulations' and the usual appearance of such cords to strongly suggest that this is indeed what his source showed. (Watercolour by Henri Boisselier, author's collection)

1811 Regulations

Headwear

The *cacciatori* and *volteggiatori* companies wore the shako of the same pattern as the *fanteria di linea*, by 1811 this would have been of the later pattern – slightly taller with slightly more of a bell shape, both barely discernable in illustrations but more obvious on surviving examples, with a white metal lozenge plate at the front embossed with the regimental number, sometimes within a bugle horn. Cockade and strap were as for the *fanteria di linea* and shako cords were white for the *cacciatori* and green for the *volteggiatori* with pompoms as for the *fanteria di linea*. The *carabinieri* wore the *fanteria leggera* pattern bearskin, which was without a front plate, with decorations as for the *granatieri*, shakos with red cords and pompom may have been worn on campaign. Fatigue caps were dark green, piped with the regimental colour and decorated with the company insignia as for the *fanteria di linea*. A contemporary illustration of a *carabinieri* in Germany in 1807 shows a red 'falling' plume on his shako.[46]

Coat

The habit coat was similar to that of the line infantry but with pointed lapels and Brandenburg cuffs. From 1812 the regulation coat changed to the short tailed habit-veste pattern, although how long it took for the coat to be issued in any numbers is unknown. Coats were dark green with collar and cuffs of the regimental facing colour and with the lapels, turnbacks and pockets in dark green piped with the regimental distinctive colour. Cuff flaps were dark green and all buttons were white metal. The turnbacks of the elite companies were decorated with insignia as for the line regiments, and in the regimental facing colour.

The regimental facing colours were:-

1º Reggimento	Yellow
2º Reggimento	Sky Blue
3º Reggimento	Orange
4º Reggimento	Crimson

1º Fanteria Leggera c. 1808. Contemporary illustration by 'CM'. (Contemporary illustration by 'CM' in the Anne S.K. Brown Military Collection, Brown University Library, reproduced with thanks)

46 The illustration is annotated as the *2º Reggimento* but the yellow facings confirm that it is of a soldier of the *1º Reggimento*.

2° *Fanteria Leggera* c. 1806. Contemporary illustration of the 2° *Reggimento* with, as with many of this series of plates, the elite companies' 'devices' in the side bar and indicating the use of bearskins for the *Carabinieri*. (Contemporary illustration by 'CM' in the Anne S.K. Brown Military Collection, Brown University Library, reproduced with thanks)

3° *Fanteria Leggera* c. 1809. Almost identical to the illustration above there are enough small differences to indicate that the artist was drawing from life. (Contemporary illustration by 'CM' in the Anne S.K. Brown Military Collection, Brown University Library, reproduced with thanks)

Cacciatore and *Carabinieri*, *1° Fanteria Leggera*, *c.* 1807
See text for discussion of these uniforms. The buff yellow may be a result of some fading of dye on the original coats, or of the artist's pigment, but could be as the coats were issued. However all sources refer to it as yellow, and the artist has used this shade elsewhere when the original sources give 'yellow' (see above). Whether the style of colpack depicted is actually what was worn or the artist's incorrect interpretation is unknown although the latter seems more likely. (Contemporary illustration from 'The Otto Manuscript' in the Anne S.K. Brown Military Collection, Brown University Library, reproduced with thanks)

The epaulettes of the elite companies were the same as used by the *fanteria di linea* and the shoulder straps of the *cacciatori* were dark green piped in the facing colour.

Waistcoats were dark green, often with non-regulation regimental colour piping at the edge and around the pockets.

Breeches, et cetera

Breeches were dark green and worn with black knee length gaiters with white metal buttons, usually with the top shaped in imitation of hussar boots and trimmed with company colour lace and with a similar colour tassel at the front. A contemporary illustration of a *carabinieri* in full dress *c.* 1807 uniquely shows white gaiters with a yellow trim at the top and a red tassel.[47] Overall trousers were issued for campaign and were white or dark green, the latter often with a facing colour stripe on the outer seam. Greatcoats were as for the *fanteria di linea*.

Cacciatore 1° Fanteria Leggera, and (probably) *Carabinieri*, *2° Fanteria Leggera*, *c.* 1807
See text for discussion of these uniforms. As stated above the buff yellow may be a result of the artist's pigment, as all sources refer to the hue as yellow, and the artist has used this shade elsewhere when the original sources give 'yellow' (see above). As with his painting of the *1° Reggimento* the colpack shape may be the artist's incorrect interpretation of the cap's shape. The difference in uniform of the *cacciatore* from the other plate above has been suggested may be by them possibly being from different battalions having slightly different uniforms.[121] (Contemporary illustration from 'The Otto Manuscript' in the Anne S. K. Brown Military Collection, Brown University Library, reproduced with thanks)

47 This is almost certainly no more than a regimental or even just a company variation. I have seen no confirmation from any other source but the distinction is unique and unusual enough to be what the artist actually saw.

48 Guy C Dempsey, *Napoleon's Soldiers: The Grande Armée of 1807 as Depicted in the Paintings of the Otto Manuscript*, (London: Arms & Armour, 1994), p.242, broadly discounts this suggestion and suggest that the figure is from the *2° Fanteria Leggera*,

Equipment

Equipment was identical to that of the *fanteria di linea*, although the regulations laid down that only the elite companies were to carry the sabre-briquet there is evidence that many of the centre companies did so as well[49].

Officers & N.C.O.s

All rank distinctions were the same pattern as those of the *fanteria di linea* with rank lace silver or white. Officers of all companies carried the curved sabre with silver sabre-strap, usually worn from a white waist belt with a silver buckle. Officers' greatcoats were dark green and double-breasted with two rows of white metal buttons. Although not strictly regulation, many officers wore hussar pattern boots with silver lace and tassels in imitation, as with so much of the Kingdom of Italy's Army, of their allies in the French Army.

2° Fanteria Leggera, 1807
Interesting study showing a number of variations from the normally illustrated uniform. Note the cuff and cuff flaps of *fanteria di linea* style, but in *3° Fanteria Leggera* colouring, on the first figure – a similar variation is recorded for the *1°* in 1807, although the red piping is unique. Note also the czapska and the yellow gaiter lace on the second, and the *di Linea* pattern gaiters on the third. This latter is a logical adaptation if there was a shortage of the correct pattern. The czapska however is confirmed from some sources as having been used by some companies in both the *2°* and *3° Reggimenti* before the issue of the shako, it was probably depot stores ex of the Cisalpine Republic. (NB Boisselier's legend states this is the *3°* but the blue facings indicate the *2°*, an error copied from the Weiland manuscript) (Watercolour by Henri Boisselier in the Author's Collection)

---

which I think is actually more probable. Although unlike Dempsey I have no problem with the theory that the uniforms could be different between the battalions, especially considering things like the existence of the blue 'provisional uniform'.

49 Yet again an emulation of the practice in the French *Régiments Légère*.

2° Fanteria Leggera, Officers *c.* 1810
Although this is titled as the *4° Reggimento*, the facings indicate that it is actually the 2°. The uniforms depicted essentially follow that normally recorded. (Watercolour by Henri Boisselier in the Author's Collection)

2° Fanteria Leggera, *c.* 1810
A companion to the plate of the Officers of the 2° *Fanteria Leggera*. The sky blue cords shown for the *cacciatore* are worthy of note. Boisselier shows an orange pompon which may be a misinterpretation from French practice. (Watercolour by Henri Boisselier in the Author's Collection)

Musicanti

The uniforms of *tamburi* and *cornetti* were essentially the same as those of the Regiment's rank and file but with the addition of red and white lace trim to the collar and cuffs and the other uniform variation worn by the *musicanti* of the line infantry. *Volteggiatore cornetti* are sometimes shown wearing the colpack with facing colour bag and company colour cords, and tassel.

Prior to 1811 some *tamburi* and *cornetti* may have worn coats of reversed colours although this was never a widespread practice.

1º Reggimento

Tamburo Maggiore c. 1807:[50] Black colpack with a yellow patch, but without a bag, with silver cords and racquets falling at the left side. No plume is indicated but it may be assumed that the cap had a cockade either at the left-hand side, although this is not actually present on the 'Zimmerman' illustration, or at the front. Dark green coat of the same cut as the rest of the Regiment with a yellow collar and cuffs, both edged with a wide silver lace. Dark green lapels edged with a wide silver lace, piped in yellow and with a further yellow piping inside, but not 'touching' the silver lace. The rank stripes on the cuff are silver, piped in yellow and the coat has silver, trefoil epaulettes on a yellow cloth (which gives the impression of them being piped in yellow). Yellow waistcoat with pockets and edge laced silver and silver batons at each button and buttonhole extending across almost the whole front. Dark green breeches with silver trefoil knots on the thighs and a broad silver lace along the outer seam. The boots are hussar pattern with silver lace and tassel. (NB all of the broad silver lace, including the rank stripes, incorporates a 'zigzag' pattern). The black waist belt has a silver buckle embossed with a hunting horn device. The *Tamburo Maggiore* baton is brown wood with a silver top and ferrule and silver cords plaited along its length and ending in silver tassels.

Tamburo Maggiore c. 1807:[51] Black bearskin without plate with double gold cords and racquets falling at the right side. A tall red plume with three dark green falling feathers each side. Dark green coat of the same cut as the rest of the Regiment with a dark green collar and cuffs piped with a wide gold lace. Yellow lapels edged with a wide white lace and laced in white across the front. The rank stripes on the cuff are gold, piped in red and the coat has gold, fringed epaulettes. Yellow waistcoat with pockets and edge laced white. Yellow breeches with white spearheads on the thighs. The boots are English pattern with buff, turned-over tops. The black waist belt has a brass buckle embossed with a grenade badge in silver and supports an infantry officer style sabre fitted silver with a gold sword-knot and strap and a black scabbard, also fitted silver. The *tamburo maggiore'* baton was brown

Tamburo Maggiore, 1º Fanteria Leggera c. 1807
See text for discussion of this uniform. It is notable though that the yellow used is not the 'buff yellow' of the artist's other paintings of this *Reggimento*. The arrangement if feathers on the colpack is eccentric – see elsewhere for my comments of the colpack shape (Contemporary illustration from 'The Otto Manuscript' in the Anne S.K. Brown Military Collection, Brown University Library, reproduced with thanks)

50 Forthoffer plate 242, *Italie, L'Infanterie Légère (1), 1801–1808*. Although no more precise date that this is given the figure almost certainly dates earlier that the 1807 one recorded in the Otto Manuscript. It appears however to be based on that shown in the Zimmerman manuscript which carries the title 'Costume des Troupes Francaises et de celles de l'Alliance Du Rhin qui ont etées a Berlin depuis le 24ième Octobre 1806 Desfiné par Zimmerman.' As the *1º Reggimento* did not arrive in Germany until 1807, this illustration must date to 1807 and it is possible that these two 1807 depictions are simply variations of the same uniform or a new uniform was received while in Germany.

51 Guy C. Dempsey Jr, *Napoleon's Soldiers : The Grande Armée of 1807 as Depicted in the Paintings of the Otto Manuscript*, (London, Arms & Armour 1994), pp.246–247..

wood with a silver top and ferrule and silver cords plaited along its length and ending in silver tassels. [The illustration does not allow for any bearskin patch or cuff flaps to be seen and, remarkably, the figure is not wearing a 'sash'.]

2° Reggimento

*Tamburo Maggiore c.*1810:[52] Black colpack with red bag piped silver and silver cords and racquets falling on the right-hand side. A tall white plume with a group of white ostrich feathers at the base and a single red and a single green ostrich feathers at the front. Dark green coat of the same cut as the Regiment with a red collar edged with a wide silver lace. Dark green lapels edged with a wide silver lace and with a similar lace on the buttonholes. The turnbacks appear to be dark green edged silver. The rank stripes on the cuff are silver and the seams of the coat's sleeves are decorated with wide silver lace. Silver, full-fringed epaulettes. Red waistcoat with pockets and edge laced silver. All buttons on both coat and waistcoat are silver. Red breeches with silver Hungarian knots on the thighs

3° Fanteria Leggera, 1811
The uniform follows the usual pattern although the plume at the left-hand side rather than the front is unusual but a not unique aspect of light infantry headwear. (Watercolour by Henri Boisselier in the Author's Collection)

3° Fanteria Leggera, Carabinieri 1807 and 1812
The uniform illustrated essentially follows the usual form as described in the text but note the lack of cords and the flounders attached directly to the patch on the left-hand figure. This figure also lacks the lacing around the top of the gaiters, which is a not uncommon variation often also seen in the French *infanterie légère*. (Watercolour by Henri Boisselier in the Author's Collection)

52 Unpublished watercolour by Henri Boisselier

4º Fanteria Leggera, Tamburo Maggiore, Tamburo, Cornetto, c. 1810
As with the French Army, the fact that these uniforms are dated '*c.* 1810' does not necessarily mean that this is how these individuals appeared in 1809 or 1811. Coats could be issued annually and the cut and colour vary with the whim or the pocket of the *Colonello*, or simply what cloth was available. (Watercolour by Henri Boisselier in the Author's Collection)

and silver lace on both inside and outside seams. Yellow Hungarian boots with silver lace and tassel. The black waist belt has a brass buckle embossed with a grenade badge in silver and supports an infantry officer's style sabre fitted brass with a silver sword-knot and strap and a black scabbard. His baton is brown wood with a silver top and bottom and silver cords plaited along its length ending in silver tassels. The *tamburo maggiore*' sash is red with silver lace edge and silver fringe along the edges, silver drumstick badge. [The illustration does not allow for the cuffs or cuff flaps to be seen.]

Zappatori

The *zappatori* of the *fanteria leggera* wore the uniform of the *carabiniere* company with the usual badges and equipment of the position added.

1º Reggimento

Zappatore *c.* 1807:[53] The *zappatore* is shown with a lower than standard, flat-topped bearskin,[54] without plate but with a red falling plume at the front, red double cords with racquets at the left. No National cockade is in evidence but it may have been at the front and thus covered by the falling plume. The coat is dark green with dark green lapels and collar, piped in a buff colour (from other evidence in the manuscript this may once have been a fairly bright yellow), and with a red crossed axe badge on each upper arm, and red, fringed epaulettes. The

53 Guy. C. Dempsey Jr, *Napoleon's Soldiers : The Grande Armée of 1807 as Depicted in the Paintings of the Otto Manuscript*, (London, Arms & Armour 1994), pp.244–245.

54 Looking like a cross between a bearskin and the colpack, this unique pattern of bearskin/colpack appears in a number of illustrations of *zappatori* of various infantry regiments in the Army.

Zappatore, 1º Fanteria Leggera, c. 1807
See text for discussion of this uniform. The buff waistcoat and piping should, I feel, be yellow (see above) although I would suggest that the gauntlets and apron may be accurately depicted. (Contemporary illustration from 'The Otto Manuscript' in the Anne S.K. Brown Military Collection, Brown University Library, reproduced with thanks)

2º Fanteria Leggera, Zappatore 1810
Rare study of a *zappatore* of the *fanteria leggera*. The reversed colours, which as with many of these uniforms may only have existed in one particular year, were relatively common in what the French called the *Tête de Colonne*. Noteworthy is the pair of pistols in his belt, again something copied from practice in the French Army. (Watercolour by Henri Boisselier in the Author's Collection)

waistcoat is the same buff as the piping and the apron, of a buff colour close to that of the waistcoat, reaches almost to the ankles. The gauntlets are the same colour as the apron. The cartridge box is worn on the stomach on a black waist belt. All belts have brass fittings.

4º Reggimento

Sergente Zappatore, c. 1811.[55] Boisselier illustrates the *sergente zappatore* in a uniform that reflects the custom in the French Army, and although the illustration is credited as the *4º Reggimento*, the colouring would seem to be more suitable for the *2º Reggimento*. The *sergente* has a black colpack with no apparent bag but with a scarlet falling plume at the front but no other visible decoration. The coat is sky blue with dark green collar and lapels but neither the cuffs (covered by the gauntlets) nor the turnbacks are visible – although it may be assumed that both are dark green. Buttons are white metal. The rank stripes are silver, edged with red, as is the *zappatore* badge on the upper arm. The epaulettes have brass straps and crescent and a red fringe. The gauntlets are white with black cuffs. The *zappatore* carries two pistols in his waist

55 Unpublished watercolour by Henri Boisselier in the Author's Collection.

belt, one each side of the buckle. Breeches are green and the short light infantry pattern gaiters are white with a red braid and tassel. The usual *zappatore* apron is white. The cartouche box belt has a large brass grenade badge on the breast where the two belts cross. The sword cannot be seen but is probably the heavy *zappatore* sword illustrated above.

Regimental Artillery Companies

All details are as for the *artiglieria* companies of the *fanteria di linea* but the coat was of *fanteria leggera* pattern with pointed lapels and 'Polish' cuffs.

Legione Reale Dalmata / Reggimento Reale Dalmata

(Royal Dalmatian legion / Regiment)

In 1806 the Kingdom of Italy annexed parts of Dalmatia and subsequently raised the *Legione Reale Dalmata* (Royal Dalmatian Legion), although there is no record that it ever comprised anything except infantry so was technically not a 'Legion'.[56] In 1808 the Legion was redesignated as the *Reggimento Reale Dalmata* (Royal Dalmatian Regiment). Following the tradition of the Venetian Republic, from whom the area had been annexed, the unit was recruited from the native Slavs. In 1808 the unit was reformed, or more accurately redesignated again, as a light infantry regiment with the same establishment as that of the other *Reggimenti Leggera* of the Kingdom of Italy. The uniform changed at the time to bring it in line with the rest of the Army of the Kingdom, although no doubt the somewhat dramatic changes took more than a little time to fully carry through the whole *Reggimento*.

Service

1809,	Tyrol
1812,	(1st, 2nd, 3rd Battalions) Russia

Headwear

In 1806 the Regiment was supplied with the 'Corsican Hat'; a wide brimmed, black felt hat with a stovepipe crown and the left side of the brim turned up.[57] The turned up side was decorated with the National cockade and cockade strap surmounted by a carrot-shaped pompom in red for the *carabinieri*, green for the *volteggiatore* and yellow for the *cacciatori*.

In 1808, when the *Legione* was reformed and renamed, the Corsican Hat was replaced by a regulation pattern shako, which had a white metal lozenge shaped plate embossed with the Iron Crown above the letters 'RD'.[58] Shako cords and pompom were of the same colouring as previously worn on the Corsican Hat. The *volteggiatore* companies continued to wear the Corsican Hat until around 1811, as is so often the case, probably wearing out old depot stocks.

Coat

The coat was the pattern as worn previously by the *Reggimento Leggera* of the Cisalpine Republic. This was a hip-length single-breasted coat cut square along the bottom and with the turnbacks at the front in the manner of the 1790s Austrian Army's coat. The upright collar was closed at the throat and cuffs were of the pointed 'Polish' style. The coat was dark green with red collar, cuffs and turnbacks. The front was closed with eight white metal buttons. Shoulder straps were dark green piped red for the centre companies and the elite companies wore red, for the *carabinieri*, or yellow, for the *volteggiatore*, fringed epaulettes. It appears that in 1808 the coat changed to the usual *fanteria leggera* cut in the same colouring.[59]

Breeches, et cetera

In 1806 the *Reggimento* wore breeches of the tight fitting 'Hungarian' pattern, similar to those worn by the Hungarian and *Grenzer* regiments of the Austrian Army. Breeches were dark green with a tight cuff that fitted over the top of the boot and laced beneath the instep. These breeches were worn with the Dalmatians' National style *Opanker* shoes; essentially these were leather open sandals, cross-gartered to mid-calf. In 1808 the *Reggimento* adopted the more usual pattern of infantry breeches in dark green, with black knee length gaiters and the normal pattern of boots.

Equipment

All equipment was as for the *fanteria leggera*, however prior to *c.* 1808, the sabre/bayonet shoulder belt of the elite companies was often replaced with a waist belt. The sword-strap of the elite companies was either red or yellow as appropriate.

56 'Legions' were a mid-eighteenth Century eccentricity that continued into the nineteenth. They supposedly contained both horse and foot units and often artillery as well. Almost all European Nations adopted the concept for many of their 'non-mainstream' units.

57 This style of headwear echoed that of the post 1806 Austrian Jaeger Regiment.

58 A modern reproduction of the uniform on display in the Museo di Risorgimento in Milan has a brass plate but the contemporary sources all show white metal.

59 I have never found formal confirmation of this although Luca Cristini also follows this line in *L'Esercito Del Regno Italico 1805–1814. Volume 1: La Fanteria*, (Lodigliano: Soldiershop, 201)0, plates L and M. Perhaps it was simply that depot stocks of the old pattern of coat had been exhausted?

Officers & N.C.O.s

The N.C.O.s of the *Reale Dalmata* wore the same uniform as the rank and file with the addition of the silver rank badges, in the form of inverted chevrons, above each cuff.

Officers, except for full dress, usually wore the surtout with regimental lace and the rank badges of the light infantry. In full dress, officers wore the habit with pointed lapels and Polish cuffs, with red facings as for the rank and file.

Musicanti

The Regiment's *musicanti* were uniformed the same as the rank and file but with the addition of red and white lace trim to the collar and cuffs. Whether this continued after 1808 I have been unable to confirm.

Battalione Cacciatori d'Istria

(Istrian Light Infantry Battalion)

History and Organisation

The fairly short-lived *Battalione Cacciatori d'Istria* was raised in 1808[60] and then absorbed into the *3° Fanteria Leggera* at the end of 1810. It was recruited in the Trieste region ostensibly only from men of Slavic origin, although it seems likely that others were accepted.

Service

The battalion does not feature in any of the Orders of Battle of the Army of the Kingdom during the period of its existence and Martinien[61] records no casualties amongst its officers.

Uniform

The *Battalione Cacciatori d'Istria* was uniformed along the same lines as the *Reggimento Leggero Dalmata* (see above) except with the regimental pattern of shako in place of the latter's hat. The dark green coats had mid-blue facings replacing the red of the *Reggimento Leggero Dalmata*. The *d'Istria* are also recorded wearing dark grey breeches in place of the green of the *Leggero Dalmata*, and one illustration shows silver-white Hungarian knots on the thighs.[62]

Musicanti

The uniform was essentially that of the rank and file although only a single shoulder belt was worn to support the sabre-briquet of regulation pattern with initially a white sword-knot and tassel but by 1809 a green one. The drums had a brass barrel with the hoops painted in white / red / white / mid-blue / white diagonals.

Compagnie Dipartmentali di Riserva

(Departmental Reserve Companies)

History and Organisation

A Decree was issued on 11 October 1811 ordering the raising of *Compagnie Dipartmentali di Riserva* in each of the Kingdom's twenty-two Departments, along the lines of those that existed in France.[63] Milan and Venice were excluded from the Decree since both already had their own 'Guard Battalions' (see above) and which served a similar purpose to that for which the new companies were intended. The companies were organised along the same lines as the *fuciliere* companies of the *fanteria di linea*, however the strength of the company varied according to the population of the Department and thus the rank and file numbered anywhere from 120 to close to 250. Each company also had a small administrative staff and was customarily commanded by a *Maggiore*.

Service

The companies saw no active service but were drafted wholesale into the Army in 1814, either as complete companies or broken up and their manpower used to bring the regular regiments up to strength. It is unlikely that everyone was re-uniformed and it is probable that many men served in their *compagnie di reserve* uniforms, particularly where a company was absorbed complete.

Headwear

The shako was of the usual regulation infantry pattern with a white metal lozenge plate bearing either the company number (the companies were numbered consecutively 1 to 22) or the letter 'R' for *Riserva*. Two patterns of pompom appear to have been used by the companies, the first, of green and white, identical to that in use by the *fucilieri* of the *fanteria di linea*, and the second a carrot-shaped pompom of red over white over green. Shako cords were white and the chin scales white metal. Fatigue caps were dark green with white piping.

Coat

The habit was dark green with white, piped red, lapels and turnbacks, the latter decorated with red grenade badges. The collar and cuffs were red piped dark green, the cuff

---

60 Luca Stefano Cristini however dates its raising as 1806. *L'Esercito Del Regno Italico 1805–1814. Volume 1: La Fanteria*, (Lodigliano: Soldiershop, 2010).

61 Aristide Martinien, *Tableaux Par Corps et par Batailles des Officiers Tués et Blessées Pendant les Guerres de l'Empire (1805–1815)*, (Paris: Henri-Charles Lavauzelle, 1899).

62 Luca Stefano Cristini, *L'Esercito Del Regno Italico 1805–1814. Volume 1: La Fanteria*, (Lodigliano: Soldiershop, 2010), plate N.

63 There is some evidence that similar companies had existed earlier and until at least 1805/06 but their uniform was not regulated, except by Department, and they seem to have been less than effectively organised.

flaps were white and unpiped. Shoulder straps were dark green piped red.[64] The horizontal pockets were piped in red. All buttons were white metal.

Breeches, et cetera

Breeches and waistcoats were white. Gaiters were black over-the-knee pattern with white metal or cloth covered buttons. The grey greatcoats were of regulation infantry pattern.

Equipment

All equipment was the same as that used by the elite companies of the *fanteria di linea*, and the sword-knot on the sabre-briquet was white.

Officers & N.C.O.s

Rank badges and distinctions were as used by the line infantry

Musicanti

Essentially the uniform was that of the *musicanti* of the line infantry with the addition of white swallow's nest epaulettes edged with red and white lace.

Reggimento Veterani E Invalidi

(Veteran and Invalids Regiment)

History and Organisation

The regiment was formed in November 1811 by the amalgamation of the pre-existing *Battaglione Veterani dell'Esercito*[65] and the *Navale Verterani Battaglione*.[66] The Regiment initially had an establishment of two battalions; a *1º Invalidi* Battalion of 480 men and a *2º Veterani* Battalion of 1,440 men. By 1813 the establishment had increased to one *Invalidi* Battalion of four companies, and two *Veterani* Battalions, each of six companies.

Service

There is no record of any field service by the Regiment or its constituent battalions and it does not feature in any of the Italian Army's orders of battle.

Uniform

Headwear

The shako was the same model as that worn by the *fucilieri* of the *fanteria di linea* with a white metal lozenge plate embossed 'VR', and with white shako cords. There is no evidence of a pompom being worn by the regiment, although with white cords being recorded a plain white pompom would seem probable.

Coat

The dark green habit had a white collar and cuffs, both piped red, red lapels and dark green cuff flaps without piping. The turnbacks and shoulder straps were dark green with red piping, the horizontal pockets were piped red, all buttons were white metal.

Breeches, et cetera

Waistcoats and breeches were white and the over-the-knee gaiters were white with white metal buttons for full dress parades in summer, and black with cloth covered buttons for campaign dress and winter. Greatcoats were of the same pattern as those of the *fanteria di linea*, probably in steel-grey.

Equipment

Equipment was the same pattern as that used by the *fucilieri* of the *fanteria di linea* with a single cross belt supporting both the black leather cartridge box, with a plain lid, and the bayonet in a brown scabbard. There were no elite companies in the *Regimentto* and sabre-briquets were not worn.

Officers & N.C.O.s

All rank badges, uniform variations, et cetera were the same as those of the officers and N.C.O.s of the *fucilieri* of the *fanteria di linea*. Officers' plumes were white.

Tamburi

Again, all uniform variations, equipment, et cetera were as for the *tamburi* of the *fucilieri* of the *fanteria di linea*

Battaglione Franca di Bersaglieri

also termed

Bersaglieri di Brescia

(Volunteer Rifle Battalion or Brescia Rifle Battalion)

History and Organisation

The *Battaglione Franca di Bersaglieri* was raised by an Order of 30 August 1813, and was to be recruited from the men of the Forestry Department skilled in the use of rifles (there were attempts, with various levels of success, to raise similar units in other Napoleonic armies). The battalion's establishment was set as four companies, each with a strength of 140 all ranks, but by 13 December

64 Although a sketch illustration in Piero Giorgio Franzoni, *Napoleone in Italia: Soldati e Uniformi*, (Franzoni, Rome, Rivista Militare 1987), p.17 shows red full-fringed epaulettes.

65 I am unsure of the exact nomenclature of this unit as I have seen some variations in Italian sources.

66 Prior to this date the two 'units' existed separately with a strength of one battalion each. Their uniform had been the same except that both battalions wore the bicorne and the Naval Veterans wore a green waistcoat and green breeches. Similarly there is no evidence that the units ever participated in the field.

1813 the *Battaglione* numbered only 142 men, sixty of whom deserted a month later at the first hint of the unit being deployed (suggestive that the men may have been conscripted, or at least recruited under some sort of 'pressure', and not actually volunteers). With ongoing recruitment difficulties the unit never went beyond organising a single company, and it seems to have "faded away" rather than being formally disbanded although it was listed amongst the units of the Army that were formally disbanded at the fall of the Kingdom in 1814.

Service

There is no record of the unit taking part in any actions, or even actually joining the army in the field.

Bersaglieri di Brescia, c1812
Note the short rifle and apparent lack of either bayonet or sabre-briquet. The method of wearing the pack at the right lower back is also shown in the Austrian Army and this may indicate the reuse of old or captured Austrian equipment. (Vinkhuijzen Collection, General Research Division, New York Public Library Digital Collections. Public Domain)

Uniform

Headwear

The battalion wore a black felt Corsican Hat, perhaps in imitation of the Austrian Jaegers who may have been the inspiration for the battalion.[67] The hat was turned up at the left side, which was decorated with a wide 'v' of green lace. The National cockade, at the upper edge of the turned up left side, was secured by a green cockade strap and surmounted by a green carrot-shaped pompom. The hat had a black leather chinstrap.

Coat

The dark green coat was of a similar cut to the 1812 pattern 'Spencer' habit-veste, with short tails and lapels closed to the waist. The lapels, collar, pointed cuffs and short turnbacks were mid-green, the lapels and cuffs piped dark green. The shoulder straps were dark green piped mid-green, the pockets were also piped mid-green. All buttons were of white metal.

Breeches, et cetera

Breeches were dark green with a facing colour stripe on the outer seam; the short gaiters were black with cloth covered buttons. On campaign the battalion wore grey overall trousers with a mid-green stripe on the outer seam. The pepper grey greatcoats, of the regulation infantry pattern, had a mid-green collar.

Equipment

According to the regulations the rank and file were to have a black leather waist belt supporting the cartridge pouch at the centre front and the sabre-briquet and bayonet on the left hip. However there are references to the use of a white shoulder belt to support a sabre-briquet with green sword-knot and bayonet, as for the *fanteria di linea*. It is improbable that both variations existed given the small size of the unit and it may be that the latter variation reflects what was available and issued as opposed to what was intended.

It had initially been planned to arm the battalion with rifles, but these were never issued and instead the unit was armed with the short dragoon pattern muskets, although many of the men are known to have carried their own hunting rifles.

Officers & N.C.O.s

N.C.O.s wore the uniform of the rank and file with the usual distinctions and stripes, in the form of inverted silver chevrons above the cuff. Senior N.C.O.s had a silver trim to the upper edge of the hat. The sword-knot was mixed green and silver.

67 Although it should also be noted that the French *Garde Impériale* raised two similar battalions around the same time – the *Flanquers Grenadiers* and the *Flanquers Chasseurs*, both of whom appear to have originally been intended to be rifle armed.

Bersaglieri di Brescia, c. 1813, as in the illustration above the pack is worn on the hip rather than on the back – although it is possible that both artists have copied from the same contemporary source. (Illustration by Henri Boisselier in the Author's collection)

Officers wore a bicorne hat with silver trim and green plume or pompom. The coat was of a similar pattern to that of the rank and file but with long tails. Epaulettes were as worn in the line infantry but all officers carried the curved sabre with silver sword-knot and tassel.

Musicanti

The *Battaglione* had, perhaps not surprisingly, *cornetti* in place of *tamburi*. These wore the uniform of the other ranks with the addition of white lace trim to the hat, collar and cuffs. The horns were brass with green cords.

Corpo Delle Guardia di Finanza

(Customs Guards Corps)

History and Organisation

The Customs Department was not formally a part of the army, however, the unit was in constant action while performing its primary duty of patrolling the borders of the Kingdom and maintaining the blockade against imported British goods under 'the Continental System' aimed at ruining Britain economically. In 1814 the unit was drafted wholesale into the Army during the campaign in the Po Valley. The rank and file were *Guardie*.

Uniform

Headwear

The *Corpo* wore a plain black bicorne hat with National cockade and white cockade strap.

Coat

Coats were light blue-grey single-breasted 'surtout' style, fastened with nine brass buttons. The collar, round cuffs (without cuff flaps), turnbacks and shoulder straps were light blue-grey piped white.

Breeches, et cetera

Breeches and waistcoats were light blue-grey. The plain-topped black leather boots reached between ankle and calf, and were apparently worn without gaiters. Greatcoats were of the same pattern as those of the *fanteria di linea*.

Equipment

All equipment was the same as that used by the centre companies of the *fanteria di linea*. The cartridge box lid carried a brass plate with the inscription 'Regno d'Italia Guardia di Finanza'.

N.C.O.s

N.C.O.s of the *Corpo Delle Guardia di Finanza* used the same rank badges as the *fanteria de linea* but the actual titles of the ranks were unique to the Corps:

Capo di I Classe (*Sergente Maggiore* / Sergeant-Major)
Capo di II Classe (*Sergente* / Sergeant)
Sotto Capo (*Brigadiere* or *Caporale* / Corporal)

The uniform was the same as that of the rank and file although all N.C.O.s additionally wore the sabre-briquet with a white sword-knot and tassel from a second cross belt.

Officers

There were two grades of officer in the *Corpo*: *Ispettori* (Inspectors) and *Subispettori* (Sub-Inspectors) but as they were technically not a part of the military, they did not wear military epaulettes of rank. Their rank was instead indicated by, respectively, a double and single edging of silver lace on the collar and turnbacks. Coats and waistcoats had all buttons silvered. Officers wore Hungarian pattern boots with silver lace and tassel. Armament was the straight, infantry pattern epée, worn in a black leather scabbard, fitted silver, and suspended from a yellow-leather waist belt fastened with a silver buckle covered by a square silvered plate.

5
Artillery and Support Units

Artiglieria
(Artillery)

History and Organisation

The Artillery of the Kingdom of Italy was created from that of the Cisalpine Republic in November 1805 and organised into two regiments. The *Reggimento di Artiglieria a Cavallo* (Horse Artillery), which comprised both the Horse Artillery companies and the Artillery Train and the *Reggimento di Artiglieria a Piedi* (Foot Artillery), which supplied the great majority of the Kingdom's artillery needs. The organisation was basically along the lines of the artillery regiments of the French Army and the guns and equipment were, mainly, the older French 'Gribeauval' pieces although there is some evidence that, at least in the earlier period, some captured Austrian pieces were used.

Reggimento di Artiglieria a Piedi

(Regiment of Foot Artillery)

The *Reggimento di Artiglieria a Piedi* was created in November 1805 with two field battalions, each of ten companies and numbered 1 to 20 straight through both battalions. Initially there were ten artillery companies in each battalion but the following year companies 17 to 20 were disbanded and the artillery support companies integrated into the battalions. Thereafter the first battalion comprised eight companies of *artiglieri* (company Nos 1 to 8) plus a company each of *braccianti* (company No.9) and Artificer Armourers (No.10). The second battalion again had eight companies of *artiglieri* (companies 11 to 18) but with a company each of Bridge Engineers (No.19) and *bombardieri* (No.20).

On 20 August 1807, a small depot battalion was authorised with a permanent establishment of one *maggiore*, five other officers, twenty-one N.C.O.s and two *tamburi*. The depot was responsible for processing recruits and passing them through to the field battalions.

By an Order of 16 January 1808 Eugène reorganised the Regiment into two battalions of artillery (the 1st and 2nd battalions) and a third battalion, which contained the support companies and had an establishment of:

2 *Bracciante* Companies
2 Bridge Engineer Companies
1 Artificer Armourer Company
1 *Bombardiere* Company
1 Depot "Company"[1]

On 7 March 1808 the Regiment absorbed the *Compagnia di Artiglieria a Piedi* of the Tuscan Army and on 7 May the two companies of the Roman Army.

The last reorganisation of the Regiment was ordered on 4 February 1811, which increased the 1st and 2nd battalions' establishments to ten companies of artillery and the 3rd battalion to:

3 *Bracciante* companies
3 Bridge Engineer companies
1 Artificer Armourers company
1 Depot 'company'

The companies of the field battalions each had eight guns: either six 12pdr artillery pieces and two eight inch howitzers or six 8pdr[2] artillery pieces and two short barrelled six inch howitzers, the latter establishment being the most common.

The number of men required to serve a gun varied according to the type of piece; a 12pdr field gun or eight inch howitzer had a crew of fifteen men of whom eight were specialist gunners; an 8pdr field gun or six inch howitzer required a crew of thirteen men, again eight were specialists, and the 4pdr field guns of the horse batteries had an eight man crew of whom five were specialists. The non-specialists were usually temporarily detached from infantry regiments for the duration of a battle, occasionally it appears that such draftees could serve with a gun for longer periods.

Regimental Staff	
1 *Colonnello*	1 *Colonnello Sotto*
1 *Maggiore*	3 *Capo Battaglione* (foot artillery)
2 *Aiutante*	6 *Aiutante-Sottufficiale*
1 *Quartiermaistro*	1 *Aquile-Alfiori*
2 *Sergente-Aquile*	
1 *Tamburo Maggiore*	
Company Establishment	
1 *Capitano*	1 *Tenente*
1 *Sotto Tenente*	1 *Sergente Maggiore*
4 *Sergenti*	8 *Caporali*
1 *Caporale furiere*	1 *Tambure*
64 *Primo Artiglieri*	46 *Artiglieri*

1 Although titled as a "company" the Depot had an inflated officer and N.C.O. establishment (see above) and a fluctuating rank and file strength as recruits came in or were passed out to the field battalions.

2 NB, This was the French "pound", not the British. A French 8pdr gun actually used a shot slightly heavier than the British 9pdr.

Watercolour 'sketch' by Henri Boisselier showing various ranks in the *Regimentto*. (Author's collection)

Over the first years of the Regiment's existence there were a number of minor alterations to the initial establishment, mainly in the number of gunners.

At the general disbandment of the Army of Italy in 1814, the *Reggimento di Artiglieria a Piedi* (and parts of the artillery of the *Guardia Reale*) was incorporated into the Austrian Infantry *Regiment IR 2 Erzherzog Ferdinand*, despite it being theoretically an 'Hungarian Regiment'![3]

Service

The Army's artillery, medical and support units fought alongside the rest of the Army at almost every engagement and skirmish and to list them all here would seem a particularly pointless exercise. Except in Russia none of these units suffered particularly heavy casualties.

An indication of the service of the Regiment can perhaps be seen in a snapshot of the locations of the Foot Artillery Regiment in the summer of 1807:[4]

1st Battalion	
1st Company	Mantua
2nd Company	Grande Armée
3rd Company	Verona
4th Company	Army of Naples
5th Company	Istria
6th Company	Ancona
7th Company	Dalmatia
8th Company	Dalmatia

3 The infantry regiments of the Austrian Army of the period were designated either "Hungarian", recruited (theoretically) only from Hungary, or "German", recruited from all other provinces of the Empire.

4 Jean-Pierre Perconte, 'Organisation et Uniformes de l'Artillerie à Pied du Royaume d'Italie, 2e Partie', in *Soldats Napoleoniens : Les Troupes Françaises, Alliés et Coalisées, No.4, Décembre 2004*, (Paris: Éditions de la Revue Napoléon, 2004), pp.37–44.

2nd Battalion	
9th Company	Ragusa
10th Company	Civitavecchia
11th Company	Pavia
12th Company	Pavia
13th Company	Dalmatia
14th Company	Dalmatia
15th Company	Grande Armée
16th Company	Venice

Bracciante Company	Pavia
Blacksmith Coy	Brescia, Milan, Verona
Bridging Coy	Grande Armée
Maintenance Coy	Venice

A comparative of the company locations on 1 February 1813[5] demonstrates that the companies of the battalion rarely served together:

1st Battalion	
Company No.1	Mantua
Company No.2	Grande Armée
Company No.3	Illyria
Company No.4	Corfu
Company No.5	Palmanova
Company No.6	Trieste
Company No.7	Grande Armée
Company No.8	Spain
Company No.9	Spain
Company No.10	Spain

2nd Battalion	
Company No.11	Venice
Company No.12	Corfu
Company No.13	Mantua
Company No.14	Grande Armée
Company No.15	Venice
Company No.16	Chioggia
Company No.17	Ancona
Company No.18	Ancona
Company No.19	Peschiera
Company No.20	Osopo
3rd Battalion	

Bracciante Coy No.1	Venice
Bracciante Coy No.2	Pavia
Bracciante Coy No.3	Mantua
Armourers Coy	Brescia
Bridging Coy No.1	Grande Armée
Bridging Coy No.2	Grande Armée
Bridging Coy No.3	Grande Armée
Depot Company	Pavia

Uniform

Headwear

In 1805 the regiment wore a black bicorne with National cockade, white cockade strap and carrot-shaped red pompom, but by an Order of 17 February 1808 this was replaced by a black shako, without peak and possibly even without the leather reinforcing top and bottom although one source shows the shako as having a red band around the upper edge. The front of the shako was decorated with a large brass crossed cannon badge, the shako cords and the carrot-shaped pompom were both red. The shako appears to have had variations with both brass chin scales and a black leather chinstrap being recorded.

By 1812 this unusual pattern of shako[6] had been replaced by the more conventional infantry pattern, with a brass lozenge plate embossed with crossed cannon below the Iron Crown or the Imperial Eagle (from French stocks?). The shako had the National cockade at the front above the plate and for full dress a red plume and cords, replaced when on campaign with a carrot-shaped red pompom.

The fatigue caps were dark green, piped red with a red tassel.

Coat

The coat for all personnel of the *Reggimento di Artiglieria a Piedi* was a dark green habit, with dark green shoulder straps piped red, red-piped horizontal pockets, red turnbacks with dark green grenade badges. Details of other facings, et cetera varied for each arm, vizt:

Artiglieri	black lapels and collar piped red. Red cuffs and cuff flaps piped dark green.
Braccianti	black collar piped red, red lapels with no piping. Red cuffs and cuff flaps piped dark green.

5 Perconte, Jean-Pierre, 'Organisation et Uniformes de l'Artillerie à Pied du Royaume d'Italie, 2e Partie'. *Soldats Napoleoniens : Les Troupes Françaises, Alliés et Coalisées, No.4, Décembre 2004.* Paris: Éditions de la Revue Napoléon, 2004), pp.37–44.

6 A guess would say that this shako was "old stock" from a warehouse somewhere and used, until stocks ran out, to save costs.

Bridge Workers	black collar piped red, sky blue lapels with no piping. Black cuffs and cuff flaps piped red.
Blacksmiths	Aurore[7] collar piped black, black lapels piped red.[8] Aurore cuffs, cuff flaps and turnbacks, all piped black. Shoulder straps and pockets were dark green piped red.

Boisselier's drawings show a gunner for the period 1812–14 in a dark green 'Spencer' coat with the same colours as the habit coat except that the turnbacks are green piped red and without badges, and the shoulder straps have been replaced with red fringed epaulettes. This would appear to follow the styles adopted in the French Foot Artillery regiments although it may not have ever been a widely issued uniform.

Breeches, et cetera

Breeches and waistcoat were dark green with white metal buttons. Black over-the-knee gaiters with white metal buttons for parade and cloth covered buttons on campaign. If the 'Spencer' coat mentioned above came into use it would be expected that the gaiters were replaced by the shorter, below-knee, pattern. The greatcoats were the same pattern as used by the infantry and are shown as dark blue in 1807 in an illustration by Massimo Fiorentino,[9] although other sources show grey, including by Fiorentino for 1812 – it may be that, as in the French Army, they were often intended to be blue but the exigencies of war caused them to be made in whatever suitable cloth was available (which would include all shades of grey and even brown).

Equipment

Equipment was of the same pattern as that used by the elite companies of the *fanteria di linea*, with a brass grenade badge on the cartridge box lid. The sword-strap was white with red knot and tassels.

Officers & N.C.O.s

All rank distinctions and badges were the same as those used by the *fanteria di linea*. *Primo Artiglieri* wore the stripe of a *caporale* in white on the left cuff only.

Officers' distinctions and badges were the same as those used by the line infantry. Officers' greatcoats were dark green with a black collar and silver buttons. All belts were black leather with brass fittings. Field officers' shabraques were of infantry officers' pattern, of dark green with silver trim and a grenade badge in the rear corners.

Musicanti

Tamburi had the same lace and uniform differencing as the *tamburi* of the *fanteria di linea*. Drums, equipment, et cetera were also the same as those used by the *fanteria di linea*.

Reggimento di Artiglieria a Cavallo

(Regiment of Horse Artillery)

The Regiment was created by a Decree of 1 November 1805 and comprised a Regimental Staff, two companies of Horse Artillery and four companies of Train, which had been the strength of the similar Regiment in the Army of the Cisalpine Republic.

The 1805 Decree laid down the establishments as:

Regimental Staff	
1 *Colonnello*	2 *Capo Squadrone*
2 *Aiutante Maggiore*	1 *Quartiermaistro*
1 *Chirurge Maggiore*	
8 *Aiutante Sottoufficiale*	1 *Tromba-Maggiori*
1 *Veterinario*	
3 *Maestro Artigiano* (master craftsmen: boot maker, tailor, saddler)	

Horse Artillery Company	
1 *Capitano Comandante*	1 *Sottocapitano*
1 *Tenente*	2 *Sotto Tenente*
1 *Capo Maresciallo*	6 *Maresciallo Delle Case*
1 *Furiere Caporale*	6 *Caporali*
2 *Trombettieri*	
1 *Sellaio* (not mounted)	1 *Marshal Ferratura* (not mounted)
30 *Primo Cannoni*	60 *Cannoni di 2 classe* (40 not mounted)

Train Company	
1 *Tenente*	2 *Sotto Tenente*
1 *Capo Maresciallo*	4 *Maresciallo Delle Case*

7 'Aurore', literally 'dawn', is a bright orange-red colour.

8 A project of April 1806 projected steel-grey lapels but there is no evidence that this was ever put into effect.

9 Jean-Pierre Perconte, 'Organisation et Uniformes de l'Artillerie à Pied du Royaume d'Italie, 2e Partie', in *Soldats Napoleoniens : Les Troupes Françaises, Alliés et Coalisées, No.4, Décembre 2004*, (Paris. Éditions de la Revue Napoléon 2004), pp.37–44.

1 *Furiere Caporale*	4 *Caporali*
2 *Trombettieri*	2 *Sellai* (not mounted)
28 *Primo Soldati*	54 *Soldati di 2° classe*

There were some minor adjustments to this organisation over time, including the addition of a *maggiore* to the Staff on 2 February 1807, and an *aiutante chirugiano* and a *chirurgo secondario-principale* to the staff on 23 February of the same year. However aside from the increase to six Train companies on 31 December 1807 none were significant until the Train was moved out into a separate Regiment in February 1811.

Service

Perconte[10] gives a table for the period 1807–1810, which I have reproduced here and which is indicative of the service of the Regiment during this period. The later service of the Regiment would have been similar.

Uniform

Headwear

The first headdress issued to the *Reggimento di Artiglieria a Cavallo* was a lancer style czapska with the lower part a black fur turban and the upper part black, trimmed with dark green along the edge and across the top. The trim was changed to red by a regulation of 1807 but this change may have taken some time to appear in the Regiment. The chin scales were brass and the peak was black leather edged in brass. At the left front upper edge of the czapska was the National cockade, secured by a white cockade strap and surmounted by a red plume, in later issues the plume had a white over red ball pompom at its base. Below the cockade was a brass badge of crossed cannon with a crown above and a small pyramid of six cannonballs below. On campaign the plume was replaced with a red carrot-shaped pompom.

***Reggimento di Artiglieria a Cavallo* service 1807–1810**			
Date	Men	Horses	
Establishment of 2 companies of Horse Artillery and 4 of Train : 624 men and 656 horses[11]			
1807, 15 October	789	1,012	444 men with 709 horses were outside Italy
1808, 16 January	716	847	
Establishment of 2 companies of Horse Artillery and 6 of Train : 824 men and 1,320 horses			
1808, 31 May	803	872	
1808, 1 July	780	1,109	47 men were outside of Italy
1808, 16 September	796	1,008	244 men at Perpignan
1808, 1 October	784	996	250 men with 351 horse at Perpignan
1808, 16 December	789	995	250 men with 342 horses in Spain
1809, 1 February	936	1,291	252 men with 345 horses in Spain
1809, 1 March	934	1,328	253 men in Spain (horses not recorded)
1809, 1 November	913	1,270	246 men with 327 horses in Spain 515 men with 793 horses in Germany
1810, 16 February	848	1,140	245 men with 327 horses in Spain
1810, 16 March	905	1,102	241 men with 327 horses in Spain
1810, 1 April	901	1,120	241 men with 327 horses in Spain
1810, 1 June	869	766	220 men with 144 horses in Spain
1810, 16 August	806	746	152 men with 139 horses in Spain
1810, 1 September	805	741	149 men with 139 horses in Spain
1810, 16 October	813	712	160 men with 157 horses in Spain and Dalmatia

The Regimental Depot was at Pavia.

10 Jean-Pierre Perconte, 'Artillerie à Cheval et Train d'Artillerie du Royaume d'Italie 1805–1814, 2e Partie,' in *Soldats Napoleoniens: Les Troupes Françaises, Alliés et Coalisées, No.15, Décembre 2007*, (Paris: Éditions de la Revue Napoléon, 2007), pp.61–69.

11 No explanation is given in the document as to why the Regiment was actually, and highly unusually, OVER establishment!

Artigliera a Cavallo, 1807 & 1810
Gunners in 1807 and 1810 and an Officer c.1807. The primary difference to note between the two gunners is the otherwise unrecorded disappearance of the red piping on the czapska, although this could simply be the continuation, unmodified, of an older item; and the change in the saddlery from the cloth and sheepskin shabraque to the simpler sheepskin only. Unusually Boisselier shows this as black, which was normally reserved for trumpeters and may reflect only a variation in a particular company. Note the alternate shape of the portmanteau; it appears that both forms were in use throughout this period.
The officer has added gold piping to his czapska, not something I have found in regulations but a not untypical sort of conceit for the period. The use of gold in place of silver lace is non-regulation and while it could be an error it is more likely to be the conceit either of a company or even of an individual officer. (Watercolour by Henri Boisselier in the Author's Collection)

Three gunners, probably dated to around 1807–1808 since the figure at right is wearing the post 1807 red piped czapska whereas the two at left wear the older pattern which have not yet been updated. It seems likely that rather than issue new czapskas it would be possible to simply 'update' the piping on them. The green upper part of the right-hand figure's czapska is not otherwise recorded but is certainly a possibility. Note also the use of overalls and surtout probably for a variation of campaign dress. (Watercolour by Henri Boisselier in the Author's Collection)

In 1811 the czapska was officially replaced with the infantry pattern of shako, identical to that in use by the foot artillery, although the czapska may have remained in use by some companies until at least the end of 1812.

The Horse Artillery's fatigue caps were dark green with red piping, often shown with a red crossed cannon badge.

Coat

In 1805 the regiment was uniformed in a dark green hussar style dolman with red collar (Weiland[12] shows a dark green collar, piped red) and 'Polish' cuffs and red frogging with five rows of brass buttons. By the end of 1806 this uniform had been replaced by a dark green coat of the same cut as that worn by the regiments of *Cacciatori a Cavallo*. The new coat had a black collar and Polish cuffs, both piped red, red turnbacks with dark green grenade badges, and red lace batons on the front. The dark green shoulder straps and the pockets were both piped in red. Some illustrations show red epaulettes in place of the shoulder straps and it may be that, like the French Horse Artillery regiments, these were taken into use quite unofficially. From 1812 the Regiment appears to have adopted the short tailed habit-veste with pointed lapels and Brandenburg cuffs with all facings identical to those of the *1° Reggimento* (foot artillery).

Breeches, et cetera

Waistcoats were dark green with white metal buttons. The breeches were also dark green, with red Hungarian knots on the thighs and a red stripe on the outer seam. The Hungarian boots had red lace and tassel and steel spurs. From at least 1811 dark green overalls with black leather inserts and cuffs were issued for campaign wear. The overalls had a wide red stripe and white metal buttons on the outer seam. Greatcoats were dark green with black collar and red lining, and were of the same pattern as used by the light cavalry. White gloves were worn for parades and white gauntlets on campaign.

A watercolour by Henri Boisselier in his series of studies of the Army of the Kingdom of Italy shows gunners, dated to 1807 in both sky blue and dark blue breeches with red side stripes and Hungarian knots on the thigh. A subsequent plate with figures dated 1811 shows the more commonly illustrated green breeches.[13]

Equipment

All equipment was the same as that used by the *Cacciatori a Cavallo* regiments, and the cartridge box lid carried either a brass crossed cannon badge or a lozenge shaped plate embossed with a crowned crossed cannon device. All belting was white and the sword-strap was white with a red knot and tassel.

Artiglieri were not routinely issued with the carbine although dragoon pattern muskets and cartridge boxes of infantry pattern were available for picket duties. *Artiglieri* were armed with a brace of pistols, carried in the usual design of holster on the saddle.

Officer and Gunner *c.* 1812. (Watercolour by Henri Boisselier in the Author's Collection)

Officers & N.C.O.s

All rank distinctions and badges were the same as those used by the *Cacciatori a Cavallo*. Additionally the *Primo Artiglieri* wore the white stripe of a *caporale* on the left cuff only.

Officers' distinctions and badges were also the same as those used by the *Cacciatori a Cavallo*. The lace batons on the 1806 coat were often piped silver, apparently an individual conceit and preference and not a regulation.

12 C. F. Weiland published his work in Weimar in 1807. The best modern reprint is Alain Pigeard (ed.), *Le Manuscrit de Weiland: Uniformes de l'Armée Français et de ses Alliés de 1806 à 1815*, (Paris: Tradition, 1998).

13 Unpublished watercolours by Henri Boisselier in the Author's Collection.

Fiorentino[14] shows a *Capitano* with the batons and breeches decoration in silver, which again may be a personal conceit albeit that it looks impressive. Officers' greatcoats were dark green with black collar and silver buttons. All belts were white (black on campaign) leather with brass fittings.

Trombettieri

Even after the adoption of the shako *trombettieri* continued to wear the czapska. The upper part was dark green with black piping and the lower turban was of white fur. *Trombettieri*' plumes are shown as both black and dark green,[15] both with a red tip. *Trombettieri* are later sometimes shown wearing the colpack with a red bag piped dark green and with the crossed cannon badge at the front. Coats were trimmed with mixed red and white lace at the collar and cuffs with a similar lace being used on the front of the 1806 coat. The fringed epaulettes were white with mixed red and white fringes and crescents. Trumpets were brass with red cords.

Fiorentino[16] shows a variation reconstructed from a description of *c.* 1807–11. The czapska is trimmed red and has a red plume from the white over red pompom described for the troop. The coat is red with black collar and cuffs, both trimmed with wide silver lace, silver batons at the front, a single baton on the collar and two on each cuff. Silver, full-fringed epaulettes.

(left to right) *Trombettiere*, *Capitano*, Gunner. Although undated this illustration is from 1811 or 1812, and unusually shows the *trombettiere* in a shako. The *capitano*, as was often, or perhaps even customarily, the case demonstrates a number of personal conceits – the gauntlets with black cuffs, the silver lace chest batons mentioned in the text, et cetera. (Watercolour by Henri Boisselier in the Author's Collection)

14 Jean-Pierre Perconte, 'Artillerie à Cheval et Train d'Artillerie du Royaume d'Italie 1805–1814, 2e Partie' in *Soldats Napoleoniens: Les Troupes Françaises, Alliés et Coalisées, No.15, Décembre 2007*, (Paris: Éditions de la Revue Napoléon, 2007), pp.61–69. An unpublished watercolour by Henri Boisselier in the author's collection also shows an officer with silver batons.

15 It is possible, perhaps even probable, that the black plume is simply a misinterpretation of the dark green.

16 Jean-Pierre Perconte, 'Artillerie à Cheval et Train d'Artillerie du Royaume d'Italie 1805–1814, 2e Partie', in *Soldats Napoleoniens: Les Troupes Françaises, Alliés et Coalisées, No.15, Décembre 2007*, (Paris: Éditions de la Revue Napoléon, 2007), pp.61–69.

Trombettiere c1812
Regulations called for a red cloth shabraque but the green is certainly more pleasing to the eye and may represent a variation in campaign dress introduced when the sheepskin shabraque was brought into use for the majority of the regiment. As with many things even if the regulations changed, as in replacing the cloth shabraque with a sheepskin one (see text) that is not a guarantee that such changes were carried out immediately. (Watercolour by Henri Boisselier in the Author's Collection)

Horse Furniture

The dark green 1805 pattern shabraque was of the same pattern as used by the *Cacciatori a Cavallo* regiments with a wide red stripe piped dark green. The rear corners were decorated with red grenade badges. The dark green valise was round with red lace on the ends. When not worn the greatcoat was strapped on top of the valise with the lining uppermost.

In 1811 the shabraque was replaced, for campaign dress, with a white sheepskin with a red dogtooth cloth edging. The battery number in white was added to the ends of the valise at around the same time.

Trombettieri' shabraques were red with white lace and grenades and when the sheepskin shabraque was introduced in 1811, it was black with red edging.

Officers' shabraques were of the same pattern as the men with the addition of a wide silver trim, piped red and silver grenades in the rear corners. Officers did not adopt the sheepskin shabraque but retained the cloth for all orders of dress.

Treno di Artiglieria

(Train of Artillery)

Headwear

The *Treno d'Artiglieria* wore the czapska, similar to that originally issued to the *Artiglieria a Cavallo*. This had a black upper part, piped black at the top and red down the vertical edges. The lower part was a black fur turban with a brass lozenge plate at the front bearing a device of crowned crossed cannon barrels over a pyramid of cannonballs. The National cockade had a white cockade strap and was surmounted by a light green carrot-shaped pompom.

In 1811 the artillery pattern peakless shako was introduced to replace the czapska. It had the same plate, cockade and pompom as the czapska but had light green cords and plume for parade dress.

Fatigue caps were mid-grey with light green piping and tassels.

Coat

The mid-grey coat was of the surtout style with short tails. The collar, Polish cuffs and turnbacks were mid-green and the vertical pockets and front of the coat leading down into the turnbacks were piped in the same colour. The front of the coat had green lace batons of the same design as the coats of the Horse Artillery, and there were two similar batons on the cuffs (one above and one below the actual cuff). The full-fringed epaulettes were mid-green, and all buttons were white metal. In 1811 the companies serving the *Artiglieria a Piedi* made some changes to their coats (how far, if at all, these changes were reflected by the other companies is unknown): the epaulettes were replaced by mid-grey shoulder straps piped in mid-green and the cuffs were changed to the Brandenburg pattern with cuff flaps, all still in mid-green, with two mid-green lace batons, worn one above the other but both on the cuff, although a painting in the collection of H. M. The King shows the cuffs without these lace batons.

Breeches, et cetera

Waistcoats were mid-grey with white metal buttons and breeches were soft buff leather with white metal buttons on the outer seams and were worn with high, cuffed riding boots with steel spurs. Members of the regiment who were not mounted wore white or mid-grey breeches and black gaiters as for the infantry. Whitened leather gauntlets were worn for parade and buff gauntlets on

Treno di Artiglieria c. 1812, *Tenente* (left) and Driver (right). Watercolour by Henri Boisselier (Author's Collection)

campaign. The light grey greatcoats were of light cavalry pattern, with a light green collar and lining.

Equipment

The drivers wore the light cavalry pattern pouch belt and cartridge box with the crossed cannon badge, and the twin shoulder belts supported an infantry pattern sabre-briquet in a black leather scabbard with light green sword-strap and a white knot with light green tassel. Short dragoon pattern muskets were carried on the saddle.

Officers & N.C.O.s

Insignia was as the same as that used by the light cavalry and *brigadieri* were equipped as for the drivers. Senior N.C.O.s and all officers carried the light cavalry sabre from the light cavalry pattern waist belt, and on campaign both favoured the bicorne hat with silver lace and tassels. Officers' uniforms followed the style of the officers of the *Artiglieria a Cavallo*. Greatcoats were dark grey with a light green collar.

Musicanti

The regiment's *trombettieri* were uniformed as for the rank and file but with the addition of white lace to the edges of the collar and cuffs and red cords and plume to both the czapska and shako. *Trombettieri* carried the light cavalry sabre with a red sword-strap and tassel. Trumpets were brass with green or red cords.

Tamburi had the same distinctions as the *trombettieri* but wore mid-grey breeches and black gaiters. All equipment, drums, et cetera were the same as that of the *tamburi* of the *fanteria di linea*.

Horse Furniture

All draught horse harness was plain brown leather with brass buckles and fittings. The outriders' saddles were brown leather with a plain grey saddle blanket and a mid-grey round valise piped in light green at the ends.

Sergenti and other senior N.C.O.s were mounted and used a mid-grey version of the 1805 pattern dragoon shabraque, with wide light green edging piped mid-grey. The pistol holsters were also light green edged white, in turn piped light green.

In 1811 the half shabraque was taken into use; the cloth was the same colouring as the 1805 issue and the white sheepskin had a light green dogtooth edge.

The square valise was mid-grey with a light green lace on the ends.

Trombettieri' shabraques were mid-grey with red trim and the sheepskin was black with a red dogtooth edging.

Officers' shabraques were of the 1805 dragoon officers' pattern in mid-grey with silver lace decorations and grenades, the silver lace was piped with light green.

All wooden items – ordnance, caissons, limbers, halter collars, et cetera were painted dark green (NB this is a true dark green, not the olive green used by the French artillery).

Guardiacosta Artiglieri Compagnia

(Coast Guard Artillery Companies)

History and Organisation

The *Guardiacosta Artiglieri Compagnia* were commissioned on 7 July 1810, initially with an establishment of seven batteries, but an eighth battery was raised in 1811. Ostensibly recruited locally to their location, the *Guardiacosta Artiglieri* were intended to offer some defence against raids by the Royal Navy. The batteries were equipped with heavy 'fixed position' guns, often of naval pattern and battery establishments varied according to the crew requirement of the particular gun or guns.

Service

The *Guardiacosta Artiglieri* was, of course, sedentary and saw little action although *Capitano* Riron of the Battery of Goro was killed by unspecified enemy action on 2 October 1813.

Uniform

Headwear

The headwear was a black felt bicorne hat with National cockade and white cockade strap, the plume and pompom were of the National colours of red over white over green, although the reverse is also shown. Fatigue caps were dark green with white piping and tassels.

Coat

The dark green habit was the same as that worn by the *Reggimento di Artiglieria a Piedi*, with dark green collar, cuff flaps and shoulder straps and black lapels and cuffs. The turnbacks, pocket piping and shoulder strap piping were mid-grey and the turnback badges were dark green grenades. All buttons were white metal.

Breeches, et cetera

Breeches and waistcoats were mid-grey and worn with black over-the-knee gaiters with white metal or cloth covered buttons. Greatcoats were of the regulation infantry pattern and usually grey.

Equipment

The sabre-briquet, with a white sword-strap and tassel, was the gunners' only personal weapon and was worn on a single shoulder belt. As always the sabre-briquet hilt was in brass and the scabbard was of black leather, fitted with brass. Highly unusually there is no record of the *Guardiacosta Artiglieri* being issued with muskets.

Officers & N.C.O.s

The uniform was of the same colouring as that of the rank and file with all rank badges and distinctions of the same pattern as those used by the foot artillery.

The *Guardiacosta Artiglieri* do not appear to have had either *tamburi* or *musicanti* and arguably there would have been no purpose for them.

Battaglioni dei Transporti

(Transport Battalions)

Headwear

The 1st Battalion was initially issued with the Corsican Hat of black felt with National cockade, white cockade strap and red over white over green carrot-shaped pompom. In 1809 this was replaced with the infantry pattern shako with brass lozenge plate embossed with the letters 'TM' surmounted by the Iron Crown. Cockade and cockade strap were as on the Corsican Hat and the pompom was tricoloured, and both carrot-shaped and round examples are recorded. Fatigue caps were red-brown with crimson piping and tassel for the 1st Battalion and yellow for the 2nd.

Coat

The coat was the short tailed habit-veste in red-brown, it had square lapels and Brandenburg cuffs with three-pointed cuff flaps. The collar and turnbacks were crimson and the lapels, cuffs, cuff flaps and shoulder straps were all red-brown piped in crimson.

The coat of the 2nd battalion, raised in 1811, was identical to that of the 1st but substituted yellow for crimson as the facing colour.

Breeches, et cetera

Waistcoats and breeches were buff leather for the 1st Battalion and red-brown for the 2nd battalion. Outriders wore high cuffed riding boots and the drivers who sat upon the wagons wore black gaiters and infantry boots. The 2nd battalion's cloth breeches had black leather inserts. The men assigned to duties with the oxen teams walked beside their charges and had black gaiters but also often wore white or red-brown overall trousers. The red-brown greatcoats were of the cavalry pattern for the mounted troops with facing colour lining and collar; dismounted men wore the infantry pattern in grey with facing colour lining and collar. Buff leather gauntlets were worn by the drivers and mounted troops.

Equipment

All rank and file wore pouch-belts and cartridge boxes of the light cavalry pattern. The belt was of whitened leather with brass fittings and the pouch is often shown decorated with a brass plate of the same design as that of the shako. Mounted men carried the light cavalry belt and sabre and the wagon drivers and foot conductors carried the infantry pattern shoulder belt with sabre-briquet and bayonet; both sabres and sabre-briquets had white sword-straps and knots. Mounted men were armed with the light cavalry carbine, Italian manufactured copies of the French *An IX*, carried on a light cavalry pattern white leather carbine belt, and dismounted men carried infantry pattern muskets.

Officers & N.C.O.s

N.C.O. rank stripes were as used by the infantry but all equipment was that of the light cavalry.

Officers almost invariably wore the bicorne with silver lace and cockade strap and white plumes. The officers' coat was the long tailed habit of the same colouring as the men's coats. Waistcoats and breeches were either red-brown or white and worn with cuffed riding boots with silvered spurs. All rank distinctions were as used by infantry officers and all equipment was as used by light cavalry officers, with all leatherwork in black. Officers' greatcoats were of cavalry pattern and were dark brown with a facing colour collar.

Musicanti

The *trombettieri* of the *Battaglioni dei Transporti* wore the same uniform as the other ranks with the addition of mixed facing colour and white lace to the collar and cuffs and white epaulettes with mixed facing colour and white crescents and fringes. Shako plumes were white tipped with the facing colour or red. The *Trombettieri* of the 1st Battalion had brass trumpets with green cords and tassels, those of the 2nd battalion used brass infantry style bugle horns with green cords.

2nd Battalion, *Trombettiere c.* 1812/1813: Headwear was a czapska but the illustration that this information comes from shows it covered with its oilskin protection so any colours are unknown. The coat was yellow with a red-brown collar and cuffs, edged with red and white lace, and plain red-brown turnbacks. The overalls were red-brown with white metal buttons and all belting was black. Horse furniture was the black sheepskin without any apparent edging.

Horse Furniture

Outriders' saddlery was of the same pattern as used by the *Treno di Artiglieria*. Those mounted conductors acting as attendants to heavy draught animals that could not be ridden had red-brown shabraques and sheepskins of the pattern used by the Artillery Train. The edging was of facing colour. Sheepskins were white with facing colour dogtooth edging. The square valise was red-brown with facing colour lace on the ends.

Trombettieri had black sheepskins with facing colour edge and the shabraques were facing colour with white lace.

Officers' shabraques were of the 1805 officers' pattern in red-brown with silver trim, piped with the regimental colour.

Harness for the heavy draught animals was plain brown leather and the wooden halter collars were painted the same dark green as the ordnance.

Battaglione dei Zappatore e Minatore del Genio

(Sappers and Miners Battalion)

History and Organisation

The *Battaglione d'Zappatore e Minatore* was raised in 1807 with an establishment of seven companies of sappers and two companies of miners. Despite its relatively small size the battalion was responsible for all engineering work for the Army but, as required, would draw additional labour from any nearby infantry unit.

Uniform

Headwear

All companies initially wore the black bicorne with National cockade, white cockade strap and carrot-shaped pompom, in yellow for the *zappatore* companies and red for the miners. By 1812 the battalion had adopted the infantry pattern shako. This lacked the usual front plate, but had white metal chin scales, National cockade and carrot-shaped pompom as had been worn on the bicorne; the full dress cords were of the pompom colour. Fatigue caps were dark green, with yellow piping for the *zappatori* and red for *minatori*.

Coat

The dark green habit had black lapels, collar, cuffs and three-pointed cuff flaps, all piped red, the red turnbacks had dark green grenade badges. The horizontal pockets were piped red. All companies wore full-fringed epaulettes, the *zappatori* in yellow and the *minatori* in red.

Breeches, et cetera

Breeches and waistcoats were dark green. Gaiters were of the over-knee pattern in black with cloth covered buttons. Greatcoats were standard infantry pattern in grey.

Equipment

All equipment was of the same pattern as that used by the foot artillery. Sword-knots were yellow for the *zappatore* companies and red for the *minatore* companies, following the company distinctive colour.

Battaglione d'Zappatore e Miniatore del Genio
'Rank and File' of the *Zappatore*. The lower left figure is shown wearing essentially regulation dress. However the figure lower right wearing white waistcoat and breeches is a variation that I have not seen otherwise recorded and it may be, given the date, an exigency of dress perhaps caused by a shortage of cloth or perhaps the date should be '1812–1813' and it has been caused by a shortage from the rapid rebuilding of the Army after the disastrous Russian campaign.
The most interesting uniform is that shown in the upper figure. This is not recorded elsewhere but comes from a contemporary picture of the unit in Germany in 1807. Given that this is from a contemporary and eyewitness source and it is of a newly raised unit it seems likely that this is, like the light blue uniform of some *Fanteria Leggera* of the same period, what can only be called an 'emergency uniform'. Yellow was, of course, the significant colour for the *zappatore* - in contrast to the red for the *Genio* - and it may be that this was a short-lived uniform at the battalion's first raising.
(Watercolour by Henri Boisselier in the Author's Collection)

Officers & N.C.O.s

All rank, badges, distinctions, et cetera were as used by the *Reggimento di Artiglieria a Piedi*. The *Capo di Battaglione* and the company *Capitani* were mounted, with shabraques of infantry pattern of dark green edged with a single wide silver lacing edged with red.

Musicanti

The company *tamburi* were uniformed the same as the rank and file but with the addition of red and white lace on the collar and cuffs. All other details and equipment was the same as for the *tamburi* of the infantry

Treno di Genie

(Engineers' Train)

History and Organisation

Raised in 1807, at the same time as the *Battaglione d'Zappatore e Minatore*, the *Treno di Genie* had an establishment of a single company and the sole (and obvious) function of moving the engineering equipment. The initial strength was only two N.C.O.s and fifteen drivers but by 1812 this had expanded to an establishment of three officers, including a *Capitano Commandante*, seventeen N.C.O.s, two *trombettieri* and fifty-six conductors with thirty-five specialist wagons. Of the fifty-six other ranks, thirty-two were mounted and twenty-four dismounted, although they actually marched and moved on the wagons. In 1813 when the Army was reformed after the Russian campaign the company was

Treno di Genie, Officers c1812, Watercolour by Henri Boisselier. (Author's Collection)

absorbed into the *Treno di Artiglieria* and the uniform consequently changed to conform to that Regiment.

Uniform

Headwear

The company initially wore the bicorne with National cockade and white strap, white tassels and a yellow carrot-shaped pompom. By around 1810 the rank and file of the company appear to have adopted the shako in place of the bicorne. The shako was regulation pattern with a white metal lozenge shaped plate below a National cockade, which was secured with a white strap and white metal button. I cannot confirm any device on the shako plate but the letters 'TG' below the Iron Crown appears likely, although a grenade below the Iron Crown is possible. Boisselier shows the shako with a red ball pompon, but I have not seen confirmation of this. The fatigue cap was dark green with yellow piping and tassel.

Coat

The coat was a dark green, long tailed surtout, with black collar and Polish cuffs and dark green turnbacks; the

Treno di Genie, Driver and Trumpeter. The driver is in regulation uniform except for the white breeches, which may be no more than an error in colouring. The *trombettiere* has red breeches which, while not shown, probably had white lace on the front thigh – either of knot or of spearhead form. (Watercolour by Henri Boisselier in the Author's Collection)

turnbacks and vertical pockets were piped black. The front of the coat was decorated with eight yellow lace batons and the collar and cuffs had narrow yellow batons as for the *Treno di Artiglieria*. The coat had yellow full-fringed epaulettes.

Interestingly, but not at all unlikely, Boisselier shows the coat in 1810 as a short tailed habit with black lapels, collar, plain cuffs without cuff flaps, and turnbacks – all piped red.

Breeches, et cetera

Waistcoats were dark green with white metal buttons and the breeches were buff leather. Mounted troops wore high cuffed riding boots with steel spurs, dismounted men had black over-the-knee gaiters with cloth covered buttons. Gauntlets were buff leather and the grey greatcoats were of cavalry pattern.

Equipment

Mounted rank and file carried the light cavalry pattern sabre with a yellow sword-strap with white knot and yellow tassel, and the light cavalry pattern cartridge box. Dismounted rank and file were armed with the infantry pattern sabre-briquet and bayonet with the dragoon pattern musket and the infantry pattern cartridge box. The dismounted troops' sabre-briquet sword-knot was the same as that of their mounted comrades.

Officers & N.C.O.s

All badges and rank distinction were the same as those used by the *Treno di Artiglieria*.

Musicanti

Trombettiere 1807. The two *trombettieri* were uniformed the same as the rank and file but with white lace edging to the collar and cuffs and they did not wear the pouch belt. The plume on the bicorne was red with a yellow tip. Trumpets were brass with green cords.

Trombettiere 1810. The 1810 uniform illustrated by Boisselier is again similar to that of the troop but with red and white lace on the cuffs, collar turnbacks, pockets and (presumably) lapels but additionally along the back between the pockets (see illustration), and with seven inverted chevrons of red and white lace on the sleeves. The trumpet cords are red and white.

Horse Furniture

Outriders' saddles were the same as those of the *Treno di Artiglieria* and the mounted conductors' shabraques were of the later dragoon pattern half shabraque of a white sheepskin with yellow dogtooth edging over a dark green cloth with white edging. The dark green valise was square, trimmed white and with the letters 'TG' on the ends.

Officers' shabraques were of the 1805 pattern with a silver lace edge piped dark green.

Pompieri Della Città di Milano

(City of Milan Company of Firemen)

History and Organisation

In 1811 a single company of *Pompieri* was raised in Milan to assist with engineering and to combat fires in the event of the City coming under siege. Although privately financed, as so often with such units the company was organised and uniformed as a military unit of 85 officers and men. In 1813 the Company provided drafts to the *Battaglione Guardia Alla Città di Milano*, although given its low establishment these cannot have been numerous.

As a small side note, the current *Corpo dei Vigili del Fuoco di Milano* is a lineal descendant of the *Pompieri* and thus is the only unit of the Army of the Kingdom of Italy still in existence (insofar as it actually was a part of the Army of Italy).

Company establishment	
1 *Capitano*	1 *Tenente*
4 *Sergente*	2 *Caporale*
2 *Tamburi*	75 *Pompieri*

Service

The Company saw no formal field service although in 1814 it was attached to the *Battaglione Guardia Alla Città di Milano* and at least a part of the unit may therefore have been present with that unit at the Battle of Pescheira.

Uniform (NB see Knötel Plate II / 45 in Chapter 3)

Headwear

The company wore a brass dragoon style helmet without the black fur turban or horsehair crest and with a red houpette and plume. The front of the helmet was embossed with the unit's title. The chin scales were brass and fitted with sun-burst bosses. Fatigue caps were light blue with red trim.

Coat

The coat was a sky blue, short tailed habit-veste, as worn by the light infantry, with sky blue lapels and turnbacks, both piped red, turnback ornaments were red grenades. The collar and 'Polish' cuffs were red and the pockets were piped red. All buttons were brass. The company wore red full-fringed epaulettes.

Breeches, Et cetera

Breeches and waistcoats were sky blue. Gaiters were black knee length, and with white metal buttons.

Equipment

All rank and file wore twin white leather shoulder belts. The first supported the cartridge pouch, with a brass badge of a grenade superimposed upon crossed axes on the lid, against the right hip, with the bayonet frog attached to the left side of the pouch; the only other unit recorded using this unusual placement of the bayonet is the *Battaglione Guardia Alla Città di Milano* (The City of Milan Guard Battalion, see above). The second belt supported the sabre-briquet, which had a red sword-strap and tassel. The company carried short, dragoon pattern, muskets.

Officers & N.C.O.s

All rank badges and distinctions were the same as those of the *fanteria di linea* but the N.C.O. rank stripes were, as was usual with the Polish cuff, in the form of inverted chevrons.

Officers carried the light infantry style curved sabre and customarily had all belts of black leather.

Tamburi

Tamburi coats were of the same pattern as the rank and file but in red with sky blue facings, and with white lace trim to the collar and cuffs. All other details as for the infantry.

Corpo di Medicina & Ambulanza Compagnia

(Medical Corps and Ambulance Companies)

The Italian Army had an organised medical corps as early as 1802 and with the formation of the Kingdom's Army in 1805 the Corps was reorganised as part of the new army.

The Corps was commanded by a Director General and consisted of three Departments: *Medici* (physicians/doctors), *Chirurgi* (surgeons), and *Farmacisti* (apothecaries), each with 1st, 2nd and 3rd Class Grades and Cadet officers.

Following the French example, four ambulance companies were raised on 27 August 1811, each with an establishment of two administrative officers, one *trombettiere* and seventy-nine 'attendants'. The companies were equipped with the French pattern two-wheeled ambulances, each drawn by two horses, harnessed in line. Although I have seen no confirmation of this I would speculate that these ambulances were painted the same dark green as the artillery pieces and wagons.

Medico Ufficiali

(Medical Officers)

Headwear

All medical officers wore the black bicorne with National cockade and silver cockade strap.

The hat of the *Ispettore Generale* (Inspector General) was faced with black velvet and had silver lace edging and tassels.

Coat

The dark green full dress surtout closed with nine silver-plated buttons, embossed with the words 'SANITA MILITARE' around the edge. The collar and cuffs were of departmental colour, red for the *chirurgi*, black for the *medici* and dark green velvet for the *farmacisti*. The *Ispettore Generale* had the collar and cuffs of his coat in black velvet. Turnbacks were dark green and the coat had horizontal pockets with three buttons. The cuffs were plain but had three buttons horizontally at the front and outside. The full dress waistcoats were red for *chirurgi* and dark green for the other officers and all had silvered buttons.

On campaign all officers wore the dark green surtout with turned-over 'Swedish' collar of departmental colour and pockets *à la Soubise* piped in the same. All buttons were silver. Waistcoats were white or dark green.

Rank Insignia

The coats of the *Ispettori Generali* were heavily embroidered with nine 32mm wide silver laurel-leaf lace batons, with pointed ends, across the front. The collar and cuffs were trimmed with the same lace, 20mm wide, and a further 5mm strip outside of that – the two separated by a narrow piping of the cuff colour. The pockets and the edges of the waistcoat were trimmed with 5mm of the lace. The undress surtout was trimmed only on the collar and cuffs.

Senior Departmental Officers wore the same uniform as the *Ispettore Generali* but with lace batons only 20mm wide.

The coats of 1st Class Officers of all three Departments again had the same lace batons but 10mm wide and extending approximately 150mm each side of the front. The collar was decorated with four 15mm wide horizontal batons and the cuffs and pockets each had three vertical batons of the same width. The undress coat was decorated with only the cuff and collar batons.

2nd Class Officers' full dress coats had only three batons on the collar and cuffs. The undress surtout was laced only on the collar.

3rd Class Officers had two batons of the lace on the collar and cuffs of the full dress coat and the undress tunic was decorated with two batons of lace on the collar only.

Medical Officer Cadets wore the undress surtout without lace but with departmental colour collar, dark green cuffs and turnbacks and white metal buttons.

Breeches, et cetera

Dark green breeches were worn in full dress and white or dark green for undress uniform and on campaign, although white or dark green trousers were more common for campaign wear. All officers wore English pattern boots, which had turned-over tops showing the buff leather lining. The dark green greatcoats were of the cavalry pattern and were lined in the facing colour, the collar was in the dark green of the coat. White gloves were worn for full dress.

Equipment

The waist belts were in black leather and supported the straight bladed epée with embossed silvered hilt, carried in a black leather scabbard with brass fittings. The sword-strap was gold with a heavy bullion fringe for the *Ispettore Generale* and the same but in silver for the Senior Officers. 1st Class Officers had silver sword-straps with finer fringe on the tassel, as worn by infantry officers. 2nd Class Officers had the same but with a narrow red stripe on the knot strap and the 3rd Class Officers had the same but with two stripes. Officer Cadets had sword-straps of mixed white silk and wool with silver fringing.

Horse Furniture

The dark green shabraques were of the *Dragoni della Guardia* pattern with brown leather saddles and a wide silver edging, piped dark green. 55mm wide for the *Ispettore Generale*, 45mm wide for the Senior Officers, 40mm for 1st Class Officers, 35mm for 2nd Class, and 30mm for 3rd Class. Cadets had the same shabraque with a 20mm wide lace. Pistol Holsters were dark green and trimmed in the same way as the shabraque. Girth straps were grey and all harness was black leather with brass fittings.

Ambulanza Compagnia

(Ambulance Companies)

Headwear

The companies wore the regulation infantry pattern shako, with a white ball pompom, black leather chinstrap and the National cockade with a white cockade strap. The shako plate was a white metal lozenge shape, embossed with the letter 'A'. Fatigue caps were red-brown, piped grey with a grey tassel and a white, or just possibly grey, 'A' at the front.

Coat

The coat was a red-brown habit-veste with squared lapels and Brandenburg cuffs. The collar, cuffs, turnbacks and shoulder straps were red-brown with grey piping and the lapels and cuff flaps dark grey piped red-brown. All buttons were white metal.

Breeches, et cetera

Breeches and waistcoats were dark grey and the high gaiters black with white metal buttons. The infantry pattern greatcoats were dark grey.

Equipment

The single white shoulder belt supported the infantry sabre-briquet with a white sword-strap.

Officers & N.C.O.s

The two *sergenti* and four *caporali* of each company wore rank insignia as used by the *fanteria di linea*.

The company was commanded by an officer known as the *Centurione*, assisted by a *Sottocenturione*; for unknown reasons these did not rank as commissioned officers and were not thus allowed the privilege of wearing epaulettes of rank or sword-straps. The *Centurione* was distinguished by a wide silver lace band around the top of the cuff and on the collar and the *Sottocenturione* had the same lace but only on his cuffs. Coats were red-brown surtout style with red-brown collar, cuffs of plain round pattern, and turnbacks all piped dark grey. All buttons were white metal. The bicorne was decorated with the cockade and silver cockade strap only. Breeches and waistcoats were white and the boots were of the English pattern. A straight epée was carried on a black leather waist belt in a scabbard of black leather fitted in white metal. Officers' shabraques were of the infantry pattern in red-brown with a wide silver edging.

Musicanti

The shakos of the *trombettieri* had a white plume tipped red and the coat was as for the rank and file with white and red lace on the collar and cuffs. *Trombettieri* were mounted and wore the light cavalry sabre, their shabraque was as for the officers but with white lace. The infantry pattern bugle horn was brass with green cords.

Unknown figure and *Carabiniere 2° Fanteria Leggera*, c. 1807
The right-hand figure although identified on the painting as of the 3° *Reggimento* is assigned by Guy Dempsey to the 2° *Reggimento* with the comment that the artist was simply mistaken – an interpretation with which I would totally agree. With respect to the left-hand figure the uniform is not that of the *artigliere*, who had black facings, UNLESS some older or non-regulation uniforms were being used from 'stock', a not unknown situation in the Army in its early period, and is very close to that of the *Reggimento Veterani E Invalidi* although there is no indication that personnel from that *Reggimento* served in Germany. (Contemporary illustration from 'The Otto Manuscript' in the Anne S.K. Brown Military Collection, Brown University Library, reproduced with thanks)

15 *soldi* coin 1808
Note the use of the Iron Crown of Lombardy
The vast majority of these coins were melted down in 1814/15 when the *'Ancien Regime'* Governments returned to power. (Author's collection)

6
Naval Units

The small navy of the Kingdom of Italy saw almost constant, albeit small-scale, service in the Mediterranean from its creation with the Kingdom in 1805 until it, and the Kingdom, were dissolved in 1814 when the remaining personnel passed into the service of the Austrian Empire. While it is not the purpose of this study to cover the ships and personnel of the Navy a number of Naval units served with the Army.[1] These units were:

Navale Artiglieri Battaglione (Battalion of Naval Gunners)
Navale Bracciante Compagnia (Naval Workers Companies)
Compagnia Due Militari Guardaciurme (Military Company of Ships Guards)
Navale Verterani Battaglione (Naval Veterans Battalion)

These units were often commanded by, or in part at least officered by, Naval Officers so it is worthwhile to cover the uniform of the *Capitano* and other ranks of the Navy. Even when serving on land or with the Army, Naval Officers appear to have retained their full naval uniform, probably as much out of pride as for any other reason (British Royal Navy Officers did the same).

Naval Officers

Officers wore the bicorn, usually 'fore and aft', with the National cockade held by a silver cockade strap on the left side, and silver tassels.

Two patterns of coat were in use by naval officers:

The first was of a surtout style in dark green with red collar, turnbacks and cuffs and seven batons of white lace with pointed ends, across the breast. All buttons were silvered and silver epaulettes following the system set out below.

The second pattern of coat, which seems to have been service dress, was again a dark green surtout but with all facings dark green piped silver. Rank was again indicated by silver epaulettes.

The system of naval officers' rank epaulettes was:

Capitano (3 years service)	Two full heavy-fringed epaulettes[2]
Capitano (under 3 years service)	As above, but on the right shoulder only
Comandante	As above, but on the left shoulder only
Tenente	As for *Comandante* but with a thinner fringing

Officers' breeches were dark green for parade and white for wear onboard ship and for service dress on land (this appears to be the reverse of what would be intuitive but it is what the sources indicate…). The green breeches had silver Hungarian knots on the thigh and the full dress boots were of Hungarian pattern with silver trimmed lace along the top and silver tassels. On board ship officers wore either sea boots or shoes and white stockings, for service on land they may have worn either the Hungarian boots or perhaps English style 'jockey boots'.

Navale Artiglieri Battaglione

(Battalion of Naval Gunners)

History, Organisation and Service

The battalion was raised to defend the coast between Rimini and the marshes of the delta of the River Po.[3] Its organisation was as four companies of gunners, one ordnance company, one apprentice company and one *bombardiere* company. Each company comprised one *sergente maggiore*, four *sergenti*, four *caporali*, a *caporole-furiere*, two *tamburi* and 95 other ranks. The absence of any officers on the company establishment as it is recorded is almost certainly an error and it should perhaps be expected that there would be three officers in addition to the above. There certainly were officers in the unit – see below.

By definition the battalion was sedentary but Martinien records *Tenente* Santolini as wounded in the Battle of Lissa on 13 March 1811, although this was a naval action so he may have been serving on board, perhaps 'on attachment'?

Uniform

Headwear

The hat was a narrow-crowned leather 'top hat' with a curled and polished brim and with black fur roll forming an inverted V trim to the front and rear of the crown.

1 Similarly the French Navy supplied a number of units, particularly artillery, for service with the French Army.
2 NB Higher ranks in the Navy had their rank indicated by varying numbers of stars on a similar pattern of epaulettes. *Capitano* and below had plain straps.
3 Why this Battalion should have been a part of the Navy and not a Coastguard Artillery unit of the Army is unknown.

The front of the hat was decorated with a large triangular brass plate embossed with crossed cannon superimposed over an anchor between two grenades. A red carrot-shaped pompom with tufted tip was worn at the left side, above the National cockade secured by a white strap with a white metal button. The dark green fatigue cap was the same pattern as that of the infantry, with red piping and tassel, and a red grenade badge.

Coat

The coat was a dark green Spencer tunic, with dark green collar, lapels and cuffs piped red and red turnbacks and cuff flaps, both piped dark green. Turnbacks could be either plain or decorated with a dark green grenade badge. Pockets were piped red. The *Bombardiere Compagnia* and *Primo Artiglieri* wore red fringed epaulettes, all other personnel had red contre-epaulettes. All buttons were white metal.

Breeches, et cetera

The Hungarian style breeches were dark green, full length and tight fitting with a cuff that fitted over the top of the shoes and strapped beneath the instep. The buttons at the sides of the calf were of white metal. The infantry pattern greatcoat was dark grey.

Equipment

All equipment was of the same pattern as that used by the *Reggimento di Artiglieria a Piedi* of the line. The cartridge box lid was decorated with a brass crossed cannon and anchor badge.

Officers & N.C.O.s

N.C.O.s wore rank badges the same as those of the foot artillery. *Caporali* had red fringed epaulettes; other N.C.O.s had epaulette fringes of mixed red and silver with a plain red strap.

Officers' distinctions would probably have been the same as those used by the Army.

Tamburi

All *tamburi*' distinctions were the same as those in the Army, as was their equipment, drums, et cetera.

Navale Bracciante Compagnia

(Naval Workers Companies)

History, Organisation and Service

The original purpose of these companies was for shipbuilding but in 1813 two companies were sent to Germany as bridge-builders for the Italian Army. Each company had, besides officers, four *sergenti*, four *caporali*, one *tamburo* and 96 *braccianti* (literally 'labourers' which says much for their original function).

Headwear

The *Bracciante Compagnia* wore the infantry pattern shako with a brass lozenge plate embossed with crossed axes and an anchor. Chin scales were brass and the National cockade, worn at the front above the plate, was surmounted by a red carrot-shaped pompom. *Braccianti 1º classe may* have had a red trim to the upper edge of the shako. Fatigue caps were dark green with red piping.

Coat

The dark green 'Spencer' habit-veste had a black collar, black lapels and cuffs piped red, red turnbacks and red cuff flaps. All buttons were white metal. One source shows dark green turnbacks piped red with white crossed axes and anchor badges.

Braccianti 1º classe wore red fringed epaulettes, *2º classe* red contre-epaulettes and the *3º classe* had dark green shoulder straps piped red.

Breeches, et cetera

The dark green breeches were worn with black knee length gaiters that had white metal buttons. The grey greatcoat was of the usual infantry pattern and worn with epaulettes the same as those worn on the coat.

Equipment

All as for the elite companies of the line infantry with white sword-strap and red knot and tassel.

Officers & N.C.O.s

The N.C.O.s wore the uniform of the company with badges and distinctions as for the line infantry.

The companies were commanded by naval officers.

Musicanti

Tamburi wore the uniform of the company with equipment and distinctions as for the army.

Compagnia Due Militari Guardaciurme

(Military Company of Ships Guards)

The *Compagnia Due Militari Guardaciurme* was originally raised as a unit of the Venetian Navy to guard galley slaves but by the time that the Venetian Navy was absorbed into the Italian Navy in 1806 it had become simply a unit of marines that supplied guards to the docks and the 'sharpshooters' for service on warships.[4]

The unit was commanded by naval officers and had an establishment of two *tamburi*, eight *sergente maggiore*,

4 The use of such 'sharpshooters' was usual in the navies of most nations. For example the French Navy used selected infantry regiments onboard its ships – see Stephen Ede-Borrett, *Swiss in the Service of France, 1798–1815*, (Warwick: Helion & Co, 2019).

fourteen *sergenti*, and fourteen *caporali*, commanding 200 *marinai* organised into eight squads.

Headwear

The *Guardaciurme* had a black shako with a white metal lozenge plate at the front embossed 'MG' (for *Militari Guardaciurme*). It had white metal chin scales and National cockade above the plate but, unusually, no pompom. The fatigue caps were dark green with light grey piping.

Coat

The infantry pattern dark green habit had collar, lapels, turnbacks and cuff flaps of light grey and cuffs and shoulder straps of dark green with light grey piping. All buttons were white metal and the pockets were piped light grey.

Breeches, et cetera

Breeches and waistcoats were light grey and the knee length black gaiters had white metal buttons. Greatcoats were grey and of the same pattern as the infantry.

Equipment

Equipment was as for the elite companies of infantry with a brass anchor on the cartridge box lid and a white sword-knot.

Officers and N.C.O.s

The N.C.O.s had infantry rank badges on uniforms following the pattern of the rank and file. Officers were Naval personnel.

Musicanti

Tamburi had distinctions as for the infantry.

Navale Verterani Battaglione

(Naval Veterans Battalion)

The Battalion was raised in 1807, and merged into the *Reggimento Veterani E Invalidi* (Veteran and Invalids Regiment) in 1811 but, in the interim, was responsible for the guarding of the Navy's bases.

Headwear

Black felt bicorne with National cockade surmounted by a carrot-shaped pompom of red over white over green. Fatigue caps were dark green with white piping.

Coat

The coat was a dark green habit with white collar, plain round cuffs, red lapels, turnbacks and shoulder straps piped dark green. The pockets were piped red. All buttons were white.

Breeches, et cetera

White waistcoats and white breeches worn with black over-the-knee gaiters with white metal buttons. Greatcoats were the infantry pattern of grey.

Equipment

All as for the elite companies of the *fanteria di linea*. Sword-knots were white with a red tassel.

Officers & N.C.O.s

All distinctions and rank badges as for the fanteria.

Tamburi

All distinctions as for the *fanteria di linea*.

Appendix I
Ordine della Corona Ferrea
(The Order of the Iron Crown)

The *Ordine della Corona Ferrea* was instituted by Article VIII of the original Constitution of the Kingdom of 5 June 1805 and was conceived as an Italian equivalent of the French *Légion d'Honneur*. The Order was to be in three classes and by its initial rules it was to comprise a maximum of 20 Grand Cross Dignitaries, 100 Commanders and 500 Knights. The Order was also to be available to French Citizens who had fought in Italy in addition to citizens of the Kingdom of Italy, indeed the nominees for the first 20 Grand Cross Dignitaries on 25 March 1806 were all French Generals (although the list included, unsurprisingly, Prince Eugène himself).

When the Kingdom was annexed by Austria in 1815 the Order was, very surprisingly, not abolished as all the other Napoleonic institutions were but became the *Kaiserlicher Orden der Eisernen Krone* (Imperial Order of the Iron Crown), one of the highest orders of merit in The Empire, and in which form it survived until 1918 and the fall of the Habsburg Monarchy.

The Order of the Iron Crown
'Medal' (top) and Breast Star (bottom)
NB as originally instituted the medal ribbon was aurore bordered in dark green, this example shows some fading to its current red hue. (Public Domain)

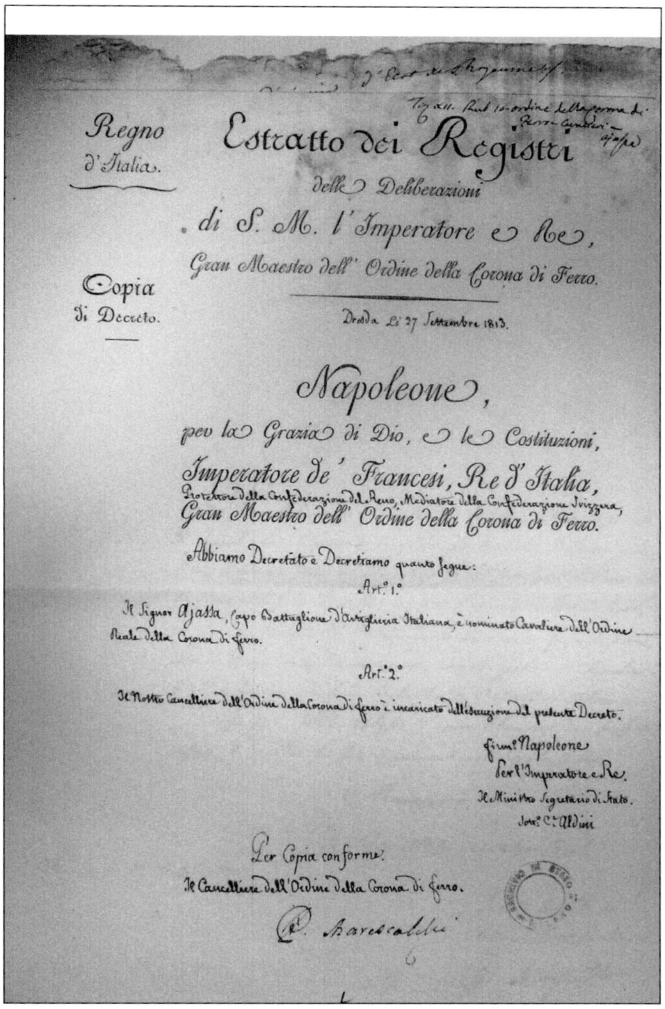

Regno d'Italia.

Estratto dei Registri delle Deliberazioni di S. M. l'Imperatore e Re, Gran Maestro dell' Ordine della Corona di Ferro.

Copia di Decreto.

Dresda li 27 Settembre 1813.

Napoleone, per la Grazia di Dio, e le Costituzioni, Imperatore de' Francesi, Re d'Italia, Protettore della Confederazione del Reno, Mediatore della Confederazione Svizzera, Gran Maestro dell' Ordine della Corona di Ferro.

Abbiamo Decretato e Decretiamo quanto segue:

Art. 1°

Il Signor Ajassa, Capo Battaglione d'Artiglieria Italiana, è nominato Cavaliere dell'Ordine Reale della Corona di Ferro.

Art. 2°

Il Nostro Cancelliere dell'Ordine della Corona di Ferro è incaricato dell'esecuzione del presente Decreto.

firm. Napoleone

Per l'Imperatore e Re,
Il Ministro Segretario di Stato,
firm. C. Aldini

Per Copia conforme:
Il Cancelliere dell'Ordine della Corona di Ferro.
Marescalchi

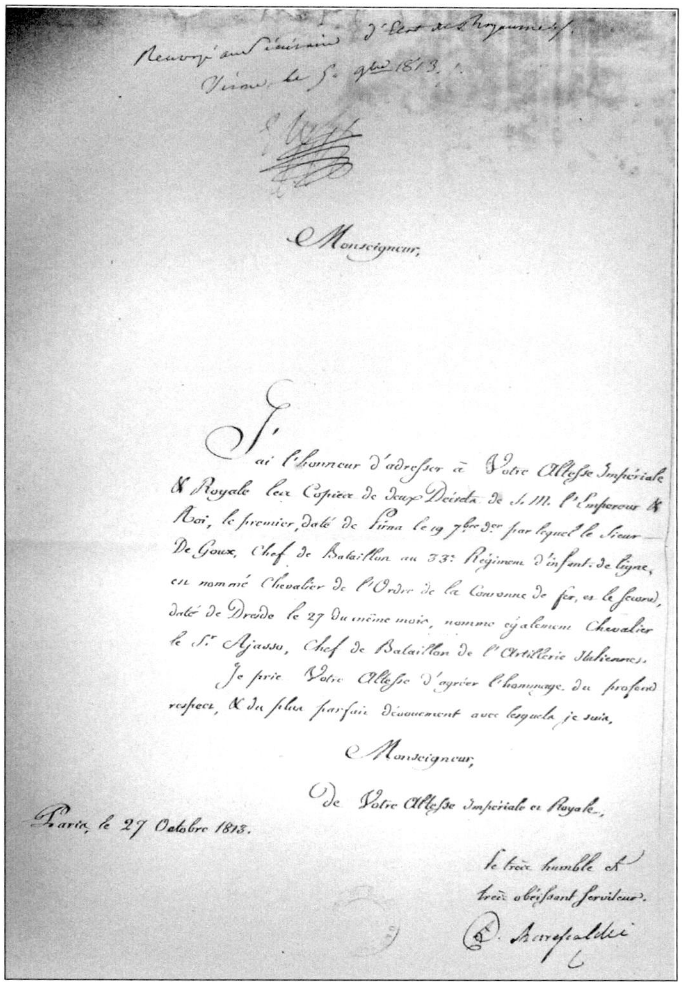

Monseigneur,

J'ai l'honneur d'adresser à Votre Altesse Impériale & Royale les Copies de deux Décrets de S. M. l'Empereur & Roi, le premier, daté de Pirna le 19 7bre der par lequel le Sieur De Goux, Chef de Bataillon au 33e Régiment d'infant. de ligne, est nommé Chevalier de l'Ordre de la Couronne de fer, et le second, daté de Dresde le 27 du même mois, nomme également Chevalier le Sr Ajassa, Chef de Bataillon de l'Artillerie Italienne.

Je prie Votre Altesse d'agréer l'hommage du profond respect, & du plus parfait dévouement avec lesquels je suis,

Monseigneur,

De Votre Altesse Impériale et Royale,

Paris, le 27 Octobre 1813.

le très humble et très obéissant serviteur.
Marescalchi

Covering letter and confirmation of the appointment of Giuseppe Ajassa of the Royal Guard Artillery as Chevalier of the Order of the Iron Crown. Dated 27 September 1813, Ajassa served until the fall of the Kingdom but (at present) his subsequent career is unknown.

Note that Napoleon, even on such documents terms himself *Imperatori des Francesi, Re d'Ialia* (Emperor of the French, King of Italy).

Ajassa was a Piedmontese and he and his wife had to marry 'At the Church Door' (my Italian correspondent equates this to 'running away to Gretna Green') since her family disapproved of him and her father would not give permission for the wedding because he was twice her age and a foreigner (they obviously came from somewhere other than Piedmont) and that despite the fact that he came from a good family and had a good career. Ajassa also received the French *Légion d'Honneur*.

Photographs courtesy of Patrick T. del C. Nisbett, a descendant of the family.

Appendix II
Illustrative Strength Returns

The Strength of the Royal Guard, 1 July 1807

Guardie D'Onore					
	1st Coy *Milano*	2nd Coy *Bologna*	3rd Coy *Brescia*	4th Coy *Romagna*	5th Coy *Venezia*
Capitano	1	1	1	1	1
Tenente	1				
Sotto Tenente	2	1	2	1	
Maresciallo d'Alloggio Capo		1	1	1	
Marescialli d'Alloggio	2	2	3	2	3
Brigadieri Furieri	1	1	1	1	1
Brigadieri	5	5	5	4	3
Guardie	49	25	60	33	44
Veterinari	1				
Maniscalchi	1	1	1	1	1
Trombe	2	2	2	1	2
Tamburi	1	1	1	1	1
Total	66	40	77	46	56

Dragoni	
Colonnello	1
Capo Squadrone	1
Capitani	6
Tenente 1ª Classe	5
Tenente 2º Classe	6
Sotto Tenente	6
Ufficiali di Sanita	3
Maresciallo d'Alloggio Capo	5
Veterinario	2
Maestro Artigiano	23
Brigadieri	37
Mariscalchi	4
Musicanti	12
Dragoni	300
Total	411

Granatieri, Cacciatori* and *Veliti		
	Granatieri & Cacciatori	*Veliti*
Colonello	1	
Maggiore	1	1
Capo Battaglione	2	2
Capitano	12	14
Tenente 1° Classe	10	15
Tenente 2° Classe	9	16
Sotto Tenente	10	12
Ufficialo di Santa	3	2
Aiut Sottufiaclo	8	10
Sergenti & Artigiano	47	28
Caporali & Zappatori	116	96
Tamburi	19	30
Musicanti	29	30
Soldati	770	1029
Total	1,036	1,255

The Italian Division at Kolberg, 1 April 1807

1° Fanteria di Linea	58 Officers and 1,508 men. Plus 297 in hospital, 1 under arrest, 9 in prison, 19 missing.
1° Fanteria Leggera	52 Officers and 1,428 men. Plus 365 in hospital, 23 under arrest, 15 in prison, 16 missing.
2° Fanteria Leggera	65 Officers and 1,568 men. Plus 265 in hospital, 2 under arrest, 9 in prison, 19 missing.
4° Compagnia d'Zappatore	3 Officers and 78 men. Plus 16 in hospital, 1 under arrest.
2° Compagnie di Artiglieria[1]	5 Officers and 54 men. Plus 4 in hospital. These companies had: 2 x 12pdr guns, 8 x 6pdr guns, 2 howitzers and a mortar.

Granatieri a Piedi and *Carabinieri a Piedi Della Guardia* in 1811 and 1812

1811, August	50 Officers, 1086 N.C.O.s and men, 32 N.C.O.s and men in hospital, 26 in prison, 6 under arrest, 10 invalids.
1812, September, Moscow	1078 officers and men, plus 56 in the depot, 25 in hospital, 6 prisoners of war, 28 "lost en route".

1 I have been unable to identify which companies these were

The Italian Contingent in IV Corps, 25 June 1812[2]

	Officers	Men	Officers' Horses	Men's Horses	Train Horses
Royal Guard Division					
Guardia Reale d'Onore, 5 companies	17	274	40	269	16
Granatieri & *Carabinieri*, and artillery co.	45	1137	3		54
Veliti, 1st & 2nd Battalions and artillery co.	43	1105	3		52
Conscritti, 1st & 2nd Battalions and artillery co.	40	1084	3		49
Dragoni, 1st & 2nd Squadrons	19	392	49	371	8
1º Dragoni di Linea ('Regina'), 1st to 4th squadrons	37	616	86	595	8
Artiglieria, 1st (Foot) & 2nd (Horse) Btns *Treno d'Artiglieria*	10	373	11	70	327
Zappatore Battalion, 4th Company (Line)	3	81			6
1º Transporti Militari, 1st & 3rd cos	3	239	4		352
Marini	3	99			
Total	220	5400	199	1305	872
15th Infantry Division					
1º Leggera, 4th Battalion	22	742			8
3º Leggera, 1st, 2nd, 3rd, 4th Battalions and artillery company	87	3039	3		61
2º di Linea, 1st, 2nd, 3rd, 4th Battalions and artillery company	86	2690	4		61
3º di Linea, 1st, 2nd, 3rd, 4th Battalions and artillery company	89	2892	3		62
Reale Dalmata, 1st, 2nd, 3rd Battalions and artillery company	65	1681	3		53
Artiglieria a Piedi, 14th Company *Artiglieria a Cavallo*, 2nd Company *Treno d'Artiglieria*, 3rd & 4th Companies *Braccianti*, 2nd Company	13	406	20	87	290
Zappatori, 6th Company	3	101			6
Transporti Militari, 2nd Company	2	152	6		286
Total	367	11703	39	87	827
15th Light Cavalry Brigade					
2º Cacciatori a Cavallo, 1st 2nd, 3rd, 4th squadrons	39	608	89	587	8
3º Cacciatori a Cavallo, 1st 2nd, 3rd, 4th squadrons	33	601	76	590	8
Total	72	1209	165	1177	16

2 As previously mentioned 'The Army of Italy', which comprised IV Corps, also contained a large number of units and personnel of the French Army.

The Strength of the Royal Guard, late 1812 / February 1813

(Germany in late 1812, Italy in February 1813)

Guardia Reale d'Onore				
	Germany		Italy	
	Officers	Men	Officers	Men
Staff	4		1	
1° Company *Milano*	3	54	1	30
2° Company *Bologna*	1	49	2	20
3° Company *Brescia*	3	53		21
4° Company *Romagna*	1	67	1	17
5° Company *Venezia*	4	60		28
Total	16	283	5	116

Dragoni & Gendarmeria				
	Germany		Italy	
	Officers	Men	Officers	Men
Staff	7	5	2	4
1st Squadron, 1 Company	4	104	1	15
1st Squadron, 3 Company	4	109		12
2nd Squadron, 2 Company	4	107		16
2nd Squadron, 4 Company	4	106		12
Total	23	431	3	59
Gendarmeria		9	1	30

Granatieri				
	Germany		Italy	
	Officers	Men	Officers	Men
Staff	12	31	1	4
1st Battalion, 1 – 4 Coy	14	521		
1st Battalion, 5 Coy			3	54
2nd Battalion, 1 – 4 Coy	17	526		
2nd Battalion, 5 Coy			3	45
Detached	1	48		
Total	44	1126	7	103

Veliti				
	Germany		Italy	
	Officers	Men	Officers	Men
Staff	11	32	1	6
1st Battalion, 1 – 4 Coy	15	482		
1st Battalion, 5 Coy			2	204
2nd Battalion, 1 – 4 Coy	16	506		
2nd Battalion, 5 Coy			2	186
Detached	2	47		
Total	44	1,067	5	396

Cacciatori				
	Germany		Italy	
	Officers	Men	Officers	Men
Staff			2	2
1st Battalion, 1 – 4 Coy	15	545		
1st Battalion, 5 Coy			3	29
2nd Battalion, 1 – 4 Coy	15	524		
2nd Battalion, 5 Coy			2	299
Detached	2	101		
Total	32	1,170	7	330

Artiglieria				
	Germany		Italy	
	Officers	Men	Officers	Men
Staff	6	3	1	2
1st Company (Horse)	5	75		
Depot (Horse)				4
1st Company (Foot)	4	102		4
2nd Company (Foot)	3	94		
1st Company (Train)	3	94		
2nd Company (Train)	2	93		
Depot (Train)				12
Total	23	461	1	22

Appendix III

The *Armée d'Italie* at the Battle of the Mincio, 8 February 1814[1]

This is an illustrative and typical Order of Battle of the Army of Italy and it can be seen that, even in 1814, the French still provided the majority of the combat troops of the Field Army. This Order of Battle also shows the relative weakness of the Italian units by this time.

Commander-in-Chief: Prince Eugène de Beauharnais, Viceroy of the Kingdom of Italy	
First Army Corps, *Général de Division* Paul Grenier	
2ᵉ Division Rouyer	
Brigade Schmitz	
9ᵉ de Ligne	2,266
52ᵉ de Ligne	1,010
67ᵉ de Ligne	1,042
Brigade d'Arnaud	
35ᵉ de Ligne	2,144
1ᵉʳ Régiment Étranger	2,144
1 Horse Battery	
1 Foot Battery	
4ᵉ *Division* Marcognet	
Brigade Jeanin	
6ᵉ de Ligne	863
20ᵉ de Ligne	1,242
102ᵉ de Ligne	849
Brigade Deconchy	
131ᵉ de Ligne	1,149
132ᵉ de Ligne	518
36ᵉ Légère	813
102ᵉ de Ligne	1,712
106ᵉ de Ligne	2,136
2 Foot Batteries	
6ᵉ *Division* Zucchi	
Brigade Saint Paul	
1° Fanteria Leggera	885
2° Fanteria Leggera	752
Volontari[2]	555
Brigade Paolucci	
4° Fanteria di Linea	560
5° Fanteria di Linea	869
1 Horse Battery (Italian)	
Cavalry Division, *Général de Division* Julien Mermet	
Brigade Perrymond	
1° Dragoni Regina	308
1ᵉʳ Hussards	795
Brigade Bonnemain	
31ᵉʳ Chasseurs à Cheval	819
4° Cacciatori a Cavallo	261
1 Horse Battery	
Italian Royal Guard, *Maggiore Generale* Giuseppe Lecci	
Infantry Brigade	
Granatieri a Piedi della Guardia	522
Carabinieri a Piedi della Guardia	1,324
Veliti della Guardia Reale	638
Cavalry Brigade	
Dragoni della Guardia Reale	289
Guardia Reale d'Onore	119 (1 company)
2 Horse Batteries (Italian)	
1 Foot Battery (Italian)	

1 Juan Carlos Carmigniani and Gilles Boué (Marie-France Renwick trans.), *Napoleon and Italy : A Military History of Napoleonic Italy, 1805–1815*, Paris: Histoire & Collections, 2016), p.269. The unit titles show that even at this late stage the majority of the Amy of Italy in the field was actually French.

2 Perconte on his site (see Bibliography) gives details of two units of *Volontari* in the period 1813-1814. The *1°* is *di Milano* and the *2° d'Italia* or *di Bologna*. These *volontari* may have been from one of these two units.

Second Army Corps, *Général de Division* Jean-Antoine Verdier	
***1er Division* Quesnel**	
Brigade Campi	
92e de Ligne	2,795
1er Légère	1,319
14e Légère	830
10e de Ligne	1,772
Brigade Soulier	
35e de Ligne	765
84e de Ligne	2,319
1 Horse Battery	
1 Foot Battery	
***3e Division* Fressinet**	
Brigade Forestier	
1er de Ligne	519
16e de Ligne	731
62e de Ligne	597
42e de Ligne	1,891
Brigade Pegot	
7e de Ligne	1,037
53e de Ligne	1,912
1 Foot Battery	

Appendix IV
Glossary of Uniform Patterns and Types

There are some uniform patterns and styles that were essentially identical throughout the Army so, rather than endlessly repeat the same description the illustrations and descriptions below will, I hope, cover most of these.

It is always worth noting that the colour of many items such as greatcoats, shako/bearskin covers, etc. often depended on the availability of materials. Thus although greatcoats may be stated as being "grey" or "dark blue", these were often issued in other 'neutral colours' such as various shades of brown, darker shades of grey, etc. The same stricture applies to items like shako covers that are seen in many other colours than the prescribed black, even in Guard units. In Spain the problems of supply produced local solutions whereby even coats were made in the local brown cloth.

The other consideration to bear in mind has already been mentioned, that of older patterns of uniform and equipment continuing to be issued from store well after they had officially been replaced. Equipment, of course, lasted much longer than cloth items such as coats. For example, although the helmets of the Guards of Honour may have been simplified it is unlikely that existing members ever needed to replace theirs, although, of course, new recruits would receive the new pattern and thus both patterns would have been seen alongside each other for a number of years, and this continuation and longevity of helmets probably accounts for the initial use of the czapska by the Light Horse Regiments.

Incidentally, the National cockade, as used by the military, had a white outer ring, then red, and green at the centre, i.e. it was the same as the French with the centre simply substituting green for blue.

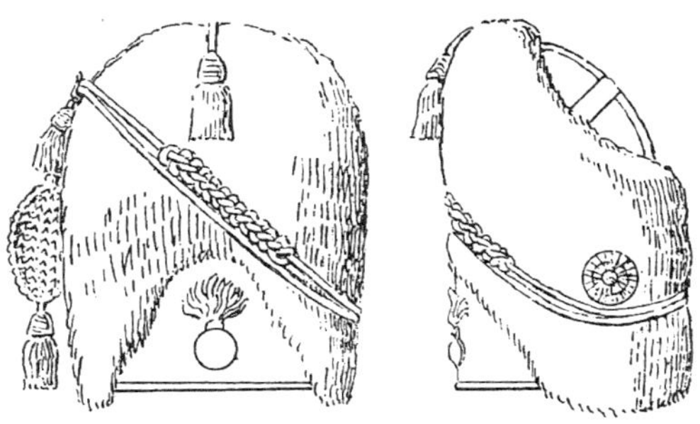

Infantry pattern bearskin with early style "cross rear patch". NB plume omitted for clarity.

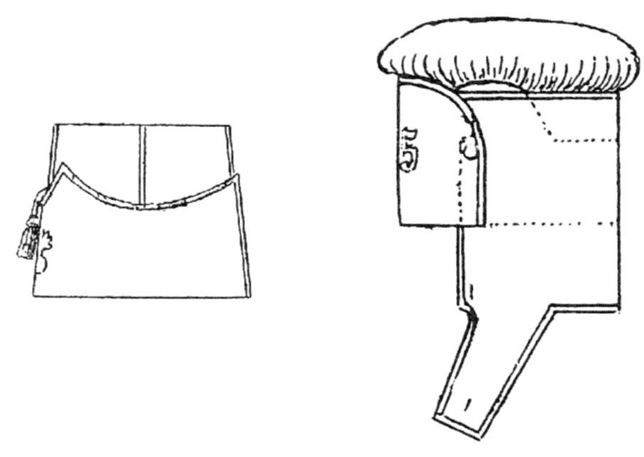

Two alternate pattern of fatigue cap in use by the Army of the Kingdom of Italy.
The left-hand illustration shows the most common pattern, here illustrated with a grenadier's badge on the front.
The right hand shows the less usual 'Pokalem' style with a regimental '5' on the front.

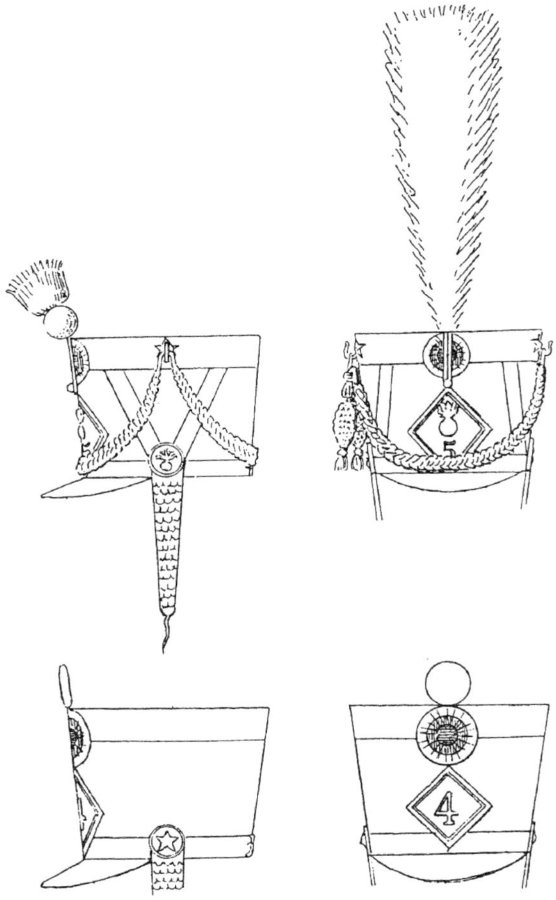

Shakos

Full dress shako with plume and cords of a grenadier company of the 5th Line. The leather reinforcing 'V' can be clearly seen although it is actually less clear on surviving examples. The ball and tuft pompom is sometimes shown for campaign use.

Shako of a fusilier of the 4th Line, devoid of all decoration as used on campaign. The 'disc' pompom is of the type shown in the illustration from the Anne S K Brown collection and in use from *c.* 1809, see colour plates.

Helmet Patterns

Left to right. Later pattern helmet of the *Gardes d'Honneur,* helmet of Dragoon Officers' pattern and helmet of Dragoon Troopers' pattern. The 'houpette' is the small tuft at the front of the crest, it should be noted that the lower "melon-shaped" part of this was the brass mount.

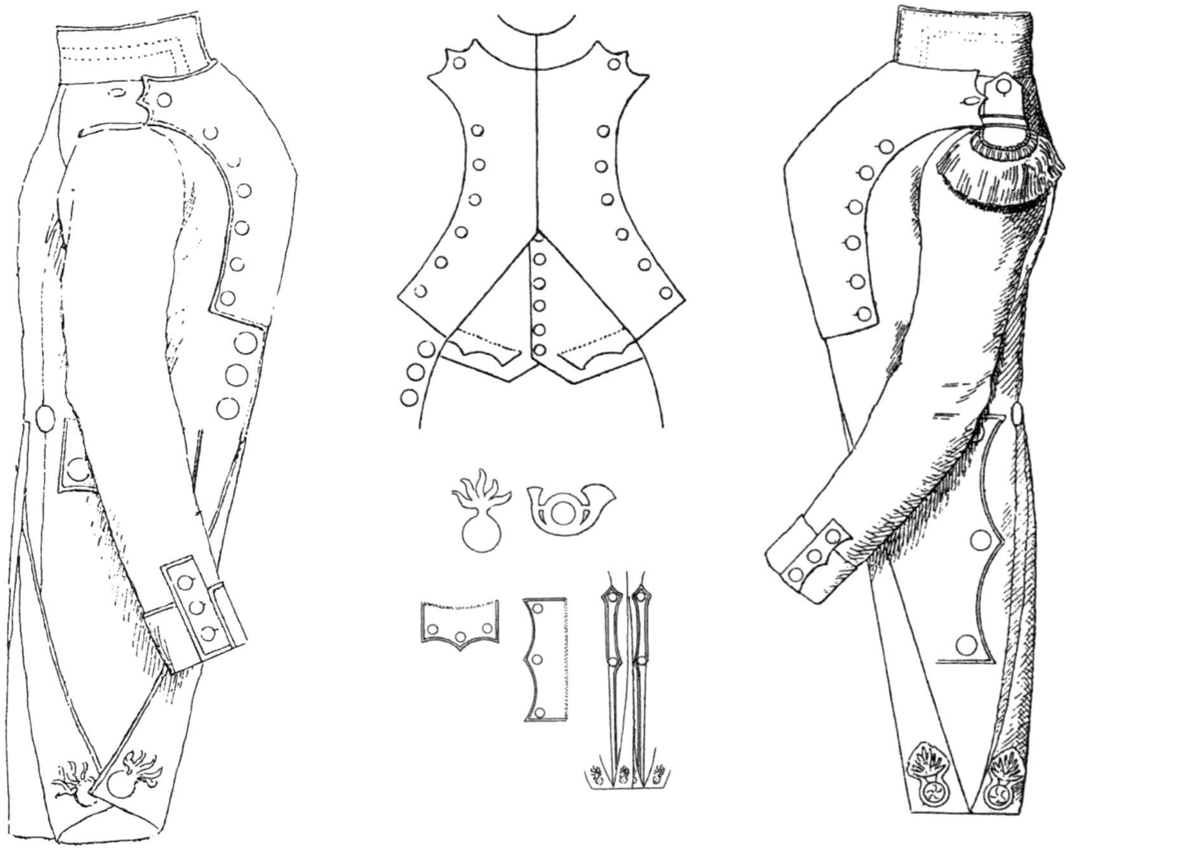

The habit coat as worn by most of the units of the Army, at left is that of a line *granatiere c.* 1805, note the square lapels and the epaulette retaining strap, the plain cuff flaps and the early style turnbacks. At right is that of a *granatiere* of the Royal Guard *c.* 1812 with Guard pattern three-pointed cuff flaps and the later 'false' turnbacks.

The smaller inset illustrations show, upper, the turnbacks badges of a *granatiere* and of a *volteggiatore* and, lower, the three pocket styles, left to right, horizontal, vertical and 'soubise'.

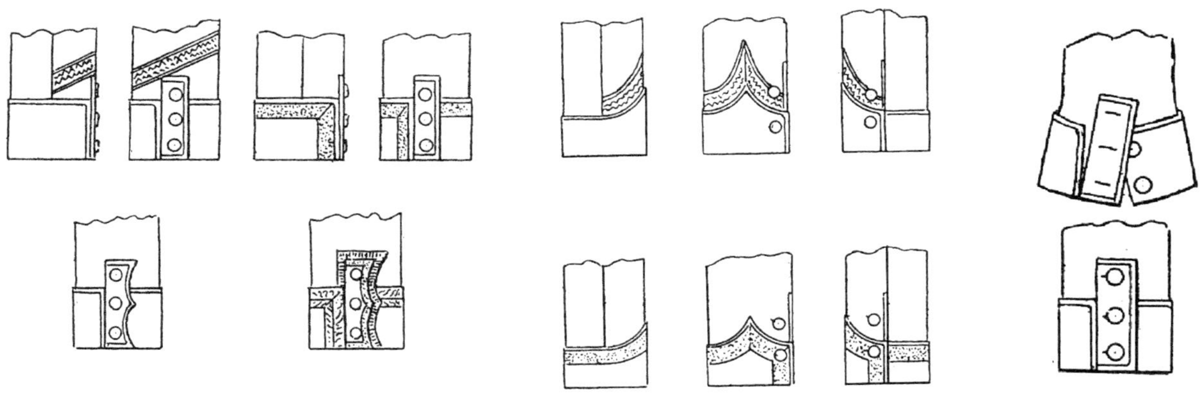

Cuff Patterns

The top row at left shows the square 'Brandenburg' cuff pattern with plain cuff flap of the line units; the first two also show an NCO stripe and the next two drummer's lace. The lower row at left shows the three-pointed flap of the Guard units, again the right-hand example shows a laced cuff, although this has the extra lace of, perhaps, the drum major.

The centre illustration shows the 'Polish' style of cuff with an N.C.O.'s stripe on the upper row and drummer's lace on the lower.

The right hand illustration shows how the cuff opened.

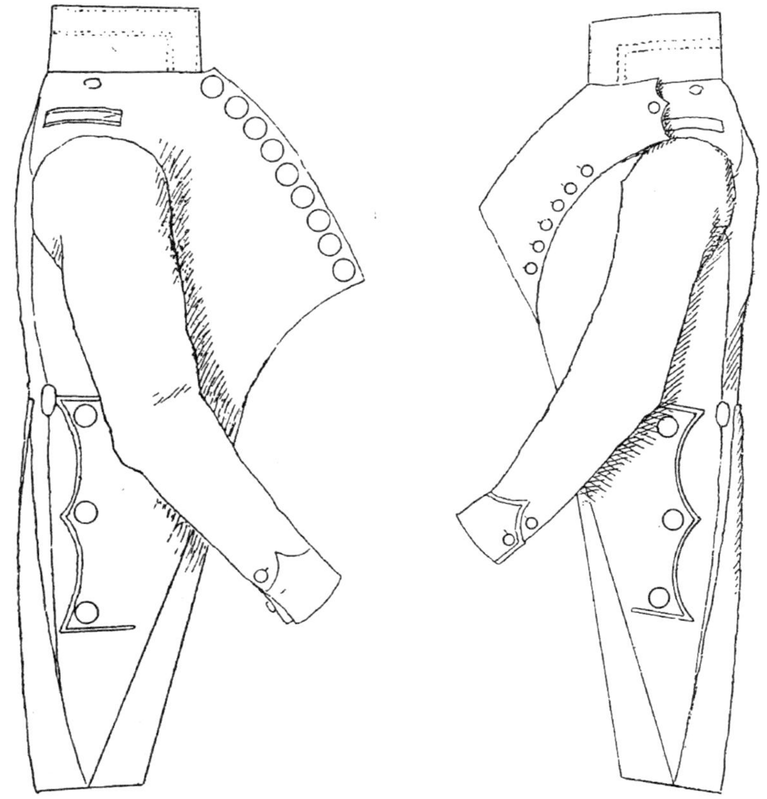

Left : Surtout coat with Polish cuffs. These coats often had vertical pockets even when the unit's habit coats used horizontal.
Right : Habit coat with pointed lapels as used by the Light Infantry Regiments.
Note the late period false turnbacks on both of these coats.

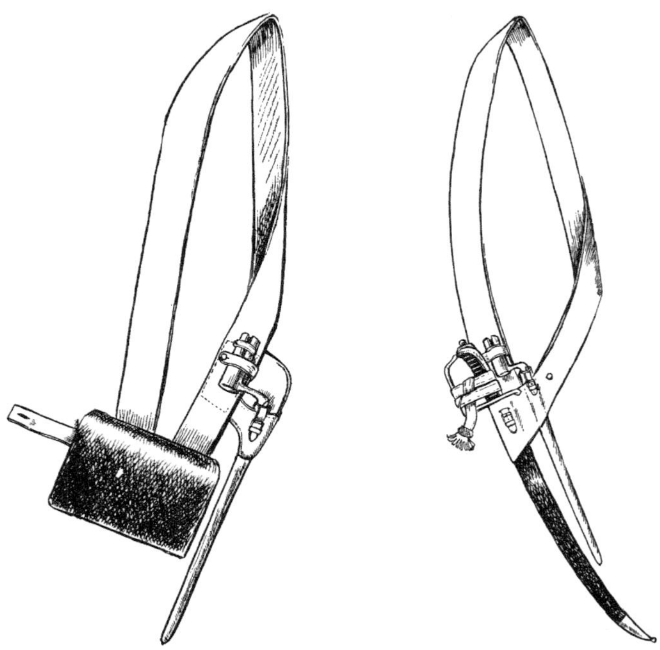

The left hand belt is that of the fusilier companies, the right hand belt is that for the elite companies.

The elite companies' second shoulder belt was identical to that of the fusiliers but without the bayonet frog and scabbard

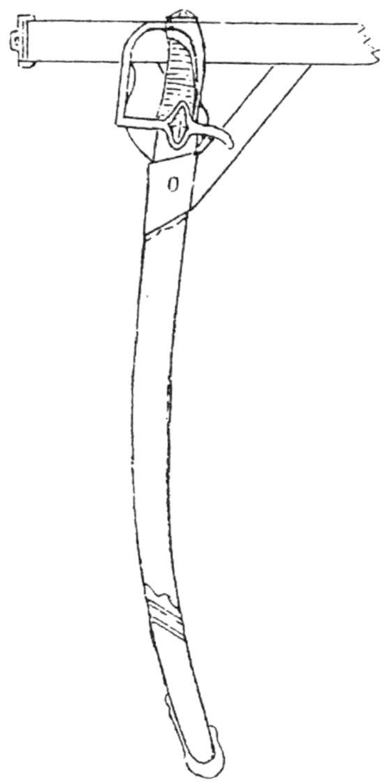

Sword and waist belt as used by many officers as well as bandsmen and, on occasion, drum majors

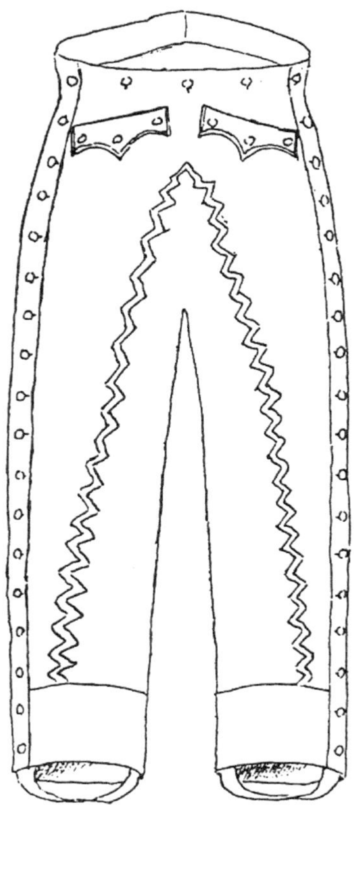

Cavalry pattern overalls worn by most mounted units. The inner part of the legs and the cuffs are black leather. The outer cloth part was of regimental colour, although dark green was commonly used by all regiments, and the outer seam, pockets and zigzag divide between the cloth and leather were of the regimental facing or piping colour.

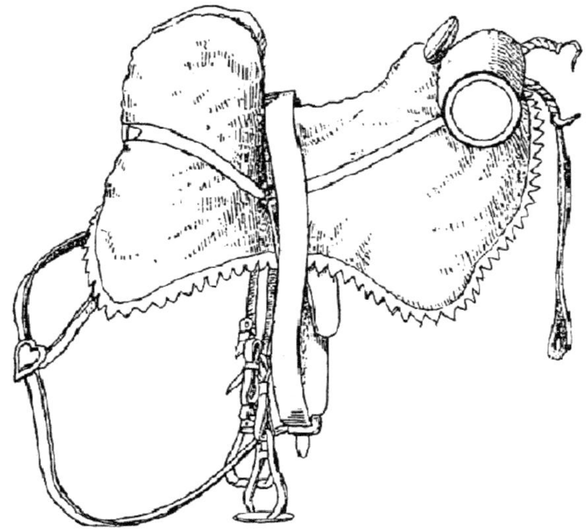

Sheepskin shabraque with the round portmanteau of the Light cavalry Regiments. The pistol holsters are hidden under the front of the saddlecloth in front of the saddle.

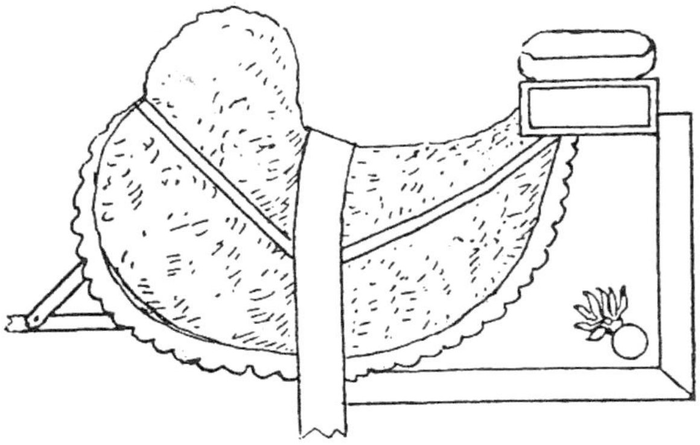

Half shabraque with square portmanteau, as used by the Line Dragoon Regiments after about 1808.

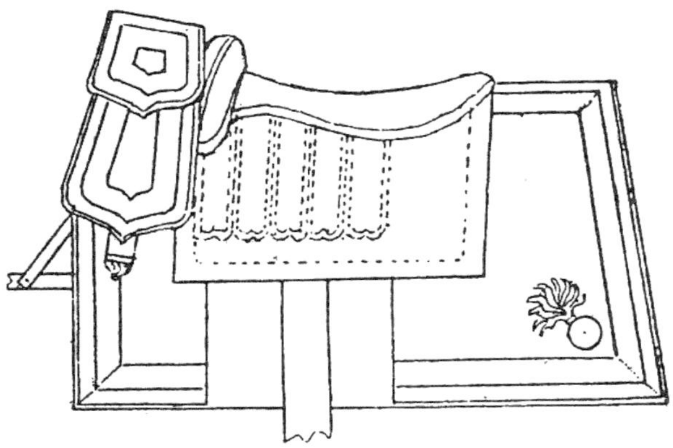

Cloth shabraque of the pattern used by the Guard Dragoons, by the Line Dragoons 1805-c1808 and by Mounted Officers of Infantry Regiments. The cavalry regiments would have used the same portmanteau as shown above.

Bibliography

Publications

Anonymous, *Uniformi De' Corpi Dell'Armata Italiana*, (Milan: 1809)

Ales, Stefano, *L'Esercito del Regno Italico : Uniformi, Equipaggiamento, Armamento* (Milan: Intergest, 1974)

Bourgeot, Vincent & Aiolfi, Xavier, *J'Étais Soldat de Napoléon : 200 ans – 200 objects* (Paris: Éditions Soixante, 2021)

Brandani, Massimo, Crociani, Pietro & Fiorentino, Massimo, *Le Uniformi Militari Italiane Del 800 – Periodo Napoleonico*, (Rome: Rivista Militaire, 1984)

Carmigniani, Juan Carlos and Boué, Gilles (Renwick, Marie-France trans.), *Napoleon and Italy : A Military History of Napoleonic Italy, 1805-1815* (Paris: Histoire & Collections, 2016)

Caude, Élisabeth (ed.), *Eugène de Beauharnais, un Prince Européen*, (Paris: Réunion des Musées Nationaux, 2022)

Cristini, Luca Stefano and Aimaretti, Guglielmo, *L'Esercito Del Regno Italico 1805-1814. Volume 1: La Fanteria*, (Lodigliano: Soldiershop, 2010)

Cristini, Luca Stefano and Aimaretti, Guglielmo, *L'Esercito Del Regno Italico 1805-1814. Volume 2: La Cavalleria*, (Lodigliano: Soldiershop, 2011)

Cristini, Luca Stefano and Aimaretti, Guglielmo, *L'Esercito Del Regno Italico 1805-1814. Volume 3: Corpi Speciali*, (Lodigliano: Soldiershop, 2011)

Crociano, Piero, *L'Esercito Italico 1805-1814: Guardia Reale*, (Parma: Albertelli, 2005)

Currie, James, *The Kingdom of Italy Infantry, 1805-1814*, No date or place of publication

Dempsey, Guy C Jr, *Napoleon's Soldiers: The Grande Armée of 1807 as Depicted in the Paintings of the Otto Manuscript*, (London: Arms & Armour, 1994)

Forthoffer, Jean-Yves, *Uniformes Napoléoniens: Armée Italienne de Napoléon, 1804-1814. Dossier de Recherches Roger Forthoffer (1920-1982) Project : Les Napoléonides 1/5* (Alsace & Strasbourg: l'Association Soldats de Temps Jadis Roger Forthoffer, 2021)

Franzoni, Pier Giorgio, *Napoleone in Italia: Soldati e Uniformi*, (Rome: Rivista Militare, 1984)

Galliani, G, Parisini, G R, Rocchiero, G M, *La Cavalleria di Linea Italica, 1796-1814*, (Genova: Interconair, 1970)

Gibellini, Valerio, *I Soldati Del Primo Tricolore: Le Uniformi*, (Rome : Rivista Militare, 1993)

Hourtoulle, F. G., *Borodino The Moskova: The Battle for the Redoubts*, (Paris: Histoire & Collections, 2000)

Hourtoulle, F. G., *Wagram: The Apogee of the Empire*, (Paris: Histoire & Collections, 2002)

Hourtoulle, F. G., *From Eylau to Friedland: 1807 The Polish Campaign*, (Paris: Histoire & Collections, 2007)

Hourtoulle, F.G., *The Crossing of the Berezina : A Victory During the Retreat*, (Paris: Histoire & Collections, 2012)

Knötel, Richard, *Mittheilungen zur Geschichte der Miltärischen Tracht, No.5 Mai 1892*, (Rathenow: Max Babeuzien, 1892)

Knötel, Herbert, Knötel, Richard, Sieg, Herbert, *Handbuch der Uniformkunde*, (Hamburg: Diepenbroick-Grüter & Schulz 1937)

Malibran, H., *Guide à l'Usage des Artistes et des Costumiers*, (Paris: Combet et Cie, 1907)

Martinien, Aristide, *Tableaux Par Corps et par Batailles des Officiers Tués et Blessées Pendant les Guerres de l'Empire (1805-1815)*, (Paris: Henri-Charles Lavauzelle, 1899)

Nafziger, George & Gioannini Marco, *The Defense of the Napoleonic Kingdom of Northern Italy, 1813-1814*, (Westport, Connecticut, USA: Praeger, 2001)

Nafziger, George (trans.), *Historical Account of the Military Operations of the Army in Italy in 1813 and 1814*, (Pisgah, Ohio, USA: Nafziger Collection, 2005)

North, Jonathan, *With Napoleon in Russia: The Illustrated Memoirs of Faber du Faur*, 1812, (London: Greenhill Books, 2001)

North, Jonathan, *Napoleon's Army in Russia: The Illustrated Memoirs of Albrecht Adam - 1812*, (London: Leo Cooper, 2005)

North, René, *Soldiers of the Peninsular War*, (London: Almark Publications, 1972)

Oliver, Michael & Partridge, Richard, *Napoleonic Army Handbook, Volume 2: The French Army and her Allies*, (London: Constable, 2002)

Oman, Carola, *Napoleon's Viceroy: Eugene de Beauharnais*, (London: Hodder & Stoughton, 1966)

Perconte, Jean-Pierre, *Organisation Militaire et Uniformes de République Cisalpine et Italiennes (1797-1805) et du Royaume d'Italie (1805-1814).* (Paris: Les Editions Jean-Pierre Perconte)

1. Les Dalmates et les Istriens au Service Italien, 1806-1814, (2007)

2. Les Chasseurs à Cheval Italiens, 1800-1814, (2008)

3. L'Infanterie de Ligne Italienne, 1799-1814, (2010)

Pigeard, Alain (ed.), *La Campagne de Russie (1812) vue par Albrecht Adam et Christian Wilhelm von Faber du Faur*, (Paris : Tradition, 1997)

Pigeard, Alain (ed.), *Le Bourgeois de Hambourg : Représentation des Uniformes de Toutes les Troupes qui ont été Casernées à Hambourg, de l'Année 1806 à l'Année 1815*, (Paris: Tradition, 1998)

Pigeard, Alain (ed.) *Le Manuscrit de Weiland: Uniformes de l'Armée Français et de ses Alliés de 1806 à 1815*, (Paris: Tradition, 1998)

Pivka, Otto von (Digby Smith), *Napoleon's Italian and Neapolitan Troops* (London: Osprey, 1979)

Rawkins, W. J., *The Italian Army, 1805-1814*, (Aylsham: Anschluss Publishing, ND)

Schneid, Frederick C., *Soldiers of Napoleon's Kingdom of Italy: Army, State, and Society, 1800-1815*, (Boulder Co.: Westview Press, 1995)

Smith, Digby, *The Napoleonic Wars Data Book.* (London: Greenhill, 1998)

Smith, Digby, *Armies of 1812* (Staplehurst: Spellmount, 2002)

Journals

Bauer, Dr Gerhard, 'Comme Les Licteurs Romains', in *Soldats Napoleoniens: Les Troupes Françaises, Alliés et Coalisées. Hors-série No.1, Avril 2003* (Paris: Éditions de la Revue Napoléon, 2003), pp.60-62

Bauer, Dr Gerhard, 'Les "Dragoni Napoleone" en 1813 : Beacoup de Pistes à Éclaircir…', in *Soldats Napoleoniens: Les Troupes Françaises, Alliés et Coalisées. Hors-série No.1, Avril 2003* (Paris: Éditions de la Revue Napoléon, 2003), pp.62-63

Boisselier, Henri, 'L'Infanterie de la Garde Royal Italienne sous Napoléon'. *Bulletin de la Société des Collectionneurs de Figurines Historiques No.3, Mai 1955*, (Paris: SCFH, 1955), pp.45-47 & pl.157-164

Carles, Lt-Col P., 'Trompettes des Gardes d'Honneur du Royaume d'Italie, 1810-1814'. *Carnet de la Sabretache No.31*, (Paris : SCFH, 1971) pp.81-82 & pl.59

Carles, Lt-Col P., 'Trompettes des Dragons de la Garde Royale Italienne'. *Carnet de la Sabretache No.9*, (Paris : SCFH, 1976), pp.7-8 & pl.3

Crociano, Piero, 'Napoleon's Italian Army'. *Tradition Magazine No.43, No.44, No.46, No.47, No.48* (London, Belmont-Maitland 197?)

Crociano, Piero and Fiorentino, Massimo, 'La Garde Royale Italienne : Les Velites 1805- 1814 (1)', in *Tradition Magazine No.153, Février 2000*, (Paris: Tradition, 2000), pp.17-22

'La Garde Royale Italienne : Les Velites 1805- 1814 (2)', in *Tradition Magazine No.162, Décembre 2000*, (Paris: Tradition, 2000), pp.16-22

Crociano, Piero and Fiorentino, Massimo, 'Les Dragons de la Garde Royale Italienne, 1805 1814 (1)', in *Tradition Magazine, No.177, Avril 2002*, (Paris, Tradition, 2002,) pp.19-22 & 30-31. 'Les Dragons de la Garde Royale Italienne, 1805 1814 (2), in *Tradition Magazine, No.178, Mai 2002*, (Paris, Tradition, 2002) pp.11-18

Crociano, Piero and Fiorentino, Massimo, '"Dragoni Napoleone", Un Nom Porté Avec Honneur', in *Soldats Napoleoniens: Les Troupes Françaises, Alliés et Coalisées. Hors-série No.1, Avril 2003* (Paris: Éditions de la Revue Napoléon, 2003), pp.51-54

Crociano, Piero, Fiorentino, Massimo and Umhey, Alfred, 'À Propos de l'"Esponton" des "Dragoni Napoleone…", in *Soldats Napoleoniens: Les Troupes Françaises, Alliés et Coalisées. Hors-série No.1, Avril 2003* (Paris: Éditions de la Revue Napoléon, 2003), pp.78-84

Crociano, Piero and Fiorentino, Massimo, 'Les Italiens en Allemagne, 1806-1808', in *Soldats Napoleoniens: Les Troupes Françaises, Alliés et Coalisées. No.10, Juin 2006* (Paris: Éditions de la Revue Napoléon, 2006), pp.55-65

Darbou, Lt-Col René 'La Cavalerie de la République Cisalpine et du Royaume : Italie, 1797-1814', in *Bulletin de la Société des Collectionneurs de Figurines Historiques No.5, Septembre 1957,* (Paris : SCFH, 1957) pp.61-69 & pl.2-11

Fiorentino, Massimo 'Eugene de Beauharnais, Prince de Venise 1807', in *Tradition No.174, Janvier 2002,* (Paris, Tradition 2002), pp.11-14

Papi, Ricardo, 'Les Chasseurs à Cheval du Royaume d'Italie, 1805-1814', in *Carnet de la Sabretache No.107,* (Paris : SCFH, 1991) pp.44-52 & pl.4-7

Papi, Ricardo, 'Le 3e Régiment de Chasseurs à Cheval Italiens', in *Soldats Napoleoniens : Les Troupes Françaises, Alliés et Coalisées, No.26, Juin 2010,* (Paris: Éditions de la Revue Napoléon, 2010), pp.58-63

Perconte, Jean-Pierre, 'Les "Napoleone" en 1813', in *Soldats Napoleoniens: Les Troupes Françaises, Alliés et Coalisées. Hors-série No.1, Avril 2003* (Paris: Éditions de la Revue Napoléon, 2003), pp.54-55

Perconte, Jean-Pierre, 'Les Uniformes des "Napoleone" en 1813', in *Soldats Napoleoniens: Les Troupes Françaises, Alliés et Coalisées. Hors-série No.1, Avril 2003* (Paris: Éditions de la Revue Napoléon, 2003), pp.56-60

Perconte, Jean-Pierre, 'Organisation et Uniformes de l'Artillerie à Pied du Royaume d'Italie, 1er Partie', in *Soldats Napoleoniens : Les Troupes Françaises, Alliés et Coalisées, No.2, 2eme Trimestre 2004,* (Paris: Éditions de la Revue Napoléon, 2004), pp. 37-45. Organisation et Uniformes de l'Artillerie à Pied du Royaume d'Italie, 2e Partie', in *Soldats Napoleoniens : Les Troupes Françaises, Alliés et Coalisées, No.4, Décembre 2004* (Paris: Éditions de la Revue Napoléon, 2004), pp.37-44

Perconte, Jean-Pierre, 'Artillerie à Cheval et Train d'Artillerie du Royaume d'Italie 1805-1814, 1er Partie', in *Soldats Napoleoniens: Les Troupes Françaises, Alliés et Coalisées, No.7, Septembre 2005* (Paris: Éditions de la Revue Napoléon, 2005), pp.45-52. 'Artillerie à Cheval et Train d'Artillerie du Royaume d'Italie 1805-1814, 2e Partie', in *Soldats Napoleoniens: Les Troupes Françaises, Alliés et Coalisées, No.15, Décembre 2007,* (Paris: Éditions de la Revue Napoléon, 2007), pp.61-69

Pigeard, Alain, 'Les Gardes d'Honneur du Royaume d'Italie' in *Tradition No.117, Janvier 1997* (Paris: Tradition, 1996) pp.12-16

Various, *Napoleon at Les Invalides: The Army Museum and Emperor's Tomb,* (Paris: Société Française de Promotion Artistique, 2007), Special Issue

Viotti, Andrea, 'The Veliti of the Italian Royal Guard, 1805-1815 [sic]'. *Campaigns Magazine No.29, July/August 1980* (Los Angeles: Campaigns, 1980) pp.52-54

Uniform Plates

Boisselier, Henri, Unpublished series of watercolours and plates on the Army of the Kingdom of Italy, all in various private collections.

CM, A series of 13 plates, painted *c.* 1806. In Anne S. K. Brown Military Collection, Brown University Library. [Artist unknown beyond 'CM'.]

Forthoffer, René, Fiches Documentaires. (Paris: Self published, 1964-1972)

Knötel, Richard, *Grosse Uniformenkude* (Rathenow: Max Babeuzien, 1890-1914). Plates: III / 17, III / 18, III / 25, III / 29, III / 45, III / 58, III / 59, VI / 42, XVI / 45

Lelièpvre, Eugene, Notes and Paintings to accompany the Historex model kits of Italian infantry.

North, Rene, 'North's Paint Your Own Cards' (London: self published, *c.*1980) Set 106

Rigondaud, Albert, 'Rigo, Le Plumet' (Paris: self published, 1960-1980), Pl.93, Pl.107, Pl.108, D.8, D.11, D.15, D.17, D.23, D.27, D.31, D.35

Pl Series 107

Websites

http://napitalia.org.uk/eng
http://www.histunif.fr
https://histunif.fr/accueil-2/le-royaume-ditalie-1805-1814

About the Author

The Author was first introduced to the glory of Napoleonic Uniforms when he was given the first Funcken 'First Empire' volume for Christmas in 1968 (at the time, only available in the original French). That initial introduction was amplified when he discovered the Willie Figures of Ted Suren. This interest has never faded and he has been particularly fascinated by the French, Italian and Austrian armies of the era (in the latter of which an ancestor of his served) ever since. Over the years he has written numerous articles on the subject in *Empires, Eagles and Lions*, *Napoleon Magazine*, and *First Empire* as well as various wargame magazines including *Wargames Illustrated* and *Miniature Wargames*. He continues to collect items of Napoleonic ephemera to clutter the house in London where he lives with his partner Mary as guests of the cats who allow them to share it.